SOFTWARE ERROR DETECTION THROUGH TESTING AND ANALYSIS

SOFTWARE ERROR DETECTION THROUGH TESTING AND ANALYSIS

J. C. Huang
University of Houston

WILEY

A JOHN WILEY & SONS, INC., PUBLICATION

Library of Congress Cataloging-in-Publication Data:

Huang, J. C., 1935–
    Software error detection through testing and analysis / J. C. Huang.
        p. cm.
    Includes bibliographical references and index.
    ISBN 978-0-470-40444-7 (cloth)
    1. Computer software–Testing.   2. Computer software–Reliability.   3. Debugging in
computer science.   I. Title.
    QA76.76.T48H72   2009
    005.1'4–dc22

                                                                        2008045493

Printed in the United States of America

10   9   8   7   6   5   4   3   2   1

To my parents

CONTENTS

PREFACE

The ability to detect latent errors in a program is essential to improving program reliability. This book provides an in-depth review and discussion of the methods of software error detection using three different techniqus: testing, static analysis, and program instrumentation. In the discussion of each method, I describe the basic idea of the method, how it works, its strengths and weaknesses, and how it compares to related methods.

I have writtent this book to serve both as a textbook for students and as a technical handbook for practitioners leading quality assurance efforts. If used as a text, the book is suitable for a one-semester graduate-level course on software testing and analysis or software quality assurance, or as a supplementary text for an advanced graduate course on software engineering. Some familiarity with the process of software quality assurance is assumed. This book provides no recipe for testing and no discussion of how a quality assurance process is to be set up and managed.

In the first part of the book, I discuss test-case selection, which is the crux of problems in debug testing. Chapter 1 introduces the terms and notational conventions used in the book and establishes two principles which together provide a unified conceptual framework for the existing methods of test-case selection. These principles can also be used to guide the selection of test cases when no existing method is deemed applicable. In Chapters 2 and 3 I describe existing methods of test-case selection in two categories: Test cases can be selected based on the information extracted form the source code of the program as described in Chapter 2 or from the program specifications, as described in Chapter 3. In Chapter 4 I tidy up a few loose ends and suggest how to choose a method of test-case selection.

I then proceed to discuss the techniques of static analysis and program instrumentation in turn. Chapter 5 covers how the symbolic trace of an execution path can be analyzed to extract additional information about a test execution. In Chapter 6 I address static analysis, in which source code is examined systematically, manually or automatically, to find possible symptoms of programming errors. Finally, Chapter 7 covers program instrumentation, in which softwarc instruments (i.e., additional program statements) are inserted into a program to extract information that may be used to detect errors or to facilitate the testing process.

Because precision is necessary, I have made use throughout the book of concepts and notations developed in symbolic logic and mathematics. A review is included as Appendix A for those who may not be conversant with the subject.

I note that many of the software error detection methods discussed in this book are not in common use. The reason for that is mainly economic. With few exceptions, these methods cannot be put into practice without proper tool support. The cost of the tools required for complete automation is so high that it often rivals that of a major programming language compiler. Software vendors with products on the mass market can afford to build these tools, but there is no incentive for them to do so because under current law, vendors are not legally liable for the errors in their products. As a result, vendors, in effect, delegate the task of error detection to their customers, who provide that service free of charge (although vendors may incur costs in the form of customer dissatisfaction). Critical software systems being built for the military and industry would benefit from the use of these methods, but the high cost of necessary supporting tools often render them impractical, unless and until the cost of supporting tools somehow becomes justifiable. Neverthless, I believe that knowledge about these existing methods is useful and important to those who specialize in software quality assurance.

I would like to take opportunity to thank anonymous reviewers for their comments; William E. Howden for his inspiration; Raymond T. Yeh, José Muñoz, and Hal Watt for giving me professional opportunities to gain practical experience in this field; and John L. Bear and Marc Garbey for giving me the time needed to complete the first draft of this book. Finally, my heartfelt thanks go to my daughter, Joyce, for her active and affectionate interest in my writing, and to my wife, Shih-wen, for her support and for allowing me to neglect her while getting this work done.

J. C. HUANG

Houston

1 Concepts, Notation, and Principles

Given a computer program, how can we determine whether or not it will do exactly what it is intended to do? This question is not only intellectually challenging, but also of primary importance in practice. An ideal solution to this problem would be to develop certain techniques that can be used to construct a formal proof (or disproof) of the correctness of a program systematically. There has been considerable effort to develop such techniques, and many different techniques for proving program correctness have been reported. However, none of them has been developed to the point where it can be used readily in practice.

There are several technical hurdles that prevent formal proof of correctness from becoming practical; chief among them is the need for a mechanical theorem prover. The basic approach taken in the development of these techniques is to translate the problem of proving program correctness into that of proving a certain statement to be a theorem (i.e., always true) in a formal system. The difficulty is that all known automatic theorem-proving techniques require an inordinate amount of computation to construct a proof. Furthermore, theorem proving is a computationally unsolvable problem. Therefore, like any other program written to solve such a problem, a theorem prover may halt if a solution is found. It may also continue to run without giving any clue as to whether it will take one more moment to find the solution, or whether it will take forever. The lack of a definitive upper bound of time required to complete a job severely limits its usefulness in practice.

Until there is a major breakthrough in the field of mechanical theorem proving, which is not foreseen by the experts any time soon, verification of program correctness through formal proof will remain impractical. The technique is too costly to deploy, and the size of programs to which it is applicable is too small (relative to that of programs in common use). At present, a practical and more intuitive solution would be to test-execute the program with a number of test cases (input data) to see if it will do what it is intended to do.

How do we go about testing a computer program for correctness? Perhaps the most direct and intuitive answer to this question is to perform an *exhaustive test*: that is, to test-execute the program for all possible input data (for which the program is expected to work correctly). If the program produces a correct result for every possible input, it obviously constitutes a direct proof that the program is correct. Unfortunately, it is in general impractical to do the exhaustive test for any nontrivial program simply because the number of possible inputs is prohibitively large.

Software Error Detection through Testing and Analysis, By J. C. Huang
Copyright © 2009 John Wiley & Sons, Inc.

To illustrate, consider the following C++ program.

Program 1.1

```
main ()
{
int i, j, k, match;

    cin >> i >> j >> k;
    cout << i << j << k;
    if (i <= 0 || j <= 0 || k <= 0
        || i+j <= k || j+k <= i || k+i <= j)
      match = 4;
    else if !(i == j || j == k || k == i)
      match = 3;
    else if (i != j || j != k || k != i)
      match = 2;
    else match = 1;
    cout << match << endl;
}
```

If, for an assignment of values to the input variables i, j, and k, the output variable match will assume a correct value upon execution of the program, we can assert that the program is correct for this particular test case. And if we can test the program for all possible assignments to i, j, and k, we will be able to determine its correctness. The difficulty here is that even for a small program like this, with only three input variables, the number of possible assignments to the values of those variables is prohibitively large. To see why this is so, recall that an ordinary integer variable in C++ can assume a value in the range $-32{,}768$ to $+32{,}767$ (i.e., 2^{16} different values). Hence, there are $2^{16} \times 2^{16} \times 2^{16} = 2^{48} \approx 256 \times 10^{12}$ possible assignments to the input triple (i, j, k). Now suppose that this program can be test-executed at the rate of one test per microsecond on average, and suppose further that we do testing 24 hours a day, 7 days a week. It will take more than eight years for us to complete an exhaustive test for this program. Spending eight years to test a program like this is an unacceptably high expenditure under any circumstance!

This example clearly indicates that an exhaustive test (i.e., a test using all possible input data) is impractical. It may be technically doable for some small programs, but it would never be economically justifiable for a real-world program. That being the case, we will have to settle for testing a program with a manageably small subset of its input domain.

Given a program, then, how do we construct such a subset; that is, how do we select test cases? The answer would be different depending on why we are doing the test. For software developers, the primary reason for doing the test is to find errors so that they can be removed to improve the reliability of the program. In that case we say that the tester is doing *debug testing*. Since the main goal of debug testing is to find programming errors, or *faults* in the Institute of Electrical and Electronics

Engineers (IEEE) terminology, the desired test cases would be those that have a high probability of revealing faults.

Other than software developers, expert users of a software system may also have the need to do testing. For a user, the main purpose is to assess the reliability so that the responsible party can decide, among other things, whether or not to accept the software system and pay the vendor, or whether or not there is enough confidence in the correctness of the software system to start using it for a production run. In that case the test cases have to be selected based on what is available to the user, which often does not include the source code or program specification. Test-case selection therefore has to be done based on something else.

Information available to the user for test-case selection includes the probability distribution of inputs being used in production runs (known as the *operational profile*) and the identity of inputs that may incur a high cost or result in a catastrophe if the program fails. Because it provides an important alternative to debug testing, possible use of an operational profile in test-case selection is explained further in Section 4.2. We discuss debug testing in Chapters 2 and 3. Chapter 4 is devoted to other aspects of testing that deserve our attention. Other than testing as discussed in Chapters 2 and 3, software faults can also be detected by means of analysis, as discussed in Chapters 5 through 7.

When we test-execute a program with an input, the test result will be either correct or incorrect. If it is incorrect, we can unequivocally conclude that there is a fault in the program. If the result is correct, however, all that we can say with certainty is that the program will execute correctly for that particular input, which is not especially significant in that the program has so many possible inputs. The significance of a correct test result can be enhanced by analyzing the execution path traversed to determine the condition under which that path will be traversed and the exact nature of computation performed in the process. This is discussed in Chapter 5.

We can also detect faults in a program by examining the source code systematically as discussed in Chapter 6. The analysis methods described therein are said to be static, in that no execution of the program is involved. Analysis can also be done dynamically, while the program is being executed, to facilitate detection of faults that become more obvious during execution time. In Chapter 7 we show how dynamic analysis can be done through the use of software instruments.

For the benefit of those who are not theoretically oriented, some helpful logico-mathematical background material is presented in Appendix A. Like many others used in software engineering, many technical terms used in this book have more than one possible interpretation. To avoid possible misunderstanding, a glossary is included as Appendix B. For those who are serious about the material presented in this book, you may wish to work on the self-assessment questions posed in Appendix C.

There are many known test-case selection methods. Understanding and comparison of those methods can be facilitated significantly by presenting all methods in a unified conceptual framework so that each method can be viewed as a particular instantiation of a generalized method. We develop such a conceptual framework in the remainder of the chapter.

1.1   CONCEPTS, TERMINOLOGY, AND NOTATION

The *input domain* of a program is the set of all possible inputs for which the program is expected to work correctly. It is constrained by the hardware on which the program is to be executed, the operating system that controls the hardware, the programming environment in which the program is developed, and the intent of the creator of the program. If none of these constraints are given, the default will be assumed.

For example, consider Program 1.1. The only constraint that we can derive from what is given is the fact that all variables in the program are of the type "short integer" in C++. The prevailing standard is to use 16 bits to represent such data in 2's-complement notation, resulting in the permissible range $-32,768$ to $32,767$ in decimal. The input domain therefore consists of all triples of 16-bit integers; that is,

$$D = \{< x, y, z > | x, y, \text{ and } z \text{ are 16-bit integers}\}$$

Input (data) are elements of the input domain, and a *test case* is an input used to perform a test execution. Thus, every test case is an input, but an input is not necessarily a test case in a particular test. The set of all test cases used in testing is called a *test set*. For example, $<3, 5, 2>$ is a possible input (or test case) in Program 1.1, and in a particular test we might choose $\{<1, 2, 3>, <4, 5, 6>, <0, 0, 5>, <5, 0, 1>, <3, 3, 3>\}$ as the test set.

This notational convention for representing program inputs remains valid even if the program accepts an input repeatedly when run in an interactive mode (i.e., sequence of inputs instead of a single input). All we need to do is to say that the input domain is a product set instead of a simple set. For example, consider a program that reads the value of input variable x, which can assume a value from set X. If the function performed by the program is not influenced by the previous value of x, we can simply say that X is the input domain of the program. If the function performed by the program is dependent on the immediately preceding input, we can make the product set $X \cdot X = \{< x_1, x_2 > | x_1 \in X \text{ and } x_2 \in X\}$ the input domain. In general, if the function performed by the program is dependent on n immediately preceding inputs, we can make the product set $X^{n+1} = \{< x_1, x_2, \ldots, x_n, x_{n+1} > | x_i \in X \text{ for all } 1 \leq i \leq n + 1\}$ the input domain. This is the property of a program with memory, often resulting from implementing the program with a finite-state machine model. The value of n is usually small and is related to the number of states in the finite-state machine.

Do not confuse a program with memory with an interactive program (i.e., a program that has to be executed interactively). Readers should have no difficulty convincing themselves that an interactive program could be memoryless and that a program with memory does not have to be executed interactively. We shall now proceed to define some terms in program testing that might, at times, have a different meaning for different people.

The composition of a test set is usually prescribed using a *test-case selection criterion*. Given such a criterion, any subset of the input domain that satisfies the criterion is a candidate. We say "any subset" because more than one subset in the input domain may satisfy the same criterion. Examples of a test-case selection criterion include $T = \{0, 1, 2, 3\}$, $T = \{< i, j, k > | i = j = k$ and $k > 1$ and $k < 10\}$, and "T is a set of inputs that cause 60% of the statements in the program to be exercised at least once during the test."

Let D be the input domain of a given program P, and let $OK(P, d)$, where $d \in D$, be a predicate that assumes the value of TRUE if an execution of program P with input d terminates and produces a correct result, and FALSE otherwise. Predicate $OK(P, d)$ can be shortened to $OK(d)$ if the omission of P would not lead to confusion.

After we test-execute the program with input d, how can we tell if $OK(d)$ is true? Two assumptions can be made in this regard. One is that the program specification is available to the tester. $OK(d)$ is true if the program produced a result that satisfies the specification. Another is the existence of an *oracle*, a device that can be used to determine if the test result is correct. The target-practice equipment used in testing the software that controls a computerized gunsight is a good example of an oracle. A "*hit*" indicates that the test is successful, and a "*miss*" indicates otherwise. The main difference between a specification and an oracle is that a specification can be studied to see how to arrive at a correct result, or the reason why the test failed. An oracle gives no clue whatsoever.

Let T be a test set: a subset of D used to test-execute a program. A test using T is said to be *successful* if the program terminates and produces a correct result for every test case in T. A successful test is to be denoted by the predicate SUCCESSFUL(T). To be more precise,

$$\text{SUCCESSFUL } (T) \equiv (\forall t)_T (OK(t))$$

The reader should not confuse a successful test execution with a successful program test using test set T. The test using T fails if there exists a test case in T that causes the program to produce an incorrect result [i.e., $\neg$SUCCESSFUL(T) $\equiv \neg(\forall t)_T(OK(t)) \equiv (\exists t)_T(\neg OK(t))$]. The test using T is successful if and only if the program executes correctly for all test cases in T.

Observe that not every component in a program is involved in program execution. For instance, if Program 1.1 is executed with input $i = j = k = 0$, the assignment statement `match = 1` will not be involved. Therefore, if this statement is faulty, it will not be reflected in the test result. This is one reason that a program can be fortuitously correct, and therefore it is insufficient to test a program with just one test case.

According to the IEEE glossary, a part of a program that causes it to produce an incorrect result is called a *fault* in that program. A fault causes the program to fail (i.e., to produce incorrect results) for certain inputs. We refer to an aggregate of such inputs as a *failure set*, usually a small subset of the input domain.

In debug testing, the goal is to find faults and remove them to improve the reliability of the program. Therefore, the test set should be constructed such that it maximizes the probability and minimizes the cost of finding at least one fault during the test. To be more precise, let us assume that we wish to test the program with a set of n test cases: $T = \{t_1, t_2, \ldots, t_n\}$. What is the reason for using multiple test cases? It is because for all practical programs, a single test case will not cause all program components to become involved in the test execution, and if there is a fault in a component, it will not be reflected in the test result unless that component is involved in the test execution.

Of course, one may argue that a single test case would suffice if the entire program were considered as a component. How we choose to define a component for test-case selection purposes, however, will affect our effectiveness in revealing faults. If the granularity of component is too coarse, part of a component may not be involved in test execution, and therefore a fault contained therein may not be reflected in the test result even if that component is involved in the test execution. On the other hand, if the granularity of the component is too fine, the number of test cases required and the effort required to find them will become excessive. For all known unit-testing methods, the granularities of the component range from a statement (finest) to an execution path (coarsest) in the source code, with one exception that we discuss in Section 7.2, where the components to be scrutinized are operands and expressions in a statement.

For debug testing, we would like to reveal at least one fault in the test. To be more precise, we would like to maximize the probability that at least one test case causes the program to produce an incorrect result. Formally, we would like to maximize

$$p(\neg OK(t_1) \vee \neg OK(t_2) \vee \cdots \vee \neg OK(t_n)) = p((\exists t)_T(\neg OK(t)))$$
$$= p(\neg(\forall t)_T(OK(t)))$$
$$= 1 - p((\forall t)_T(OK(t)))$$

The question now is: What information can be used to construct such a test set?

It is well known that programmers tend to forget writing code to make sure that the program does not do division by zero, does not delete an element from an empty queue, does not traverse a linked list without checking for the end node, and so on. It may also be known that the author of the program has a tendency to commit certain types of error or the program is designed to perform certain functions that are particularly difficult to implement. Such information can be used to find test cases for which the program is particularly error-prone [i.e., the probability $p(\neg OK(t_1) \vee \neg OK(t_2) \cdots \vee \neg OK(t_n))$ is high]. The common term for making use of such information is *error guessing*. The essence of that technique is described in Section 3.4.

Other than the nature or whereabouts of possible latent faults, which are unknown in general, the most important information that we can derive from the program and use to construct a test set is the degree of similarity to which two inputs are processed by the program. It can be exploited to enhance the effectiveness of a test set. To see why that is so, suppose that we choose some test case, t_1, to test the program first, and we wish to select another test case, t_2, to test the program further. What relationship must hold between t_1 and t_2 so that the joint fault discovery probability is arguably enhanced?

Formally, what we wish to optimize is $p(\neg OK(t_1) \vee \neg OK(t_2))$, the probability of fault discovery by test-executing the program with t_1 and t_2. It turns out that this probability can be expressed in terms of the conditional probability $p(OK(t_2) \mid OK(t_1))$:

the probability that the program will execute correctly with input t_2 given the fact that the program executed correctly with t_1. To be exact,

$$p(\neg OK(t_1) \vee \neg OK(t_2)) = p(\neg(OK(t_1) \wedge OK(t_2)))$$
$$= p(\neg(OK(t_2) \wedge OK(t_1)))$$
$$= 1 - p(OK(t_2) \wedge OK(t_1))$$
$$= 1 - p(OK(t_2) \mid OK(t_1))p(OK(t_1))$$

This equation shows that if we can choose t_2 to make the conditional probability $p(OK(t_2) \mid OK(t_1))$ smaller, we will be able to increase $p(\neg OK(t_1) \vee \neg OK(t_2))$, the probability of fault discovery.

The value of $p(OK(t_2) \mid OK(t_1))$ depends on, among other factors, the degree of similarity of operations performed in execution. If the sequences of operations performed in test-executing the program using t_1 and t_2 are completely unrelated, it should be intuitively clear that $p(OK(t_2) \mid OK(t_1)) = p(OK(t_2))$, that is, the fact that the program test-executed correctly with t_1 does not influence the probability that the program will test-execute correctly with test case t_2. Therefore, $p(OK(t_2) \wedge OK(t_1)) = p(OK(t_2))p(OK(t_1))$. On the other hand, if the sequences of operations performed are similar, then $p(OK(t_2) \mid OK(t_1)) > p(OK(t_2))$, that is, the probability that the program will execute correctly will become greater given that the program test-executes correctly with input t_1. The magnitude of the difference in these two probabilities, denoted by

$$\delta(t_1, t_2) = p(OK(t_2) \mid OK(t_1)) - p(OK(t_2))$$

depends on, among other factors, the degree of commonality or similarity between the two sequences of operations performed by the program in response to inputs t_1 and t_2.

For convenience we shall refer to $\delta(t_1, t_2)$ henceforth as the (*computational*) *coupling coefficient* between test cases t_1 and t_2, and simply write δ if the identities of t_1 and t_2 are understood. The very basic problem of test-case selection can now be stated in terms of this coefficient simply as follows. Given a test case, find another that is as loosely coupled to the first as possible!

Obviously, the value of this coefficient is in the range $0 \le \delta(t_1, t_2) \le 1 - p(OK(t_2))$, because if $OK(t_1)$ implies $OK(t_2)$, then $p(OK(t_2) \mid OK(t_1)) = 1$, and if the events $OK(t_1)$ and $OK(t_2)$ are completely independent, then $p(OK(t_2) \mid OK(t_1)) = p(OK(t_2))$. The greater the value of $\delta(t_1, t_2)$, the tighter the two inputs t_1 and t_2 are coupled, and therefore the lower the joint probability of fault discovery (through the use of test cases t_1 and t_2). Asymptotically, $\delta(t_1, t_2)$ becomes zero when the events of successful tests with t_1 and t_2 are absolutely and completely independent, and $\delta(t_1, t_2)$ becomes $1 - p(OK(t_2)) = p(\neg OK(t_2))$ when a successful test with t_1 surely entails a successful test with t_2.

Perhaps a more direct way to explain the significance of the coupling coefficient $\delta(t_1, t_2)$ is that

$$
\begin{aligned}
p(\neg OK(t_1) \vee \neg OK(t_2)) &= 1 - p(OK(t_2) \mid OK(t_1)) p(OK(t_1)) \\
&= 1 - (p(OK(t_2) \mid OK(t_1)) - p(OK(t_2)) \\
&\quad + p(OK(t_2))) p(OK(t_1)) \\
&= 1 - (\delta(t_1, t_2) + p(OK(t_2))) p(OK(t_1)) \\
&= 1 - \delta(t_1, t_2) p(OK(t_1)) - p(OK(t_2)) p(OK(t_1))
\end{aligned}
$$

The values of $p(OK(t_1))$ and $p(OK(t_2))$ are intrinsic to the program to be tested; their values are generally unknown and beyond the control of the tester. The tester, however, can select t_1 and t_2 with a reduced value of the coupling coefficient $\delta(t_1, t_2)$, thereby increasing the fault-discovery probability $p(\neg OK(t_1) \vee \neg OK(t_2))$.

How can we reduce the coupling coefficient $\delta(t_1, t_2)$? There are a number of ways to achieve that, as discussed in this book. One obvious way is to select t_1 and t_2 from different input subdomains, as explained in more detail later.

1.2   TWO PRINCIPLES OF TEST-CASE SELECTION

Now we are in a position to state two principles. The *first principle of test-case selection* is that in choosing a new element for a test set being constructed, preference should be given to those candidates that are computationally as loosely coupled as possible to all the existing elements in the set. A fundamental problem then is: Given a program, how do we construct a test set according to this principle? An obvious answer to this question is to select test cases such that the program will perform a distinctly different sequence of operations for every element in the set.

If the test cases are to be selected based on the source code, the most obvious candidates for the new element are those that will cause a different execution path to be traversed. Since almost all practical programs have a large number of possible execution paths, the next question is when to stop adding test cases to the test set. Since the purpose of using multiple test cases is to cause every component, however that is defined, to be exercised at least once during the test, the obvious answer is to stop when there are enough elements in the test set to cause every component to be exercised at least once during the test.

Thus, the *second principle of test-case selection* is to include in the test set as many test cases as needed to cause every contributing component to be exercised at least once during the test. (*Remark: Contributing* here refers to the component that will make some difference to the computation performed by the program. For brevity henceforth, we omit this word whenever the term *component* is used in this context.)

Note that the first principle guides us as to what to choose, and the second, as to when to stop choosing. These two principles are easy to understand and easy to apply, and therefore become handy under situations when no existing method is applicable. For example, when a new software system is procured, the user organization often needs to test it to see if it is reliable enough to pay the vendor and release the system for production runs. If an operational profile is available, the obvious choice is to perform operational testing as described in Section 4.2. Otherwise, test-case selection becomes a problem, especially if the system is fairly large. Source code is generally not available to the user to make use of the methods presented in Chapter 2, and detailed design documents or specifications are not available to use the methods presented in Chapter 3. Even if they are available, a typical user organization simply does not have the time, resources, and technical capability to deploy the methods. In that event, the two principles can be utilized to select test cases. The components to be exercised could be the constituent subsystems, which can be recognized by reading the system user manual. Two inputs are weakly coupled computationally if they cause different subsystems to be executed in different sequences. Expert users should be able to apply the two principles readily to achieve a high probability of fault detection. In short, if one finds it difficult to use any existing method, use the two principles instead.

Next, in practical application, we would like to be able to compare the cost-effectiveness of test sets. In the literature, the effectiveness of a test set is measured by the probability of discovering at least one fault in the test (see, e.g., [FHLS98]). It is intuitively clear that we can increase the fault-discovery capability of a test set simply by adding elements to it. If we carry this idea to the extreme, the test set eventually would contain all possible inputs. At that point, a successful test constitutes a direct proof of correctness, and the probability of fault discovery is 100%. The cost of performing the test, however, will become unacceptably high. Therefore, the number of elements in a test set must figure prominently when we compare the cost-effectiveness of a test set. We define the *cost-effectiveness of a test set* to be the probability of revealing a fault during the test, divided by the number of elements in the test set.

A test set is said to be *optimal* if it is constructed in accordance with the first and second principles for test-case selection and if its size (i.e., the number of elements contained therein) is minimal. The concept of path testing (i.e., to choose the execution path as the *component* to be exercised during the test) is of particular interest in this connection because every feasible execution path defines a subdomain in the input domain, and the set of all subdomains so defined constitutes a partition of the input domain (in a set-theoretical sense; i.e., each and every element in the domain belongs to one and only one subdomain). Therefore, a test set consisting of one element from each such subdomain is a good one because it will not only cause every component to be exercised at least once during the test, but its constituent elements will be loosely coupled as well. Unfortunately, path testing is impractical in general because most programs in the real world contain loop constructs, and a loop construct expands into a prohibitively large number of execution paths. Nevertheless, the idea of doing path testing remains of special interest because many known test-case selection methods can be viewed as an approximation of path testing, as we demonstrate later.

1.3   CLASSIFICATION OF FAULTS

In the preceding section we said that a test case should be selected from a subdomain or a subset of inputs that causes a component to be exercised during the test. Is there a better choice if there is more than one? Is there any way to improve the fault-detection probability by using more than one test case from each subdomain? The answer depends on the types of faults the test is designed to reveal. What follows is a fault classification scheme that we use throughout the book.

In the abstract, the intended function of a program can be viewed as a function f of the nature $f : X \rightarrow Y$. The definition of f is usually expressed as a set of subfunctions $f_1, f_2, \ldots, f_m$, where $f_i : X_i \rightarrow Y$ (i.e., f_i is a function f restricted to X_i for all $1 \leq i \leq m$), $X = X_1 \cup X_2 \cup \cdots \cup X_m$, and $f_i \neq f_j$ if $i \neq j$. We shall use $f(x)$ to denote the value of f evaluated at $x \in X$, and suppose that each X_i can be described in the standard subset notation $X_i = \{x \mid x \in X \wedge C_i(x)\}$.

Note that, above, we require the specification of f to be *compact* (i.e., $f_i \neq f_j$ if $i \neq j$). This requirement makes it easier to construct the definition of a type of programming fault in the following. In practice, the specification of a program may not be compact (i.e., f_i may be identical to f_j for some i and j). Such a specification, however, can be made compact by merging X_i and X_j.

Let (P, S) denote a program written to implement the function f described above, where P is the condition imposed on the input and S is the sequence of statements to be executed. Furthermore, let D be the set of all possible inputs for the program. Set D is the computer-implemented version of set X mentioned above. No other constraints are imposed. The definition of set D, on the hand, will be constrained by programming language used and by the hardware on which the program will be executed. For example, if it is implemented as the short integers in C++, then D is a set of all integers representable by using 16 bits in 2's-complement notation. The valid input domain (i.e., the set of all inputs for which the program is expected to work correctly) is seen to be the set $\{d \mid d \in D \text{ and } P(d)\}$. The program should be composed of n paths:

$$(P, S) = (P_1, S_1) + (P_2, S_2) + \cdots + (P_n, S_n)$$

Here (P_i, S_i) is a subprogram designed to compute some subfunction f_j. $P \equiv P_1 \vee P_2 \vee \cdots \vee P_n$, and P is in general equal to T (true) unless the programmer places additional restrictions on the inputs. We shall use $S(x)$ to denote the computation performed by an execution of S with x as the input.

Two basic types of fault may be committed in constructing the program (P, S). The program created to satisfy a specification must partition its input domain into at least as many subdomains as that required by the specification, each of which must be contained completely in some subdomain prescribed by the specification. Otherwise, there is a domain fault. If there is an element in the input domain for which the program produces a result different from that prescribed by the specification, and the input is in a subdomain that is contained completely in a subdomain prescribed by the specification, there is a computational fault. To be more precise, we can restate the definitions as follow.

1. *Computational fault.* The program has a computational fault if $(\exists i)(\exists j)((P_i \supset C_j \wedge S_i(x) \neq f_j(x))$.
2. *Domain fault.* The program has a domain fault if $\neg(\forall i)(\exists j)(P_i \supset C_j)$.

In words, if the program specification says that the input domain should consist of m subdomains $X_1, X_2, \ldots, X_m$, the program should partition the input domain into n subdomains $D_1, D_2, \ldots, D_n$, where n must be greater than or equal to m if the partition prescribed by the specification is compact. The partition created by the program must satisfy the condition that every $D_i = \{d \mid d \in D$ and $P_i(d)\}$ be contained completely in some X_j, $X_1 \cup X_2 \cup \ldots \cup X_m = X$, and $D_1 \cup D_2 \cup \ldots \cup D_n = D$. Otherwise, there is a domain fault.

If there is a subdomain D_i created by the program that is contained completely in some X_j prescribed by the specification, then for every input in D_i, the value computed by S_i must be equal to that computed by f_j. Otherwise, there is a computation fault.

It is possible that a program contains both domain and computational faults at the same time. Nevertheless, the same element in the input domain cannot be involved in both kinds of fault. If the program is faulty at a particular input, it is either of domain or computational type, but not both.

Previously published methods of program-fault classification include that of Goodenough and Gerhart [GOGE77], Howden [HOWD76], and White and Cohen [WHCO80]. All three include one more type of fault, called a *subcase fault* or *missing-path fault*, which occurs when the programmer fails to create a subdomain required by the specification [i.e., if $\neg(\forall i)(\exists j)(C_i \subset P_j)$]. Since such a fault also manifests as a computational fault, we chose, for simplicity, not to identify it as a fault of separate type.

In Chapters 2 and 3 we discuss test-case selection methods that are designed particularly for revealing the domain faults. In such methods, the components to be exercised are the boundaries of subdomains embodied by the predicates found in the source code or program specification.

1.4   CLASSIFICATION OF TEST-CASE SELECTION METHODS

It was observed previously that when a program is being test-executed, not all constituent components would be involved. If a faulty component is not involved, the fault will not be reflected in the test result. A necessary condition, therefore, for revealing all faults in a test is to construct the test set in such a way that every contributing component in the program is involved (exercised) in at least one test execution!

What is a *component* in the statement above? It can be defined in many different ways. For example, it can be a statement in the source code, a branch in the control-flow diagram, or a predicate in the program specification. The use of different components leads to the development of different test-case selection methods. As shown in Chapters 2 and 3, many test-case selection methods have been developed.

If the component used is to be identified from the source code, the resulting test-case selection method is said to be *code-based*. The most familiar examples of such a method are the statement test, in which the program is to be tested to the extent that every statement in its source code is exercised at least during the test, and the branch test, in which the program is to be tested to the extent that every branch in its control-flow diagram is traversed at least once during the test. There are several others that cannot be explained as simply. All the methods are discussed in detail in Chapter 2.

If the component used is to be identified from the program specification, the resulting test-case selection method is said to be *specification-based*. Examples of the components identifiable from a program specification include predicates, boundaries of input/output variables, and subfunctions. Chapter 3 is devoted to a discussion of such methods.

It is possible that certain components can be identified from either the source code or the program specification. The component defined in the subfunction testing method discussed in Chapter 3 is an example.

Since a component can be also a subdomain consisting of those and only those inputs that cause that component to be exercised during the test, a test-case selection method that implicitly or explicitly requires execution of certain components in the program during the test can also be characterized as being *subdomain-based* [FHLS98]. The test methods and all of their derivatives, discussed in Chapters 2 and 3, are therefore all subdomain-based.

Are there any test-case selection methods that are not subdomain-based? There are at least two: random testing [DUNT84, CHYU94, BOSC03] and operational testing [MUSA93, FHLS98]. The first, although interesting, is not discussed in this book because its value has yet to be widely recognized. The second is important in that it is frequently used in practice. Because it is neither code- nor specification-based, we choose to discuss it in Section 4.2.

1.5 THE COST OF PROGRAM TESTING

Software testing involves the following tasks: (1) test-case selection; (2) test execution; (3) test-result analysis; and if it is debug testing, (4) fault removal and regression testing.

For *test-case selection*, the tester first has to study a program to identify all input variables (parameters) involved. Then, depending on the test-case selection method used, the tester has to analyze the source code or program specification to identify all the components to be exercised during the test. The result is often stated as a condition or predicate, called the *test-case selection criterion*, such that any set of inputs that satisfies the criterion is an acceptable test set. The tester then constructs the test cases by finding a set of assignments to the input variables (parameters) that satisfies the test-case selection criterion. This component of the cost is determined by the complexity of the analysis required and the number of test cases needed to satisfy the criterion.

A commonly used test-case selection criterion is the statement test: testing the program to the extent that every statement in the source code is exercised at least once during the test. The critics say that this selection criterion is far too simplistic and ineffectual, yet it is still commonly used in practice, partly because the analysis required for test-case selection is relatively simple and can be automated to a great extent.

The process of test-case selection is tedious, time consuming, and error prone. The most obvious way to reduce its cost is through automation. Unfortunately, some parts of that process are difficult to automate. If it is specification based, it requires analysis of text written in a natural language. If test cases satisfying a selection criterion are to be found automatically, it requires computational power close to that of a mechanical theorem prover.

For operational testing, which we discuss in Section 4.2, the cost of test-case selection is minimal if the operational profile (i.e., the probability distribution of inputs to be used in production runs) is known. Even if the operational profile had to be constructed from scratch, the skill needed to do so is much less than that for debug testing. That is one of the reasons that many practitioners prefer operational testing. It should be pointed out, however, that a real operational profile may change in time, and the effort required to validate or to update an existing profile is nontrivial.

Test execution is perhaps the part of the testing process that is most amenable to automation. In addition to the machine time and labor required to run the test, the cost of test execution includes that of writing the test harness (i.e., the additional nondeliverable code needed to produce an executable image of the program).

The cost of *test-result analysis* depends largely on the availability of an oracle. If the correctness of test results has to be deduced from the specification, it may become tedious, time consuming, and error prone. It may also become difficult to describe the correctness of a test result if it consists of a large aggregate of data points, such as a graph of a photographic image. For that reason, the correctness of a program is not always unequivocally definable.

A class of computer programs called *real-time programs* have hard time constraints; that is, they not only have to produce results of correct values but have to produce them within prescribed time limits. It often requires an elaborate test harness to feed the test cases at the right time and to determine if correct results are produced in time. For that reason, a thorough test of a real-time software system is usually done under the control of an environment simulator. As the timing aspect of program execution is not addressed in this work, testing of real-time programs is beyond the scope of this book.

Finally, it should be pointed out that, in practice, the ultimate value of a test method is not determined solely by the number of faults it is able to reveal or the probability that it will reveal at least one fault in its application. This is so because the possible economical consequence of a fault could range from nil to catastrophic, and the value of a program often starts to diminish beyond a certain point in time. A test method is therefore of little value in practice if the faults it is capable of revealing are mostly inconsequential, or if the amount of time it takes to complete the test is excessive.

2 Code-Based Test-Case Selection Methods

We start by discussing a family of test methods that can be used to do debug testing, and the test cases are to be selected based on the information that can be extracted from the source code. In debug testing, as explained in Chapter 1, we want to maximize the probability that at least one fault will be revealed by the test. That is, if we use a test set of n elements, say, $T = \{t_1, t_2, \ldots, t_n\}$, we want to maximize the probability

$$
\begin{aligned}
p(\neg \mathrm{OK}(t_1) \vee \neg \mathrm{OK}(t_2) \vee \cdots \vee \neg \mathrm{OK}(t_n)) &= p((\exists t)_T(\neg \mathrm{OK}(t))) \\
&= p(\neg(\forall t)_T(\mathrm{OK}(t))) \\
&= 1 - p((\forall t)_T(\mathrm{OK}(t)))
\end{aligned}
$$

How do we go about constructing such a test set? We can do it incrementally by letting $T = \{t_1\}$ first. If there is any information available to find a test case that has a high probability of revealing a fault in the program, make it t_1. Otherwise, t_1 can be chosen arbitrarily from the input domain.

We then proceed to add another test case t_2 to T so that the probability of fault discovery is maximal. That probability can be expressed as

$$
\begin{aligned}
p(\neg \mathrm{OK}(t_1) \vee \neg \mathrm{OK}(t_2)) &= p(\neg(\mathrm{OK}(t_1) \wedge \mathrm{OK}(t_2))) \\
&= p(\neg(\mathrm{OK}(t_2) \wedge \mathrm{OK}(t_1))) \\
&= 1 - p(\mathrm{OK}(t_2) \wedge \mathrm{OK}(t_1)) \\
&= 1 - p(\mathrm{OK}(t_2) \mid \mathrm{OK}(t_1)) p(\mathrm{OK}(t_1))
\end{aligned}
$$

As explained in Chapter 1, this can be achieved by finding another test case, t_2, such that t_1 and t_2 are as loosely coupled as possible; that is, $\delta(t_1, t_2)$, the coupling coefficient between t_1 and t_2, is minimal. The value of $\delta(t_1, t_2)$ is a function of the degree of exclusiveness between the sequences of operations to be performed by the program in response to test cases t_1 and t_2.

Software Error Detection through Testing and Analysis, By J. C. Huang
Copyright © 2009 John Wiley & Sons, Inc.

Now if we proceed to find t_3, the third element for the test set, the fault discovery probability to maximize is

$$p(\neg OK(t_1) \vee \neg OK(t_2) \vee \neg OK(t_3))$$
$$= p(\neg(OK(t_1) \wedge OK(t_2) \wedge OK(t_3)))$$
$$= p(\neg(OK(t_3) \wedge OK(t_2) \wedge OK(t_1)))$$
$$= 1 - p(OK(t_3) \wedge OK(t_2) \wedge OK(t_1))$$
$$= 1 - p(OK(t_3) \mid OK(t_2) \wedge OK(t_1))p(OK(t_2) \wedge OK(t_1))$$

Again, this probability can be maximized by minimizing the conditional probability $p(OK(t_3) \mid OK(t_2) \wedge OK(t_1))$, that is, the probability that the program will execute correctly with t_3 given that the program executed correctly with t_1 and t_2. Obviously, this can be accomplished by selecting t_3 such that neither $OK(t_1)$ nor $OK(t_2)$ will have much, if any, impact on the probability $p(OK(t_3))$. That is, t_3 should be chosen such that both $\delta(t_1, t_3)$ and $\delta(t_2, t_3)$ are minimal.

This process can be repeated to add inputs to the test set. In general, to add a new element to the test set $T = \{t_1, t_2, \ldots, t_i\}$, the $(i + 1)$th test case t_{i+1} is to be selected to maximize the probability

$$p(\neg OK(t_1) \vee \cdots \vee \neg OK(t_i) \vee \neg OK(t_{i+1}))$$
$$= p(\neg(OK(t_1) \wedge \cdots \wedge OK(t_i) \wedge OK(t_{i+1})))$$
$$= p(\neg(OK(t_{i+1}) \wedge OK(t_i) \wedge \cdots \wedge OK(t_1)))$$
$$= 1 - p(OK(t_{i+1}) \wedge OK(t_i) \wedge \cdots \wedge OK(t_1))$$
$$= 1 - p(OK(t_{i+1}) \mid OK(t_i) \wedge \cdots \wedge OK(t_1))p(OK(t_i) \wedge \cdots \wedge OK(t_1))$$

This probability can be maximized by minimizing the conditional probability $p(OK(t_{i+1}) \mid OK(t_i) \wedge \cdots \wedge OK(t_1))$, that is, by selecting t_{i+1} in such a way that $\delta(t_1, t_{i+1}), \delta(t_2, t_{i+1}), \ldots, \delta(t_i, t_{i+1})$ are all minimal. In practice, there are several different ways to do this, each of which led to the development of a different test-case selection method, discussed in this and the following chapters.

In studying those methods, keep in mind that program testing is a very practical problem. As such, the value of a debug test method is predicated not only on its capability to reveal faults but also by the cost involved in using it. There are three components to the cost: the cost of finding test cases, the cost of performing test execution, and the cost of analyzing the test results. The number of test cases used has a direct impact on all three components. Therefore, we always strive to use as few test cases as possible. The amount of training and mental effort required to construct a test set is a major factor in determining the cost of test-set construction. Therefore, in developing a test method, whenever alternatives are available to accomplish a certain task, we invariably choose the one that is most cost-effective. In some studies, the cost of debug testing includes the cost of removing the faults detected as well. This is rightly so, because the main purpose of debug testing is to improve the reliability of a software system by detecting and removing latent faults in the system.

To facilitate understanding of the test-case selection methods discussed below, it is useful to think that every method for debug testing is developed as follows. First, a type of programming construct, such as a statement or branch predicate, is identified as the essential component of a program each component of which must be exercised during the test to reveal potential faults. Second, a test-case selection criterion is established to guide the construction of a test set. Third, an analysis method is devised to identify such constructs in a program and to select test cases from the input domain so that the resulting test set is reasonable in size and its elements are loosely coupled computationally. Those are the essential elements of every debug test method.

2.1   PATH TESTING

In path testing, the component to be exercised is the execution path. The test-case selection criterion is defined to select test cases such that every feasible execution path in the program will be traversed at least once during the test. Path testing is interesting in that every feasible execution path defines a subdomain in the input domain, and the resulting set of subdomains constitutes a partition of the input domain. That is, the intersection of any two subdomains is an empty set, and the union of all subdomains is the input domain. In other words, every input belongs to one and only one subdomain, and the subdomains are not overlapping.

If two test cases are selected from the same subdomain, they will be tightly coupled computationally because they will cause the program to test-execute along the same execution path and thus perform the same sequence of operations. On the other hand, if two test cases are selected from different subdomains of this sort, they will cause the program to test-execute along two different execution paths and thus perform different sequences of operations. Therefore, they will have a smaller coupling coefficient, as explained previously. Any subset of the input domain that contains one and only one element from each subdomain defined by the execution paths in the program will satisfy the test-case selection criterion, and the test cases will be loosely coupled.

Path testing is not practical, however, because almost all real-world programs contain loop constructs, and each loop construct often expands into a very large number of feasible execution paths. Besides, it is costly to identify all subdomains, find an input from each, and determine the corresponding correct output the program is supposed to produce. Despite its impracticality, we choose to discuss path testing first because all test-case selection methods discussed in the remainder of the chapter can be viewed as an approximation of path testing. Originally, these methods were developed independently based on a variety of ideas as to what is important in a program. The two test-case selection principles developed in Section 1.2 provide a unified conceptual framework based on which of these methods can be described as different instantiations of a generalized method—path testing. Instead of exercising all execution paths, which is impractical in general, only a sample of them will be exercised in these methods. Basically, these methods differ in the ways in which the paths are sampled. These methods are made more practical by reducing the number of test cases to be used, conceivably at the cost of inevitable reduction in the fault-discovery capabilities.

2.2 STATEMENT TESTING

In a *statement test* the program is to be tested to the extent that every executable statement in the program is exercised at least once during the test. The merit of a statement test can be explained simply as follows. In general, not every statement in the program is involved in a program execution. If a statement is faulty, and if it is not involved in a test execution, the fault will never be reflected in the test result. To increase the fault-discovery probability, therefore, we should use a test set that causes every statement in the program to be exercised at least once during the test. Consider the C++ program that follows.

Program 2.1

```
Main()
{
    float a, b, e, w, p, q, u, v;

    cin >> a >> b >> e;
    w = b - a;
    while (w > e) {
        p = a + w / 3;
        u = f(p);
        q = b - w / 3;
        v = f(q);
        if (u < v)
            a = p;
        else
            b = q;
        w = b - a;
    }
    max = (a + b) / 2;
    cout << max << endl;
}
```

To see the control structure of this program, it is useful to represent it with a directed graph, called a *program graph*, in which every edge is associated with a pair of the form $</\backslash C, S>$, where C is the condition under which that edge will be traversed and S is the sequence of statements that will be executed in the process.[1]

---

[1]This graphic representation scheme makes it possible to represent a program, or its execution paths, by using a regular expression over its edge symbols if only syntactic structure is of interest, or a regular expression over the pairs of the form $<C, S>$ if the computation performed by its execution paths is of interest. This cannot be achieved through the use of flowcharts.

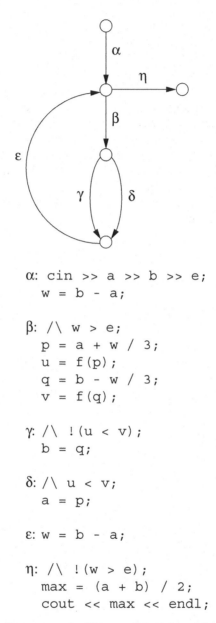

```
α: cin >> a >> b >> e;
   w = b - a;

β: /\ w > e;
   p = a + w / 3;
   u = f(p);
   q = b - w / 3;
   v = f(q);

γ: /\ !(u < v);
   b = q;

δ: /\ u < v;
   a = p;

ε: w = b - a;

η: /\ !(w > e);
   max = (a + b) / 2;
   cout << max << endl;
```

Figure 2.1 Program graph of Program 2.1. (Adapted from [HUAN75].)

The left component /\C may be omitted if C is always true. The program graph of Program 2.1 is shown in Figure 2.1. This program is designed to find the abscissa within the interval (a, b) at which a function f(x) assumes the maximum value. The basic strategy used is that given a continuous function that has a maximum in the interval (a, b), we can find the desired point on the x-axis by first dividing the interval

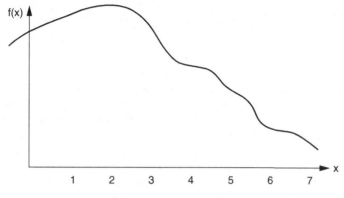

Figure 2.2   Function plot of $f(x)$.

into three equal parts. Then compare the values of the function at the dividing points $a + w/3$ and $b - w/3$, where w is the width of the interval being considered. If the value of the function at $a + w/3$ is less than that at $b - w/3$, the leftmost third of the interval is eliminated for further consideration; otherwise, the rightmost third is eliminated. This process is repeated until the width of the interval being considered becomes less than or equal to a predetermined small constant e. When that point is reached, the location at which the maximum of the function occurs can be taken as the center of the interval, $(a + b)/2$, with an error of less than $e/2$.

Now suppose that we wish to test this program for three different test cases, and assume that the function $f(x)$ can be plotted as shown in Figure 2.2. Let us first arbitrarily choose e to be equal to 0.1, and choose the interval (a, b) to be $(3, 4)$, $(5, 6)$, and $(7, 8)$. Now suppose that the values of max for all three cases are found to be correct in the test. What can we say about the design of this test?

Observe that if the values of function $f(x)$ are monotonously decreasing in all three intervals chosen, the value of u will always be greater than v, as we can see from the function plot. Consequently, the statement a=p in the program will never be executed during the test. Thus if this statement is for some reason written erroneously as, say, a=q or b=p, we will never be able to discover the fault in a test using the three test cases mentioned above. This is so simply because this particular statement is not "exercised" during the test. The point to be made here is that our chances of discovering faults through program testing can be improved significantly if we select the test cases in such a way that every statement will be executed at least once.

How do we construct a test set for statement testing? A simple answer to this question is to find, for each statement in a program, a test case that will cause that statement to be exercised during the test. In this way, each statement defines a subdomain (i.e., a subset of inputs that causes the statement to be exercised). Since an input that causes a statement to be exercised may cause other statements to be exercised also, the subdomains so defined are overlapping. Therefore, if we are to construct the test set simply by selecting one element from each such subdomain, the result may contain pairs of elements that are tightly coupled (i.e., causing the same sequence of operations to be performed, as explained elsewhere). This renders the test set less efficient in the sense that it takes more elements to achieve the same goal.

In practice, rarely can we afford to do a full statement test, simply because it requires too many test cases. Software development contracts that require statement testing often reduce the coverage requirement to 60% or less to make the cost of testing more acceptable. The tester is always under pressure to meet the test requirements by using as few test cases as possible. A minimal set of test cases can be constructed by finding a minimal set of execution paths that has the property that every statement is on some path in that set. Then find a test case to traverse each path therein. The test set so constructed will not only have a minimal number of elements but will also have loosely coupled elements (because different elements cause the program to traverse different execution paths), and therefore will be more compact and effective.

Another point to be made in this connection: Although the subdomains defined by the statements in a program are overlapping in nature, the elements of a required test set for statement testing need not be selected from overlapping subdomains, as suggested or implied in some literature (see, e.g., [FHLS98]).

What is described above is a proactive approach to test-case selection, meaning that we look actively for elements in the input domain that satisfy the selection criterion. It requires nontrivial analytical skill to do the analysis, and could be time consuming unless software tools are available to facilitate its applications. If the program to be tested is relatively small, the test-case designer may be able to find the majority of required test cases informally. Also, some test cases may be available from different sources, such as program designers or potential end users and there is no reason not to make good use of them. In that case, the only thing left to be done is to determine to what extent coverage has been achieved, and if the coverage is not complete, what additional test cases are needed to complete the task. The answer can readily be found by instrumenting the program with software counters at a number of strategic points in the program, as explained in Chapter 7. The software instruments not only provide accurate coverage information but also definitive clues about additional test cases needed to complete the task. This is important because in practice the tester has not only the responsibility to achieve the test coverage prescribed by the stakeholders but also to produce verifiable evidence that the coverage required has indeed been achieved. The software instruments do provide such evidence.

There is another way to determine if a particular statement in a program has been exercised during the test. Given a program, create a mutant of that program by altering one of its executable statements in some way. The program and the mutant are then test-executed with test cases. Unless the mutant is logically equivalent to the original program, it should produce a test result different from that of the original program when a test case causes the altered statement to be exercised during the test. Thus, to do the statement test, we can create a mutant with respect to every executable statement in the program, and then test the program together with all mutants until the program differentiates itself from all the mutants in the sense that it produces at least one test result different from that of every mutant.

Compared to the method of instrumenting the program with counters, it is advantageous, in that it will ask for additional test cases to reveal a fault if the program happens to be fortuitously correct with respect to the test case used. Unfortunately, its cost-effectiveness is dismal because in general it requires a huge number of test executions to complete a job. We discuss this topic in more detail in Section 2.7.

It must be emphasized here, however, that a statement test gives no assurance that the presence of a fault will definitely be reflected in the test result. This fact can be demonstrated using a simple example. For instance, if a statement in the program, say, x=x+y is somehow erroneously written as x=x-y, and if the test case used is such that it sets $y = 0$ prior to the execution of this statement, the test result certainly will not indicate the presence of this fault. This is so because although the statement is exercised during the test, the statement x=x-y is fortuitously correct at $y = 0$.

The inadequacy of testing a program only to the extent that every statement is executed at least once is actually more fundamental than what we described above. There is a class of common programming faults that cannot be discovered in this way. For instance, a C++ programmer may mistakenly write

```
if (B)
    s1;
    s2;
```

instead of

```
if (B) {
    s1;
    s2;
    }
```

In this case the program produces correct results as long as the input data cause B to be true when this program segment is entered. The requirement of having every statement executed at least once is satisfied trivially in this case by using a test case that makes B true. Obviously, the fault will not be revealed by such a test case.

The problem is that a program may contain paths from the entry to the exit (in its control flow) which need not be traversed in order to have every statement executed at least once. Since the present test requirement can be satisfied without having such paths traversed during the test, it is only natural that we will not be able to discover faults that occur on those paths.

2.3   BRANCH TESTING

A practical solution to the problem just mentioned is to require that every edge or branch (we use these two terms interchangeably throughout) in the program graph be traversed at least once during the test. In accordance with this new test requirement, we will have to use a new test case that makes B false, in addition to the one that satisfies B, in order to have every branch in the program graph traversed at least once.

Hence, our chances of discovering the fault will be greatly improved, because the program will probably produce an erroneous result for the test case that makes B false.

Observe that this new requirement of having every branch traversed at least once is more stringent than the earlier requirement of having every statement executed at least once. In fact, satisfaction of the new requirement implies satisfaction of the preceding one. This is so because every statement in the program is associated with some edge in the program graph. Thus, every statement has to be executed at least once in order to have every branch traversed at least once (provided that there is no inaccessible code in the program text). Satisfaction of the requirement stated previously, however, does not necessarily entail satisfaction of the new requirement. The question now is: How do we go about branch testing?

The main task is to find a test set that will cause all branches in the program to be traversed at least once during the test. To find such a set of test cases:

1. Find S, a minimal set of paths from the entries to the exits in the program graph such that every branch is on some path in S.
2. Find a path predicate for each path in S.
3. Find a set of assignments to the input variables each of which satisfies a path predicate obtained in step 2.

This set is the desired set of test cases.

In step 1 it is useful to construct the program graph and use the method described in Appendix A to find a regular expression describing all the paths between the entry and the exit of the program. Find a minimal subset of paths from that regular expression such that every edge symbol in the program graph occurs at least once in the regular-expression representation of that subset. A set of inputs that will cause every path in that subset to be traversed at least once is the desired set of test cases. It is entirely possible that some paths so chosen may turn out to be infeasible. In that case it is necessary to seek an alternative solution.

For example, consider Program 2.1. From its program graph shown in Figure 2.1, we can see that the set of all paths between the entry and the exit can be described by the regular expression $\alpha(\beta(\delta + \gamma)\varepsilon)^*\eta$. It contains subsets $\alpha\beta\delta\varepsilon\beta\gamma\varepsilon\eta$, $\alpha\beta\gamma\varepsilon\beta\delta\varepsilon\eta$, $(\alpha\beta\gamma\varepsilon\eta + \alpha\beta\delta\varepsilon\eta)$, and others that consist of all edge symbols. Any of these can be chosen as the subset of paths to be traversed if it represents a feasible path.

Just as in statement testing, test cases can be selected informally or obtained from other sources. Again, the program can be instrumented with software counters to monitor the coverage achieved as described in Chapter 7. All we need to do is to place a counter on every decision-to-decision path in the program. Examine the counter values after the test. If all are nonzero, it means that every branch in the program has been traversed at least once during the test. Otherwise, use the locations of the zero-count instruments as a guide to find additional test cases to complete the test.

2.4   HOWDEN'S AND McCABE'S METHODS

The branch test described above can be seen as a method for choosing a sample of execution paths to be exercised during the test. There are at least two other methods for selecting a sample of paths to be tested.

Boundary–Interior Method

The Howden method, called *boundary–interior testing* [HOWD75], is designed to circumvent the problem presented by a loop construct. A *boundary test* of a loop construct causes it to be entered but not iterated. An *interior test* causes a loop construct to be entered and iterated at least once. A boundary–interior test combines these two to reduce the number of paths that need to be traversed during the test. If an execution path is expressed in a regular expression, the path to be exercised in the boundary–interior test is described by replacing every occurrence of the form α^* with $\lambda + \alpha$, where λ is the identity under the operation of concatenation. The examples listed in Table 2.1 should clarify this definition.

In practice, the paths prescribed by this method may be infeasible because certain types of loop construct, such as a "for" loop in C++ and other programming languages, has to iterate a fixed number of times every time it is executed. Leave such a loop construct intact because it will not be expanded into many paths.

Semantically speaking, the significance of having a loop iterated zero and one times can be explained as follows. A loop construct is usually employed in the source code of a program to implement something that has to be defined recursively: for example, a set D of data whose membership can be defined recursively in the form

1. $d_0 \in D$.   (*initialization clause*)
2. If $d \in D$ and $P(d)$, then $f(d)$ is also an element of D.   (*inductive clause*)
3. Those and only those obtainable by a finite number of applications of clauses 1 and 2 are the elements of D.   (*extremal clause*)

Here P is some predicate and f is some function. In this typical recursive definition scheme, the initialization clause is used to prescribe what is known or given, and the inductive clause is used to specify how a new element can be generated from those given. (The extremal clause is understood and usually omitted.) Obviously, set D is defined correctly if the initialization and inductive clauses are stated correctly. When

TABLE 2.1   Examples

Paths in the Program	Paths to Be Traversed in the Test
ab^*c	$ac + abc$
$a(b + c)^*d$	$ad + abd + acd$
ab^*cd^*e	$ace + abce + acde + abcde$

D is used in a program, it will be implemented as a loop construct of the form

$$d := d_0;$$

while $P(d)$ **do begin** S; $d := f(d)$ **end**;

where S is a program segment designed to make use of the elements of the set.

Obviously, a test execution without entering the loop will exercise the initialization clause, and a test execution that iterates the loop only once will exercise the inductive clause. Therefore, we may say that boundary–interior testing is an abbreviated form of path testing. Instead of exercising all possible execution paths generated by a loop construct, it is designed to circumvent the problem by exercising only those paths that involve initialization clauses and inductive clauses of inductive definitions implemented in the source code.

McCabe's Method

The McCabe method is based on his complexity measure [MCCA76], which requires that at least a maximal set of linearly independent paths in the program be traversed during the test.

A graph is said to be *strongly connected* if there is a path from any node in the graph to any other node. It can be shown [BERG62] that in a strongly connected graph $G = < E, N >$, where E is the set of edges and N is the set of nodes in G, there can be as many as $v(G)$ elements in a set of linearly independent paths, where

$$v(G) = |E| - |N| + 1$$

The number $v(G)$, also known as *McCabe's cyclomatic number*, is a measure of program complexity [MCCA76].

Here we speak of a program graph with one entry and one exit. It has the property that every node can be reached from the entry, and every node can reach the exit. In general, it is not strongly connected but can be made so by adding an edge from the exit to the entry. For example, we can make the program graph in Figure 2.1 strongly connected by adding an edge μ (dashed line), as depicted in Figure 2.3. Since there are seven edges and five nodes in this graph, $v(G) = 7 - 5 + 1 = 3$ in this example. Note that for an ordinary program graph without that added edge, the formula for computing $v(G)$ should be

$$v(G) = |E| - |N| + 2$$

Next, for any path in G, we can associate it with a $1 \times |N|$ vector, where the element on the ith column is an integer equal to the number of times the ith edge is used in forming the path. Thus, if we arrange the edges in the graph above in the order $\alpha\beta\delta\varepsilon\gamma\mu\eta$, the vector representation of the path $\alpha\beta\gamma\varepsilon\eta$ is $<1\ 1\ 0\ 1\ 1\ 0\ 1>$ and that of $\beta\gamma\varepsilon\beta\gamma\varepsilon$ is $<0\ 2\ 0\ 2\ 2\ 0\ 0>$. We write $<\alpha\beta\gamma\varepsilon\eta> = <1\ 1\ 0\ 1\ 1\ 0\ 1>$ and $<\beta\gamma\varepsilon\beta\gamma\varepsilon> = <0\ 2\ 0\ 2\ 2\ 0\ 0>$.

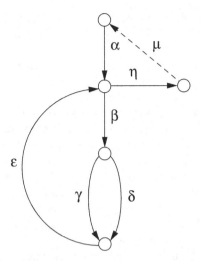

Figure 2.3 Augmented program graph.

A path is said to be a *linear combination* of others if its vector representation is equal to that formed by a linear combination of their vector representations. Thus, path $\beta\gamma\epsilon\eta$ is a linear combination of $\beta\gamma$ and $\epsilon\eta$ because

$$< \beta\gamma\epsilon\eta > = < \beta\gamma > + < \epsilon\eta >$$
$$= <0\ 1\ 0\ 0\ 1\ 0\ 0> + <0\ 0\ 0\ 1\ 0\ 0\ 1>$$
$$= <0\ 1\ 0\ 1\ 1\ 0\ 1>$$

and path $\alpha\eta$ is a linear combination of $\alpha\beta\delta\epsilon\eta$ and $\beta\delta\epsilon$ because

$$< \alpha\eta > = < \alpha\beta\delta\epsilon\eta > - < \beta\delta\epsilon >$$
$$= <1\ 1\ 1\ 1\ 0\ 0\ 1> - <0\ 1\ 1\ 1\ 0\ 0\ 0>$$
$$= <1\ 0\ 0\ 0\ 0\ 0\ 1>$$

A set of paths is said to be *linearly independent* if no path in the set is a linear combination of any other paths in the set. Thus, $\{\alpha\beta\delta\epsilon\eta, \alpha\beta\gamma\epsilon\eta, \alpha\eta\}$ is linearly independent but $\{\alpha\beta\delta\epsilon\eta, \alpha\beta\delta\epsilon\beta\delta\epsilon\eta, \alpha\eta\}$ is not (because $<\alpha\beta\delta\epsilon\eta> + <\alpha\beta\delta\epsilon\eta> - <\alpha\beta\delta\epsilon\beta\delta\epsilon\eta> = <\alpha\eta>$).

A *basis set* of paths is a maximal set of linearly independent paths. In graph G given above, since $v(G) = 3$, $\{\alpha\beta\delta\epsilon\eta, \alpha\beta\gamma\epsilon\eta, \alpha\eta\}$ constitutes a basis set of paths. That is to say, in McCabe's method, three paths, denoted by $\alpha\beta\delta\epsilon\eta$, $\alpha\beta\gamma\epsilon\eta$, and $\alpha\eta$, must be exercised during the test.

The merit of exercising linearly independent paths in a program can be explained readily in the conceptual framework of this book. According to the definition given above, two paths in a program graph are linearly independent if they have little in common structurally, which means that the operations to be performed along these two paths will have little in common. Now, if t_1 and t_2 are the inputs that cause these two paths to be traversed, it implies that the distance between t_1 and t_2 [i.e., $\delta(t_1, t_2) = p(\text{OK}(t_2) \mid \text{OK}(t_1)) - p(\text{OK}(t_2))$ as defined in Section 1.1] would be greater than if the two paths are not linearly independent. The test cases in a basis set are therefore as loosely coupled as possible as far as can be determined by their dependencies. Thus, to test a program with a basis set is to exercise a finite subset of execution paths in the program that yield a maximal probability of fault discovery.

To construct such a test set, we need to construct a set of linearly independent paths first. We can start by putting any path in the set. We then add to this set another path that is linearly independent of the existing paths in the set. According to graph theory, we will have to terminate this process when the number of paths in the set is equal to McCabe's cyclomatic number because we will not be able to find an additional path that is linearly independent of the existing paths. We then find an input for each path in the set. The result is the test set desired.

Note that although $v(G)$ is fixed by the graph structure, the membership of a basis set is not unique. For example, $\{\alpha\beta\delta\varepsilon\eta, \alpha\beta\delta\varepsilon\beta\gamma\varepsilon\eta, \alpha\eta\}$ is also a basis set in G. That is, in McCabe's method, the set of paths to be traversed is not unique. The set of paths to be traversed can be $\{\alpha\beta\delta\varepsilon\eta, \alpha\beta\delta\varepsilon\beta\gamma\varepsilon\eta, \alpha\eta\}$ instead of $\{\alpha\beta\delta\varepsilon\eta, \alpha\beta\gamma\varepsilon\eta, \alpha\eta\}$, mentioned previously.

It is interesting to observe that $v(G)$ has the following properties:

1. $v(G) \geq 1$.
2. $v(G)$ is the maximum number of linearly independent paths in G, and it is the number of execution paths to be traversed during the test.
3. Inserting or deleting a node with an outdegree of 1 does not affect $v(G)$.
4. G has only one path if $v(G) = 1$.
5. Inserting a new edge in G increases $v(G)$ by 1.
6. $v(G)$ depends only on the branching structure of the program represented by G.

2.5 DATA-FLOW TESTING

Data-flow testing [LAKO83, GUGU02] is also an approximation of path testing. The *component* that will be exercised during the test is a segment of feasible execution path that starts from the point where a variable is defined and ends at the point where that definition is used. It is important to exercise such segments of execution paths because each is designed to compute some subfunction of the function implemented by the program. If such a segment occurs in more than one execution path, only one of them needs to be exercised during the test.

For the purpose of this discussion, the concept of data-flow analysis can be explained simply as follows. When a program is being executed, its component, such as a statement, will act on the data or variables involved in three different ways: define, use (reference), or undefine. Furthermore, if a variable is used in a branch predicate, we say it is *p-used*; and if it is used in a statement that computes, we say it is *c-used*.

To clarify the idea, let us consider Program 2.2. In this program, variables x and y are defined on line 2, variable z is defined on line 3, variable y is p-used on lines 4 and 5, variable x is c-used on line 6 while variable z is c-used first and then defined, variable y is c-used and then defined on line 7, variable x is c-used and then defined on line 8, and finally, variable z is c-used on line 9.

Program 2.2

```
     main()
     {
1    int x, y, z;

2    cin >> x >> y;
3    z = 1;
4    while (y != 0) {
5    if (y % 2 == 1)
6        z = z * x;
7    y = y / 2;
8    x = x * x;
     }
9    cout << z << endl;
     }
```

This program computes x^y by a binary decomposition of y for the integer $y = 0$, where x and y are both integers. It can be represented conveniently by the directed graph shown in Figure 2.4, in which every edge is associated with a branch predicate followed by a sequence of one or more statements. The program graph represents the control flow of the program. A branch in the graph will be traversed if the branch predicate is evaluated as being true when the control reaches the beginning node of that edge.

A path in the program graph can be described by a string of edge symbols, such as $\alpha\beta\delta\varepsilon\eta$ or $\alpha\beta\gamma\varepsilon\eta$ for short, or sequences of predicates and statements associated with the edges, such as

```
αβδεη:    cin >> x >> y;
          z = 1;
          /\ y != 0;
          /\ y % 2 == 1;
          z = z * x;
          y = y / 2;
          x = x * x;
          /\ !(y != 0);
          cout << z << endl;
```

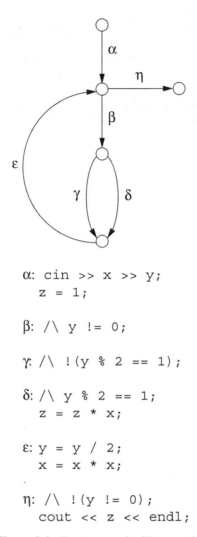

α: `cin >> x >> y;`
  `z = 1;`

β: `/\ y != 0;`

γ: `/\ !(y % 2 == 1);`

δ: `/\ y % 2 == 1;`
  `z = z * x;`

ε: `y = y / 2;`
  `x = x * x;`

η: `/\ !(y != 0);`
  `cout << z << endl;`

Figure 2.4 Program graph of Program 2.2.

and

αβγεη: `cin >> x >> y;`
         `z = 1;`
         `/\ y != 0;`
         `/\ !(y % 2 == 1);`
         `y = y / 2;`
         `x = x * x;`
         `/\ !(y != 0);`
         `cout << z << endl;`

These sequences of branch predicates and statements, called *symbolic traces*, are useful in describing the execution paths of a program. They show not only how the control flow will traverse the program but also what will be done in the process.

A path in a program graph is said to be *definition-clear* with respect to a variable, say x, if it begins at a point where x is defined and contains no statement that causes x to be undefined or redefined. For instance, the execution path between lines 2 and 5 in the following symbolic trace is definition-clear for variable z, and the path between lines 1 and 5 is definition-clear for variable x. Since for our purposes there is no need to be so precise as using the line numbers to indicate the beginning and end of a segment, it suffices to say that path $\alpha\beta\delta$ is definition-clear for both variables x and z. The path between lines 5 and 9 (i.e., path $\delta\varepsilon\eta$) is definition-clear for variable z.

$\alpha\beta\delta\varepsilon\eta$:

```
1    cin >> x >> y;
2    z = 1;
3    /\ y != 0;
4    /\ y % 2 == 1;
5    z = z * x;
6    y = y / 2;
7    x = x * x;
8    /\ !(y != 0);
9    cout << z << endl;
```

A path is *loop-free* if every edge on the path occurs only once. For example, path $\alpha\beta\delta\varepsilon\eta$ is loop-free, but the paths $\alpha\beta\delta\varepsilon\beta\delta\varepsilon\eta$ and $\alpha\beta\delta\varepsilon\beta\gamma\varepsilon\eta$ are not.

A *simple path* is a path in which at most one node occurs twice (if the path is described in terms of nodes) or at most one edge occurs twice (if the path is described in terms of edges). Roughly speaking, a simple path in a program is a path that either does not form a loop, or if it does, it iterates the loop only once and then ends upon exit from the loop. Thus, paths $\alpha\beta\delta\varepsilon\eta$ and $\alpha\beta\delta\varepsilon\beta$ are both simple paths, whereas $\alpha\beta\delta\varepsilon\beta\delta$ is not.

A *du path* of a variable, say x, is a simple path that is definition-clear with respect to x. For example, on path $\alpha\beta\delta\varepsilon\eta$ the paths formed by lines 12345 and 7345 are du paths with respect to variable x, and the paths formed by lines 2345 and 567345 are du paths with respect to variable z.

The definitions, uses, and du paths that exist in Program 2.2 are summarized in Table 2.2. Note that $\alpha\beta\gamma\varepsilon\eta$ is also a du path for variable z defined in α, but is omitted because it represents an infeasible execution path. Now we are ready to enumerate a number of test-case selection criteria that can be formulated based on the data flow in a program.

All-du-Path Testing

All-du-path testing requires that every du path from every definition of every variable in the program to every use of that definition be traversed at least once during the test. The rationale behind this requirement is that some meaningful computation must have

TABLE 2.2   Variables in Program 2.2 and Their Data-Flow Attributes

Variable	Defined in:	p-Used in:	c-Used in:	du Paths:
x	α		δ, ε	$\alpha\beta\delta, \alpha\beta\delta\varepsilon, \alpha\beta\gamma\varepsilon$
	ε		δ, ε	$\varepsilon\beta\delta, \varepsilon\beta\gamma\varepsilon$
y	α	$\beta, \gamma, \delta, \eta$	ε	$\alpha\beta, \alpha\beta\gamma, \alpha\beta\delta, \alpha\eta, \alpha\beta\delta\varepsilon, \alpha\beta\gamma\varepsilon$
	ε	$\beta, \gamma, \delta, \eta$	ε	$\varepsilon\beta, \varepsilon\beta\gamma, \varepsilon\beta\delta, \varepsilon\eta, \varepsilon\beta\delta\varepsilon, \varepsilon\beta\gamma\varepsilon$
z	α		δ, η	$\alpha\beta\delta, \sout{\alpha\beta\gamma\varepsilon\eta}$
	δ		δ, η	$\delta\varepsilon\beta\delta, \delta\varepsilon\eta$

been performed in the interim, the correctness of which can be tested by exercising that path segment in the test.

To do an all-du-path test for Program 2.2, therefore, is to find a small set of test cases that would traverse paths that include all path segments listed in the rightmost column of Table 2.2. It is obvious that those path segments would be included in some paths generated by iterating the loop in Program 2.2 zero, one, and two times, consisting of paths $\alpha\eta$, $\alpha\beta\delta\varepsilon\eta$, $\alpha\beta\gamma\varepsilon\eta$, $\alpha\beta\delta\varepsilon\beta\delta\varepsilon\eta$, $\alpha\beta\delta\varepsilon\beta\gamma\varepsilon\eta$, $\alpha\beta\gamma\varepsilon\beta\delta\varepsilon\eta$, and $\alpha\beta\delta\varepsilon\beta\gamma\varepsilon\eta$. These are syntactic paths, meaning that they exit based on a syntactic analysis of the program. In general, not all of them are semantically feasible. We can verify their feasibility by analyzing their symbolic traces as shown in Section 5.3. The analysis therein shows that paths $\alpha\beta\gamma\varepsilon\eta$, $\alpha\beta\gamma\varepsilon\beta\gamma\varepsilon\eta$, and $\alpha\beta\delta\varepsilon\beta\gamma\varepsilon\eta$ are infeasible. Therefore, only the remaining paths $\alpha\eta$, $\alpha\beta\delta\varepsilon\eta$, $\alpha\beta\delta\varepsilon\beta\delta\varepsilon\eta$, and $\alpha\beta\gamma\varepsilon\beta\delta\varepsilon\eta$ could be used as candidate paths for test-case selection.

To minimize the effort in selecting the execution paths to be traversed, we can consolidate the requirements prescribed by the rightmost column of Table 2.2 by dropping all path segments that are a subpath of another. For example, we can drop subpath $\beta\delta$ if $\alpha\beta\delta\varepsilon$ is already a member because traversal of the latter implies traversal of the former. We then proceed to construct a table with one row for each path segment that needs to be exercised and one column for each candidate execution path, as illustrated in Table 2.3. A check mark indicates that the path segment listed in the row heading is covered (i.e., is a subpath of) the candidate execution path listed in the column heading.

TABLE 2.3   Path Matrix for Table 2.2 Showing the Covering Execution Paths

	$\alpha\eta$	$\alpha\beta\delta\varepsilon\eta$	$\alpha\beta\delta\varepsilon\beta\delta\varepsilon\eta$	$\alpha\beta\gamma\varepsilon\beta\delta\varepsilon\eta$
$\alpha\beta\delta\varepsilon$		$\checkmark$	$\checkmark$	
$\alpha\beta\gamma\varepsilon$				$\checkmark$
$\varepsilon\beta\delta\varepsilon$			$\checkmark$	$\checkmark$
$\varepsilon\beta\gamma\varepsilon$				
$\alpha\eta$	$\checkmark$			
$\varepsilon\eta$		$\checkmark$	$\checkmark$	$\checkmark$
$\delta\varepsilon\beta\delta$			$\checkmark$	
$\delta\varepsilon\eta$		$\checkmark$	$\checkmark$	$\checkmark$

TABLE 2.4   Expanded Version of Table 2.3

	αη	αβδεη	αβδεβδεη	αβγεβδεη	αβδεβγεβδεη
αβδε		√	√		
αβγε				√	
εβδε			√	√	
εβγε					√
αη	√				
εη		√	√	√	
δεβδ			√		
δεη		√	√	√	

We shall henceforth refer to Table 2.3 simply as a *path matrix*. This matrix indicates that the du path $\varepsilon\beta\gamma\varepsilon$ will not be covered by any candidate execution paths that we have chosen. An additional feasible execution path has to be chosen to cover this segment. As shown in Section 5.3, the path $\alpha\beta\delta\varepsilon\beta\gamma\varepsilon\beta\delta\varepsilon\eta$ turns out to be a feasible execution path that contains $\varepsilon\beta\gamma\varepsilon$ as a subpath. Thus, we expand the path matrix to become Table 2.4.

Any candidate test-execution path is said to be *indispensable* if its removal from the matrix will leave some path segment uncovered. Obviously, every candidate path in Table 2.4 is indispensable. Indispensable candidate paths are the paths that must be exercised during the test. To do a du-path test for Program 2.2, therefore, is to test-execute the program along the paths listed in Table 2.4, which can be achieved by choosing y to be 0, 1, 2, 3, and 5, together with any normal value for x, as the test cases. To be more precise, a possible test set would be $T = \{<x, 0>, <x, 1>, <x, 2>, <x, 3>, <x, 5>\}$ for any valid integer x.

All-Use Testing

All-use testing requires that at least one definition-clear path from every definition of every variable to every use of that definition be traversed during the test. Clearly, it is a watered-down version of all-du-path testing because the requirement of "all" paths is now replaced by "at least one." We can use the same technique to find the execution paths that need to be exercised. For ease of comparison, the same table will be used to find the path segments that need to be exercised. Since the requirement is less stringent, the change will be indicated by crossing out the path segments no longer needed, as shown in Table 2.5. Remember that the solution is not unique. For example, the path segment crossed out in Table 2.5 could be $\alpha\beta\delta\varepsilon$ instead.

Next, we map the data in Table 2.5 into a path matrix to yield Table 2.6. Note that a test path is no longer needed, and the path segments covered by $\alpha\beta\delta\varepsilon\eta$ will be covered by $\alpha\beta\delta\varepsilon\beta\delta\varepsilon\eta$ and $\alpha\beta\gamma\varepsilon\beta\delta\varepsilon\eta$. Table 2.6 shows that only three paths need to be exercised in an all-use test, and it can be done by using the test set $T = \{<x, 0>, <x, 2>, <x, 3>\}$, where x can be any valid integer.

TABLE 2.5   Table 2.2 Revised for All-Use Testing

Variable	Defined in:	p-Used in:	c-Used in:	du Paths:
x	α		δ, ε	$\alpha\beta\delta, \alpha\beta\delta\varepsilon$, ~~$\alpha\beta\gamma\varepsilon$~~
	ε		δ, ε	$\varepsilon\beta\delta, \varepsilon\beta\gamma\varepsilon$
y	α	$\beta, \gamma, \delta, \eta$	ε	$\alpha\beta, \alpha\beta\gamma, \alpha\beta\delta, \alpha\eta, \alpha\beta\delta\varepsilon$, ~~$\alpha\beta\gamma\varepsilon$~~
	ε	$\beta, \gamma, \delta, \eta$	ε	$\varepsilon\beta, \varepsilon\beta\gamma, \varepsilon\beta\delta, \varepsilon\eta, \varepsilon\beta\delta\varepsilon$, ~~$\varepsilon\beta\gamma\varepsilon$~~
z	α		δ, η	$\alpha\beta\delta$
	δ		δ, η	$\delta\varepsilon\beta\delta, \delta\varepsilon\eta$

TABLE 2.6   Path Matrix for Table 2.5 Showing the Covering Execution Paths

	$\alpha\eta$	~~$\alpha\beta\delta\varepsilon\eta$~~	$\alpha\beta\delta\varepsilon\beta\delta\eta$	$\alpha\beta\gamma\varepsilon\beta\delta\eta$	~~$\alpha\beta\gamma\varepsilon\beta\delta\eta$~~
$\alpha\beta\delta\varepsilon$		$\checkmark$	$\checkmark$		
~~$\alpha\beta\gamma\varepsilon$~~					
$\varepsilon\beta\delta\varepsilon$			$\checkmark$	$\checkmark$	
~~$\varepsilon\beta\gamma\varepsilon$~~					
$\alpha\eta$	$\checkmark$				
$\varepsilon\eta$		$\checkmark$	$\checkmark$	$\checkmark$	
$\delta\varepsilon\beta\delta$			$\checkmark$		
$\delta\varepsilon\eta$		$\checkmark$	$\checkmark$	$\checkmark$	

All-p-Use/Some-c-Use Testing

All-p-use/some-c-use testing requires that at least one definition-clear path from every definition of every variable to every p-use (i.e., the definition is used in a predicate) of that definition be traversed during the test. If there is no p-use of that definition, replace "every p-use" in the sentence above with "at least one c-use" (i.e., the definition is used in a computation). The longest path segments in the rightmost column become shorter (Table 2.7). Thus, we reconstruct the path matrix to yield Table 2.8. Table 2.8 shows that only three paths, $\alpha\eta$, $\alpha\beta\gamma\varepsilon\beta\delta\eta$, and $\alpha\beta\delta\varepsilon\beta\gamma\varepsilon\beta\delta\eta$, need be traversed to exercise all the path segments listed in the rightmost column of Table 2.7. That can be achieved by using test set $T = \{<x, 0>, <x, 2>, <x, 5>\}$.

All-c-Use/Some-p-Use Testing

All-c-use/some-p-use testing requires that at least one definition-clear path from every definition of every variable to every c-use of that definition be traversed during the test. If there is no c-use of that definition, replace "every c-use" in the sentence above with "at least one p-use." In the present example, the path segments that need to be exercised are identified in the rightmost column of Table 2.9. The path matrix of Table 2.10 shows that all path segments can be covered by three execution paths, $\alpha\beta\delta\varepsilon\beta\delta\eta$, $\alpha\beta\gamma\varepsilon\beta\delta\eta$, and $\alpha\beta\delta\varepsilon\beta\gamma\varepsilon\beta\delta\eta$. To do an all-c-use/some-p-use, therefore, is to use a test set $\{<x, 2>, <x, 3>, <x, 5>\}$ to traverse these paths during the test.

TABLE 2.7   Table 2.2 Revised for All-p-Use/Some-c-Use Testing

Variable	Defined in:	p-Used in:	c-Used in:	du Paths:
x	α		δ, ~~ε~~	$\alpha\beta\delta$, ~~$\alpha\beta\gamma\varepsilon$~~
	ε		δ, ~~ε~~	$\varepsilon\beta\delta$, ~~$\varepsilon\beta\gamma\varepsilon$~~
y	α	$\beta, \gamma, \delta, \eta$	~~ε~~	$\alpha\beta$, $\alpha\beta\gamma$, $\alpha\beta\delta$, $\alpha\eta$, ~~$\alpha\beta\delta\varepsilon$~~, ~~$\alpha\beta\gamma\varepsilon$~~
	ε	$\beta, \gamma, \delta, \eta$	~~ε~~	$\varepsilon\beta$, $\varepsilon\beta\gamma$, $\varepsilon\beta\delta$, $\varepsilon\eta$, ~~$\varepsilon\beta\delta\varepsilon$~~, ~~$\varepsilon\beta\gamma\varepsilon$~~
z	α		δ, ~~η~~	$\alpha\beta\delta$
	δ		~~δ~~, η	~~$\delta\varepsilon\beta\delta$~~, $\delta\varepsilon\eta$

TABLE 2.8   Path Matrix for Table 2.7 Showing the Covering Execution Paths

	$\alpha\eta$	$\alpha\beta\delta\varepsilon\eta$	$\alpha\beta\delta\varepsilon\beta\delta\varepsilon\eta$	$\alpha\beta\gamma\varepsilon\beta\delta\varepsilon\eta$	$\alpha\beta\delta\varepsilon\beta\gamma\varepsilon\beta\delta\varepsilon\eta$
$\alpha\beta\delta$		√	√		√
$\alpha\beta\gamma$				√	
$\varepsilon\beta\delta$			√	√	√
$\varepsilon\beta\gamma$					√
$\alpha\eta$	√				
$\varepsilon\eta$		√	√	√	√
$\delta\varepsilon\eta$		√	√	√	√

TABLE 2.9   Table 2.2 Revised for All-c-Use/Some-p-Use Testing

Variable	Defined in:	p-Used in:	c-Used in:	du Paths:
x	α		δ, ε	$\alpha\beta\delta$, $\alpha\beta\delta\varepsilon$, $\alpha\beta\gamma\varepsilon$
	ε		δ, ε	$\varepsilon\beta\delta$, $\varepsilon\beta\gamma\varepsilon$, $\varepsilon\beta\delta\varepsilon$
y	α	$\beta, \gamma, \delta, \eta$	ε	~~$\alpha\beta$, $\alpha\beta\gamma$, $\alpha\beta\delta$, $\alpha\eta$,~~ $\alpha\beta\delta\varepsilon$, $\alpha\beta\gamma\varepsilon$
	ε	$\beta, \gamma, \delta, \eta$	ε	~~$\varepsilon\beta$, $\varepsilon\beta\gamma$, $\varepsilon\beta\delta$, $\varepsilon\eta$,~~ $\varepsilon\beta\delta\varepsilon$, $\varepsilon\beta\gamma\varepsilon$
z	α		δ, η	$\alpha\beta\delta$
	δ		δ, η	$\delta\varepsilon\beta\delta$, $\delta\varepsilon\eta$

TABLE 2.10   Path Matrix for Table 2.9 Showing the Covering Execution Paths

	$\alpha\beta\delta\varepsilon\eta$	$\alpha\beta\delta\varepsilon\beta\delta\varepsilon\eta$	$\alpha\beta\gamma\varepsilon\beta\delta\varepsilon\eta$	$\alpha\beta\delta\varepsilon\beta\gamma\varepsilon\beta\delta\varepsilon\eta$
$\alpha\beta\delta\varepsilon$	√	√		√
$\alpha\beta\gamma\varepsilon$			√	
$\varepsilon\beta\delta\varepsilon$		√	√	√
$\varepsilon\beta\gamma\varepsilon$				√
$\delta\varepsilon\beta\delta$		√		
$\delta\varepsilon\eta$	√	√	√	√

TABLE 2.11   Table 2.2 Revised for All-Definition Testing

Variable	Defined in:	p-Used in:	c-Used in:	du Paths:
x	α		δ, ε	$\alpha\beta\delta$, ~~$\alpha\beta\delta\varepsilon$~~, ~~$\alpha\beta\gamma\varepsilon$~~
	ε		δ, ε	$\varepsilon\beta\delta$, ~~$\varepsilon\beta\gamma\varepsilon$~~
y	α	$\beta, \gamma, \delta, \eta$	ε	$\alpha\beta$, ~~$\alpha\beta\gamma$~~, ~~$\alpha\beta\delta$~~, ~~$\alpha\eta$~~, ~~$\alpha\beta\delta\varepsilon$~~, ~~$\alpha\beta\gamma\varepsilon$~~
	ε	$\beta, \gamma, \delta, \eta$	ε	$\varepsilon\beta$, ~~$\varepsilon\beta\gamma$~~, ~~$\varepsilon\beta\delta$~~, ~~$\varepsilon\eta$~~, ~~$\varepsilon\beta\delta\varepsilon$~~, ~~$\varepsilon\beta\gamma\varepsilon$~~
z	α		δ, η	$\alpha\beta\delta$
	δ		δ, η	$\delta\varepsilon\beta\delta$, ~~$\delta\varepsilon\eta$~~

TABLE 2.12   Path Matrix for Table 2.11 Showing the Covering Execution Paths

	$\alpha\beta\delta\varepsilon\eta$	$\alpha\beta\delta\varepsilon\beta\delta\varepsilon\eta$	$\alpha\beta\gamma\varepsilon\beta\delta\varepsilon\eta$
$\alpha\beta\delta$	$\checkmark$	$\checkmark$	
$\varepsilon\beta\delta$		$\checkmark$	$\checkmark$
$\delta\varepsilon\beta\delta$		$\checkmark$	

All-Definition Testing

All definition testing requires that for every definition of every variable in the program, at least one du path emanating from that definition be traversed at least once during the test. This requirement allows us to modify Table 2.2 as shown in Table 2.11. The du paths in Table 2.11 can be translated into the path matrix shown in Table 2.12, which shows that an all-definition test can be done by traversing just one path, $\alpha\beta\delta\varepsilon\beta\delta\varepsilon\eta$, which can be done by test-executing the program with $<x, 3>$, x being any valid integer.

All-p-Use Testing

The requirement of all-p-use testing is derived from the all p-use/some c-use by dropping the "some c-use" requirement. Table 2.13 is obtained by making all necessary modifications to the rightmost column of Table 2.2. Based on Table 2.13, we construct the path matrix shown in Table 2.14. Table 2.14 shows that all path segments in the rightmost column of Table 2.13 can be exercised by traversing three paths: $\alpha\eta$, $\alpha\beta\gamma\varepsilon\beta\delta\varepsilon\eta$, and $\alpha\beta\delta\varepsilon\beta\gamma\varepsilon\beta\delta\varepsilon\eta$. That can be accomplished by using three test cases: $<x, 1>$, $<x, 2>$, and $<x, 5>$.

All-c-Use Testing

The criterion of all-c-use testing is derived from that of the all c-use/some p-use by dropping the "some-p-use" requirement. This criterion transforms Table 2.2 into Table 2.15. The rightmost column of Table 2.15 could be exercised by a number of execution paths as shown in Table 2.16, which shows that paths $\alpha\beta\delta\varepsilon\beta\delta\varepsilon\eta$, $\alpha\beta\gamma\varepsilon\beta\delta\varepsilon\eta$, and $\alpha\beta\delta\varepsilon\beta\gamma\varepsilon\beta\delta\varepsilon\eta$ are essential and are sufficient to cover the rest

TABLE 2.13   Table 2.2 Revised for All-p-Use Testing

Variable	Defined in:	p-Used in:	c-Used in:	du Paths:
x	α		δ, ε	~~αβδ, αβδε, αβγε~~
	ε		δ, ε	~~εβδ, εβγε~~
y	α	β, γ, δ, η	ε	αβ, αβγ, αβδ, αη, ~~αβδε, αβγε~~
	ε	β, γ, δ, η	ε	εβ, εβγ, εβδ, εη, ~~εβδε, εβγε~~
z	α		δ, η	~~αβδ~~
	δ		δ, η	~~δεβδ, δεη~~

TABLE 2.14   Path Matrix for Table 2.13 Showing the Covering Execution Paths

	αη	αβδεη	αβδεβδεη	αβγεβδεη	αβδεβγεβδεη
αβδ		√	√		√
αβγ				√	
εβδ			√	√	√
εβγ					√
αη	√				
εη		√	√	√	√
δεη		√	√	√	√

TABLE 2.15   Table 2.2 Revised for All-c-Use Testing

Variable	Defined in:	p-Used in:	c-Used in:	du Paths:
x	α		δ, ε	αβδ, αβδε, αβγε
	ε		δ, ε	εβδ, εβγε
y	α	β, γ, δ, η	ε	~~αβ, αβγ, αβδ, αη, αβδε, αβγε~~
	ε	β, γ, δ, η	ε	~~εβ, εβγ, εβδ, εη, εβδε, εβγε~~
z	α		δ, η	~~αβδ~~
	δ		δ, η	δεβδ, δεη

TABLE 2.16   Path Matrix for Table 2.15 Showing the Covering Execution Paths

	αβδεη	αβδεβδεη	αβγεβδεη	αβδεβγεβδεη
αβδε	√	√		√
αβγε			√	
εβδε		√	√	
εβγε				√
δεβδ		√		
δεη	√	√	√	

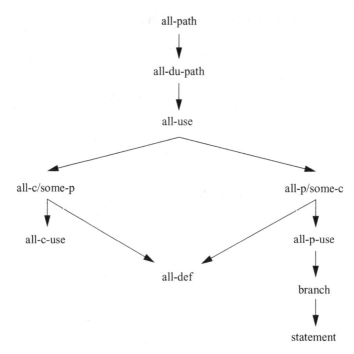

Figure 2.5   Coverage relation among test-case selection criteria.

of the path segments in the rightmost column of Table 2.15. Hence, the test cases required are $<x, 2>$, $<x, 3>$, and $<x, 5>$.

It is interesting to observe that the data-flow testing criteria discussed above are related in some way. In fact, they are related by the coverage relation mentioned elsewhere. One test-case selection criterion is said to cover another if satisfaction of that criterion implies that of the other. Figure 2.5 shows the coverage relationship among test-case selection criteria based on data flow and the structure of the source code [FRWE88].

2.6   DOMAIN-STRATEGY TESTING

Recall that in the branch testing the components to be exercised during the test are the branch predicates found in the source code, which define the line segments that form the borders of subdomains created by the program. We select a test case arbitrarily from each side of the border to see if the functions defined on the two adjacent subdomains are computed correctly.

In this section we show that for each branch predicate, a trio of test cases, located on or near the borderline it defines, can be chosen to test if the borderline is implemented correctly by the program. The method, as it is outlined here, will work only if the predicate is linear, representing a straight line in n-dimensional space.

This method, known as *domain-strategy testing* [WHCO80], is designed to detect domain faults. It is based on geometrical analysis of the domain boundary defined by the source code, exploiting the fact that points on or near the border are most sensitive to domain faults. The method works only if the program has the following properties:

1. The program contains only simple linear predicates of the form $a1v1 + a2v2 + \cdots + akvk$ ROP C, where the v_i's are variables, the ai's and C are constants, and ROP is a relational operator.
2. The path predicate of every path in the program is composed of a conjunction of such simple linear predicates.
3. Coincidental (fortuitous) correctness of the program will not occur for any test case.
4. The path corresponding to each adjacent domain computes a different subfunction.
5. Functions defined in two adjacent subdomains yield different values for the same test point near the border.
6. Any border defined by the program is linear, and if it is incorrect, the correct border is also linear.
7. The input space is continuous rather than discrete.

The essence of domain-boundary geometrical analysis to be performed in test-case selection can be stated as follows. For simplicity, we use examples in two-dimensional space to illustrate the idea involved.

- Each border is a line segment in a k-dimensional space, which can be open or closed, depending on the type of relational operator used in the predicate.
- A *closed border segment* of a domain is actually part of that domain and is formed by a predicate consisting of a $\geq$, $=$, or $\leq$ relational operator.
- An *open border segment* of a domain forms part of the domain boundary but does not constitute part of that domain and is formed by using a $<$, $>$, or $\neq$ relational operator.

For example, let domain A in a two-dimensional space be defined by the predicate $x \geq 1$, and let the domain immediately adjacent to it on the left be domain B. Domain B is defined by the predicate $x < 1$. The straight line described by $x = 1$ is the border of these two domains. The line $x = 1$ is a closed border and a part of domain A. To domain B, however, it is an open border and is not part of that domain. The test points (cases) selected will be of two types, defined by their relative position with respect to the given border. An *on test point* lies on the given border, while an *off test point* is a small distance ε from, and lies on the open side of, the given border.

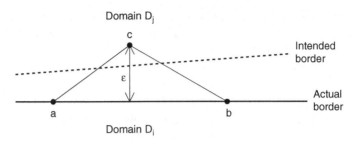

Figure 2.6 Test points for a border.

Continuing the example given above, let ε be 0.01. Then with respect to a border defined by the predicate $x = 1$, test points such as <1.00, 2.00> or <1.00, 3.14> would be candidates for *on* test points, and <0.99, 2.14> or <0.99, −4.11> would be that for *off* test points. When testing a closed border of a domain, the *on* test points are in the domain being tested, and each *off* test point is in an adjacent domain. When testing an open border, each *on* test point is in an adjacent domain, while the *off* test points are in the domain being tested.

This is indeed the case in the earlier example. In testing domain B with open border $x = 1$, the *on* points, such as <1.00, 2.00> and <1.00, 3.14>, will be in domain A, and the *off* points, such as <0.99, 2.14> and <0.99, −4.11>, will be in domain B itself. Three test points will be selected for each border segment in an on–off–on sequence, as depicted in Figure 2.6.

The test will be successful if test points a and b are computed by the subfunction defined for domain D_i, and test point c is computed by the subfunction defined for the neighboring domain D_j. This will be the case if the correct border is a line that intersects line segments ac and bc at any point except c. To verify that the actual border is identical to the border intended, we need to select test point c in such a way that its distance from the given border is ε, an arbitrarily small number.

The strategy is reliable for all three types of domain faults depicted in Figure 2.7. The domain border may be placed erroneously in parallel below (Figure 2.7a) or above (Figure 2.7b) the intended (correct) one, or may intersect with it as shown in Figure 2.7c. Observe that in Figure 2.7a, $f_i(c)$ will be computed as $f_j(c)$; in Figure 2.7b, $f_j(a)$ and $f_j(b)$ will be computed as $f_i(a)$ and $f_i(b)$, respectively; and in Figure 2.7c, $f_j(b)$ will be computed as $f_i(b)$ instead. Since it is assumed that $f_i(p) \neq f_j(p)$ for any point p near the border, all three types of domain faults can be detected by using this strategy.

Recall that two important assumptions were made at the outset: (1) All path predicates are numerical and linear, and (2) functions defined in two adjacent subdomains yield different values for the same test point near the border. The percentage of real-world programs that satisfy assumption 1 probably varies widely in different application areas. Assumption 2 is contrary to requirements in most practical applications: The common requirement is to have the functions defined in adjacent subdomains to produce approximately the same, if not identical, values near

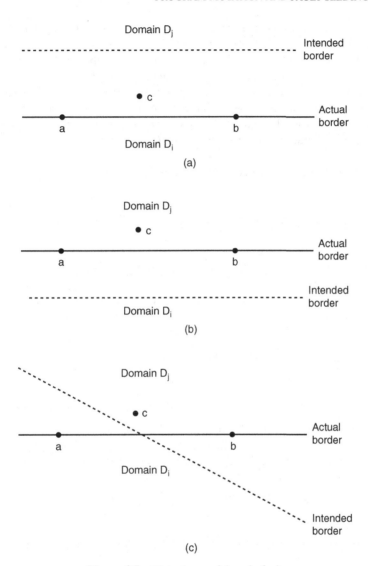

Figure 2.7   Three types of domain fault.

the border. The applicability of this test strategy therefore appears to be somewhat limited.

2.7   PROGRAM MUTATION AND FAULT SEEDING

Our final software testing method, commonly known as *program mutation*, embodies a drastically different concept. Unlike the methods presented in preceding sections, it tells us neither the algorithm to use for choosing test cases from the input domain, nor the components to be exercised during the test; it only prescribes when to stop testing. We start by describing the method as it is commonly described in the literature, and then discuss it in the conceptual framework used in this book.

A mutant of a program P is defined as a program P' derived from P by making one of a set of carefully defined syntactic changes in P. Typical changes include replacing one arithmetic operator by another, one statement by another, and so on [BDLS78, DELS78]. To illustrate, consider the following C++ program:

```
main()   // compute sine function //
{
    int i;
    float e, sum, term, x;

    cin >> x >> e;
    cout << "x = " << x << "e = " << e;
    term = x;
    for (i = 3; i <= 100 && term > e; i = i + 2) {
        term = term * x * x / (i * (i - 1));
        if (i % 2 == 0) sum = sum + term;
        else sum = sum - term;
    }
    cout << "sin(x)= " << sum << endl;
}
```

Listed below are some possible mutants of this program:

```
// a mutant obtained by changing variable//
// x to a constant 0 //
main()   // compute sine function //
{
    int i;
    float e, sum, term, x;

    cin >> x >> e;
    cout << "x = " << x << "e = " << e;
    term = 0 ;
    for (i = 3; i <= 100 && term > e; i = i + 2) {
        term = term * x * x / (i * (i - 1));
        if (i % 2 == 0) sum = sum + term;
        else sum = sum - term;
    }
    cout << "sin(x)= " << sum << endl;
}
```

```
// a mutant obtained by changing a relational //
// operator in i <= 100 to i >= 100 //
main()   // compute sine function //
{
int i;
float e, sum, term, x;
    cin >> x >> e;
    cout << "x = " << x << "e = " << e;
    term = x;
    for (i = 3; i >= 100 && term > e; i = i + 2) {
        term = term * x * x / (i * (i - 1));
        if (i % 2 == 0) sum = sum + term;
        else sum = sum - term;
    }
    cout << "sin(x)= " << sum << endl;
}
```

```
// a mutant obtained by changing constant 0 to 1 //
main()   // compute sine function //
{
    int i;
    float e, sum, term, x;

    cin >> x >> e;
    cout << "x = " << x << "e = " << e;
    term = x;
    for (i = 3; i <= 100 && term > e; i = i + 2) {
        term = term * x * x / (i * (i - 1));
        if (i % 2 == 1) sum = sum + term;
        else sum = sum - term;
    }
    cout << "sin(x)= " << sum << endl;
}
```

Program mutation had been utilized by DeMillo et al. as the basis for an interactive program testing system [DELS78]. The basic idea involved can be explained as follows. Let P' be a mutant of some program P. A test case t is said to *differentiate* P' from P if an execution of P and P' with t produced different results. If t failed to differentiate P' from P, either P' is functionally equivalent to P or t is ineffective in revealing the changes (faults) introduced into P'. Thus, a test method can be formulated as follows. Given a program P that implements function f:

1. Generate M, a set of mutants of P, by using a set of mutation operations.
2. Identify and delete all mutants in M that are equivalent to P.
3. Find T, a set of test cases that as a whole differentiate P from every mutant in M, to test-execute P and all mutants in M.

These three steps constitute an M *mutant test*. The test is *successful* if the program executes correctly for every test case [i.e., $P(t) = f(t)$ for all $t \in T$, where f is the intended function of P]. A successful M mutant test implies that the program is free of any faults introduced into P in the process of constructing M. If we can assume that P was written by a competent programmer who had a good understanding of the task to be performed and was not capable of making any mistakes other than those introduced in constructing M, we can conclude that P is correct. The significance of a successful M mutant test is discussed further by Budd et al. in [BDLS80].

How can M be constructed in practice? Budd et al. suggested that a set of syntactic operations can be used to construct the desired mutants systematically [BDLS78]. The definition of such operations obviously would be language dependent. For Fortran programs, the mutation operations may include the following:

1. *Constant replacement:* replacing a constant, say C, with $C + 1$ or $C - 1$ (e.g., statement $A = 0$ becomes $A = 1$ or $A = -1$.
2. *Scalar replacement:* replacing one scalar variable with another (e.g., statement $A = B - 1$ becomes $A = D - 1$).
3. *Scalar for constant replacement:* replacing a constant with a scalar variable (e.g., statement $A = 1$ becomes $A = B$).
4. *Constant for scalar replacement:* replacing a scalar variable with a constant (e.g., statement $A = B$ becomes $A = 5$).
5. *Source constant replacement:* replacing a constant in the program with another constant found in the same program (e.g., statement $A = 1$ becomes $A = 11$, where the constant 11 appears in some other statement).
6. *Array reference for constant replacement:* replacing a constant with an array element [e.g., statement $A = 2$ becomes $A = B(2)$].
7. *Array reference for scalar replacement:* replacing a scalar variable with an array element [e.g., statement $A = B + 1$ becomes $A = X(1) + 1$].
8. *Comparable array name replacement:* replacing a subscripted variable with the corresponding element in another array of the same size and dimension [e.g., statement $A = B(2, 4)$ becomes $A = D(2, 4)$].
9. *Constant for array reference replacement:* replacing an array element with a constant [e.g., statement $A = X(1)$ becomes $A = 5$].
10. *Scalar for array reference replacement:* replacing a subscripted variable with a nonsubscripted variable [e.g., statement $A = B(1) - 1$ becomes $A = X - 1$].

11. *Array reference for array reference replacement:* replacing a subscripted variable by another [e.g., statement $A = B(1) + 1$ becomes $A = D(4) + 1$].

12. *Unary operator insertion:* insertion of one of the unary operators, such as $-$ (negation), in front of any data reference (e.g., statement $A = X$ becomes $A = -X$).

13. *Arithmetic operator replacement:* replacing an arithmetic operator (i.e., $+$, $-$, $*$, $/$, $**$) with another (e.g., statement $A = B + C$ becomes $A = B - C$).

14. *Relational operator replacement:* replacing a relational operator (i.e., $=$, $<>$, $<=$, $<$, $>=$, $>$) with another (e.g., expression $X = Y$ becomes $X <> Y$).

15. *Logical connector replacement:* replacing a logical connector (i.e., .AND., .OR., .XOR.) with another (e.g., expression A .AND. B becomes A .OR. B).

16. *Unary operator removal:* deleting any unary operator (e.g., statement $A = -B/C$ becomes $A = B/C$).

17. *Statement analysis:* replacing a statement with a trap statement that causes the program execution to be aborted immediately (e.g., statement GOTO 10 becomes CALL TRAP).

18. *Statement deletion:* deleting a statement from the program.

19. *Return statement:* replacing a statement in a subprogram by a RETURN statement.

20. *Goto statement replacement:* replacing the statement label of a GOTO statement by another (e.g., statement GOTO 20 becomes GOTO 30).

21. *DO statement end replacement:* replacing the end label of a DO statement with some other label (e.g., statement DO 5 I $= 2,10$ becomes DO 40 I $= 2,10$).

22. *Data statement alteration:* changing the values of variables assigned by a DATA statement (in FORTRAN) (e.g., statement DATA Y /22/ becomes DATA Y /31/).

A mutant in M is created by applying one mutation operation to one statement in the program. The set M consists of all possible mutants constructed by applying every mutation operation to every applicable statement in the program. In the second step of the mutant test method, after all possible mutants are generated, one needs to identify and to remove mutants that are functionally equivalent to the program. In general, determining the equivalency of two programs is an unsolvable problem. Although a mutant differs from the original program by only one statement, determination of equivalency may become problematic in practice. This difficulty remains a major obstacle in making program mutation a practical method for program testing.

Observe that a mutant of program P is created by altering a statement in P. A test case would not differentiate the mutant from P unless this particular statement is involved in the test execution. Thus, to find a test case to differentiate a mutant is to find an input to P that causes the statement in question to be exercised during the test. Of course, causing the statement to be exercised is only a necessary condition.

For some input, a nonequivalent mutant may produce an output fortuitously identical to that of *P*. A sufficient condition, therefore, is that the mutant and *P* do not produce the same output for that input.

For example, consider a C++ program that includes the following statement:

```
while (fahrenheit <= upper) {
   celsius = (5.0 / 9.0) * (fahrenheit - 32.0);
   fahrenheit = fahrenheit + 10.0;
   }
```

A mutant obtained by replacing constant 5.0 with 4.0, for instance, thus includes the following statement:

```
while (fahrenheit <= upper) {
   celsius = (4.0 / 9.0) * (fahrenheit - 32.0);
   fahrenheit = fahrenheit + 10.0;
}
```

Obviously, any test case satisfying `fahrenheit > upper` will not be able to differentiate this mutant because the mutated statement in the loop body will not be executed at all. To differentiate this mutant, the test case must cause that statement to be exercised. In addition, the test case must cause the mutant to produce a different output. A test case that set `fahrenheit = upper = 32.0` just before the loop will not do it (because the factor `fahrenheit - 32.0` will become zero, and the variable `celsius` will be set to zero regardless of the constant used there). Such a test case may satisfy the need for a statement-coverage test because it causes the statement in question to be executed, but not the need for this mutation test because it would cause the mutant to produce an output fortuitously identical to that of the original program.

An *M* mutant test is therefore at least as thorough as a statement test (i.e., a test in which every statement in the program is exercised at least once). This is so because there is no program statement that can be made absolutely fault-free, even if it is written by a competent programmer. This means that if the *M* mutant test is to be effective, *M* should contain at least one mutant from every statement in the program. This, in turn, means that the set of test cases used should have every statement in the program exercised at least once so that all mutants can be differentiated from the program.

As mentioned previously, an *M* mutant test may be more thorough than a statement test because if a test case failed to differentiate a nonequivalent mutant in *M*, additional test cases must be employed. These additional test cases make it possible to detect faults of the type induced by the mutation operation used.

Mutation testing is attractive because it is an interesting idea, it is relatively easy to do, and it can be used to replace statement testing, as explained above. Given the opportunity to choose between statement testing and mutation testing, most proud software engineers probably would be tempted to choose the latter. We would like to point out, however, that there is an enormous difference in the amount of effort required in deploying these two processes. The analysis presented below should be of interest to those who need to make the choice.

Suppose that a given program P has m mutants and that n test cases are used to differentiate all mutants. The number of *mutant tests* (i.e., test executions of mutants) needed depends on the number of mutants that each test case is able to differentiate and the order in which the test cases are used. In the best case, the first test case differentiates all but $n - 1$ mutants with m test executions. The second test case differentiates one mutant with $n - 1$ test executions. The third test case differentiates one mutant with $n - 2$ executions, and so on. In general, the ith test case differentiates one mutant with $n - i + 1$ test executions (for all $1 < i \leq n$). Thus, the total number of mutant tests required will be

$$m + (n - 1) + (n - 2) + \cdots + 1 = m + \frac{(n - 1) + 1}{2}(n - 1) = m + \frac{n(n - 1)}{2}$$

In the worst case, each of the first $n - 1$ test cases differentiates only one mutant, and the last test case differentiates the remaining $m - (n - 1)$ mutants. The total number of mutant tests required will be

$$m + (m - 1) + (m - 2) + \cdots + (m - (n - 1)) = mn - [1 + 2 + \cdots + (n - 1)]$$
$$= mn - \frac{n(n - 1)}{2}$$

These two figures represent two extreme cases. On average, the number of test executions required will be

$$\frac{m + n(n - 1)/2 + mn - n(n - 1)/2}{2} = \frac{m + mn}{2} = \frac{m(n + 1)}{2}$$

The numbers of test executions required for the 10 programs studied in [BDLS80] are tabulated in Table 2.17 for reference.

Note that in other test methods, the number of test executions required is equal to the number of test cases used. In the mutant test, additional test executions of mutants have to be carried out with the same test cases. The last three columns in Table 2.17 indicate the minimum, maximum, and average number of test executions required. Take program 8 as an example. Only five test cases (and hence test executions) are required to complete a statement test. For a mutant test, somewhere between 6327 and 31,575 additional test executions are required. Assuming that each test execution can be completed in 10 seconds (including the time needed to analyze the test result), these additional test executions will consume somewhere between 18 and 87 hours of time. This is far more costly to use than are competing methods.

Finally, we note that the technique of program mutation is closely related to that of fault seeding, which can be used to assess the effectiveness of a test by inserting a

TABLE 2.17 Number of Mutant Tests Required

Program	Program Size (Number of Statements)	Number of Mutants	Test Cases Needed	Number of Mutant Tests Required		
				Minimum	Maximum	Average
1	30	900	4	906	3,594	2,250
2	31	773	7	794	5,390	3,092
3	16	383	7	404	2,660	1,532
4	62	5,033	34	5,529	170,626	88,078
5	28	3,348	13	3,426	43,446	23,436
6	57	8,026	17	8,162	136,306	72,234
7	43	1,028	40	1,808	40,340	21,074
8	55	6,317	5	6,327	31,575	18,951
9	34	945	9	981	8,469	4,725
10	19	567	12	633	6,738	3,686

number of concocted faults into the program and then test-executing the program to see how many of the seeded faults will be revealed.

To illustrate, suppose that 10 faults were inserted into the program before the test. If eight of the inserted faults and four of the native (nonseeded) faults were detected by the test, it is reasonable to conclude that the test is 80% effective, at least for the type of faults represented by those inserted. Based on the fact that eight out of 10 seeded faults were detected in the test, we should be able to conclude that four out of five nonseeded faults were detected, assuming that the detection rate is the same. Of course, we do not know whether or not the detection rate is the same. But statistically speaking, the detection rate should be close if the type of nonseeded fault is identical to that of a seeded fault.

Program mutation can be viewed as a systematic method of fault seeding. Concocted faults are seeded into the program by applying mutation rules to create mutants. The program is test-executed until all seeded faults are discovered. At that point we would have a reasonably sound basis to claim that all latent faults of the types representable by the mutation rules have been detected.

2.8 DISCUSSION

We have discussed many methods for test-case selection in this chapter. By this time the reader may have become anxious regarding how to choose among them. Unfortunately, there is no short answer to this question. We introduce a few more methods in Chapters 3 and 4 and then address this question in Section 4.7.

A practitioner may be tempted to find the answer by applying all methods to some example programs. The problem is that it would be overly tedious and time consuming to do it manually, and there is no set of software tools to enable us to do it automatically. There are a number of reasons why such tools are not available on the market, despite the fact that software reliability has been widely recognized to be a major problem in the industry for many years. Principally, the cost of building a complete set of such software tools is prohibitively high. Its complexity, and thus its cost, would rival those of a high-end language compiler. Presently only those software houses building products for a mass market can afford to build such tools, but they do not have an economic incentive to do so. No one will spend millions of dollars to build a testing tool system if the task of testing can be delegated to customers free of charge. Those who build safety-critical software for military and industrial applications definitely could benefit from such tools, but the amount of investment required remains unjustifiably large.

There are at least two technical reasons that make this tool so costly to build and to maintain. The first is that to automate all the test-case selection methods completely, the tool must be able to find an aggregate of inputs that satisfies some predicate. To get the taste of it, let us consider the program depicted in Figure 2.1. Now suppose that we wish to select test cases to do statement testing and find that it is necessary to find a test case that will traverse path $\alpha\beta\gamma\varepsilon\eta$, which is represented by the following symbolic trace:

```
w = b - a;
/\ w > e;
p = a + w / 3;
u = f(p);
q = b - w / 3;
v = f(q);
/\ !(u < v);
b = q;
w = b - a;
/\ !(w > e);
max = (a + b) / 2;
cout << max << endl;
```

This symbolic trace can be simplified to

```
/\ b - a > e;
/\ !(f((b + 2a) / 3) < f((a + 2b) / 3)));
/\ 2(b - a) / 3 <= e;
w = b - a;
p = a + w / 3;
u = f(p);
q = b - w / 3;
v = f(q);
b = q;
w = b - a;
max = (a + b) / 2;
cout << max << endl;
```

To cause this path to be traversed in an execution, we need to find an input of a, b, and e that will make the following predicate true:

$$b - a > e \wedge f\left(\frac{b + 2a}{3}\right) \geq f\left(\frac{a + 2b}{3}\right) \wedge \frac{2(b - a)}{3} \leq e$$

Since we do not have the exact specification of function f, we need to rewrite the part involving f into a more definitive statement. It is observed that $a < b$ is always true because a and b represent the lower and upper boundaries of an interval on the x-axis. Hence, it is always true that $(b + 2a)/3 < (a + 2b)/3$. Now from the function plot shown in Figure 2.2, we see that $f(x_1) \geq f(x_2)$ is true if $x_1 < x_2$ and $x_1 > 2$, that is, if $(b + 2a)/3 \geq 2$ or $b + 2a \geq 6$. In other words, the predicate now becomes

$$b - a > e \wedge b + 2a \geq 6 \wedge \frac{2(b - a)}{3} \leq e$$

This is expression (A) in Appendix A. A way to find values of a, b, and e from a logical point of view is discussed therein. This problem of solving a set of inequalities is closely related to that studied in the field of linear programming in mathematics. Interested readers may wish to investigate the possibility of exploiting the results obtained in that field for test-case selection purposes.

Basically, we need a software tool with the computational capability of a theorem prover to perform the task illustrated above. In addition, the tool needs to have the processing capability of a compiler to perform the necessary analysis of the program to be tested. The combined functional requirements for logical manipulation and program analysis would put its development cost on a par with that of a modern high-end compiler.

The second reason for the high cost of building and maintaining such a tool is that it has a short life span and requires high maintenance. All real-world programming languages and paradigms evolve throughout their lifetime. The evolution is always progressing in the direction of making it easier to write complex programs. Every new feature adds a new dimension to the problem of program analysis and makes the tasks to be performed by the tool more difficult. Its impact on the automated test-case selection tool would not be limited to the need for frequent adaptive maintenance. It could make the necessary changes to the tool so extensive that it renders the tool hopelessly obsolete in a short time period. This fact, plus a legal system that makes it possible to sell faulty software with impunity, make investment in building advanced testing tools utterly unattractive.

Many software testing tools are available in the market place. Although all claim to have test-coverage monitoring capability, we have not been able to find out exactly how those tools work, and if the test coverage turns out to be insufficient, what kind of information the tools will provide the user to help finding additional test cases to achieve the desired coverage. It is important to choose a tool capable of generating useful information for the selection of additional test cases. Total automation of this process is difficult, but a tool capable of pinpointing the paths or branches not traversed can be built with relative ease. The reader may wish to build such a tool, as outlined below.

First, the tool must have a good graphic user interface to facilitate analysis. Given the source code of a program, the tool should be able to construct its program graph together with its source code. For example, given Program 2.1, the tool should construct and display its program graph as shown in Figure 2.1.

Second, the user should be able to specify on the program graph a path for which the tool is to construct its symbolic trace. The path can be specified graphically as exemplified in Figure 2.8, which contains the program graph shown in Figure 2.1. For the sake of argument, let us say that the user has specified a point on branch γ with a mouse click. The tool should verify this action by generating a block arrow pointing to that location as shown in Figure 2.8. The user can specify a path, for example, by using the following convention. If no points are specified, the paths desired are the default to all the paths between the entry and the exit. If only one point is specified, the paths desired are understood to be all the paths between the entry and that point. If two points are specified, all the paths between those two points are indicated.

In response to the path specified in Figure 2.8, the tool should produce the symbolic trace for path $\alpha\beta\gamma$ as follows:

```
cin >> a >> b >> e;
w = b - a;
/\ w > e;
p = a + w / 3;
u = f(p);
q = b - w / 3;
v = f(q);
/\ !(u < v);
b = q;
```

The symbolic trace can also be generated by parsing the source code as shown in [PRAK99]. The information contained in the trace so generated may not be as specific as that contained in the trace generated by a software instrument. This is so because certain information, such as the value assumed by the index variable of an array element at some point in control flow, may not be known until execution time. But on many occasions it suffices to use traces that are generated statically.

By using the procedure or the symbolic-trace analyzer described in Chapter 5, we can simplify this symbolic trace to the following:

```
cin >> a >> b >> e;
/\ b - a > e;
/\ !(f(a + (b - a) / 3) < f(b - (b - a) / 3));
w = b - a;
p = a + w / 3;
u = f(p);
q = b - w / 3;
v = f(q);
b = q;
```

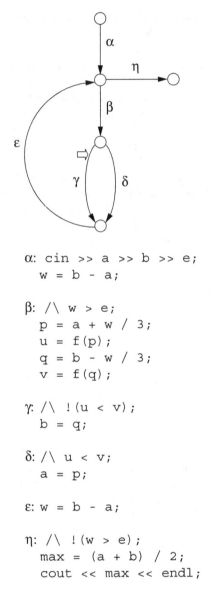

```
α: cin >> a >> b >> e;
   w = b - a;

β: /\ w > e;
   p = a + w / 3;
   u = f(p);
   q = b - w / 3;
   v = f(q);

γ: /\ !(u < v);
   b = q;

δ: /\ u < v;
   a = p;

ε: w = b - a;

η: /\ !(w > e);
   max = (a + b) / 2;
   cout << max << endl;
```

Figure 2.8   Marking of the branch selected by the user.

From this simplified trace we can see that any values of a, b, and e satisfying the predicate b − a > e and !(f(a + (b − a)/3) < f(b − (b − a)/3)) will cause path αβγ to be traversed. This is the feature we can use to select additional test cases to traverse a particular path if desired.

Also, design a tool to perform data-flow analysis of a symbolic trace. Given the symbolic trace of an execution path, say αβγεη in Figure 2.8, the tool should be able to produce the following display (where "d" represents "define" and "r" represents "reference"):

	Actions Taken on Variables:								
	a	b	e	max	p	q	u	v	w
`cin >> a >> b >> e;`	d	d	d						
`w = b - a;`	r	r							d
`/\ w > e;`			r						r
`p = a + w / 3;`	r				d				r
`u = f(p);`					r		d		
`q = b - w / 3;`		r				d			r
`v = f(q);`						r		d	
`/\ !(u < v);`							r	r	
`b = q;`		d				r			
`w = b - a;`	r	r							d
`/\ !(w > e);`			r						r
`max = (a + b) / 2;`	r	r		d					
`cout << max << endl;`				r					

The user can make use of this information to select test cases for data-flow testing. It shows that every variable is defined and used at least once on this path, that variables a, b, p, q, and max are c-used; that variables e, u, and v are p-used; and that variable w is both c- and p-used. Path $\alpha\beta\gamma\varepsilon\eta$ covers all definitions of all variables except one definition of variable a.

EXERCISES

2.1 A program could be fortuitously correct; that is, even though it is faulty, it produces correct results for some inputs. Give two example code segments and circumstances under which they become fortuitously correct.

2.2 A common problem in applying the test-case selection methods discussed in this chapter is to find elements of the input domain that will satisfy a path predicate, such as $b - a > 0.01 \wedge b + 2a \geq 6 \wedge 0.01 \geq 2(b - a)/3$. In general, it is tedious and time consuming to do so. To get a feeling for this problem, time yourself to see how long it takes for you to find two different sets of nonzero values for variables a and b that satisfy this predicate.

2.3 Survey the field to see if there are any algorithms or software packages that can be used to find inputs that satisfy path predicates, such as the one in Exercise 2.2.

2.4 There are many software testing tools on the market. Do any of them offer direct help for the solution to Exercise 2.2? If so, describe their technical capabilities and limitations.

2.5 Is it possible for the same variable to have a p-use and a c-use in the same statement in a C++ program?

2.6 Consider a program with the path domain D_i in a two-dimensional space defined by the following predicates:

$$x - 2 >= 0$$
$$x + y > 0$$
$$2x - y >= 0$$

Find three test cases (i.e., three on–off–on points) needed for testing the correctness of the boundary defined by the predicate $x - 2 >= 0$, assuming that the smallest real number on the machine is 0.001.

2.7 The following assumptions were made in developing the domain strategy testing method.

- *Assumption (f)*: The path corresponding to each adjacent domain computes a different function.
- *Assumption (g)*: Functions defined in two adjacent subdomains yield different values for the same test point near the border.

Explain why these assumptions are necessary and what would happen if these assumptions were not satisfied.

2.8 Given a program and a set of its mutants, how should we select test cases so that the number of test cases required for differentiating all mutants from the original program is minimal?

2.9 Study old software RFQs (requests for quotation) issued by the federal government or industrial concerns in the United States to see what real-world software test requirements were prevalent in the past decade.

3 Specification-Based Test-Case Selection Methods

Having explained how to select test cases based on the source code, we now turn our attention to the question of how to select test cases based on program specification. Critics of code-based test-case selection methods often claim that specification-based methods are better because if the source code did not implement some part of the specification, a code-based method will never yield a test case to reveal what is missing. That is very true, because we select test cases to cause certain components to be exercised, and if the components are not there, we will not include the necessary elements in the test set. But there is another fact that the critics have overlooked. Programmers are not only capable of neglecting to incorporate needed parts into the program but are equally capable of writing uncalled-for code segments. For example, programmers often partition the input domain into more subdomains than necessary when they write the code. If we select test cases based on the program specification only, no representative element will be selected from some of those subdomains, and therefore the resulting test set will be inadequate.

Obviously, selecting test cases based on the specification or source code alone will leave certain types of faults undetectable. It is more accurate to say that the code- and specification-based methods complement one another. One should be used in conjunction with the other to achieve an optimal fault detection rate. As for the cost involved, note that computerization is the most effective way to reduce the cost and time required to test a program. It is much more difficult to mechanize a specification-based method than a code-based method because in practice most software specifications are written in a natural language, and natural language processing is in general much more problematic than programming language processing.

The basic problem in the development of a specification-based method is the same as that in the code-based methods discussed in Chapter 2. It involves identification of the components to be exercised during the test and selection of test cases that are computationally as loosely coupled among one another as possible. There are some differences, however. Notably, the components now have to be found in the specifications instead of the source code, and unless the specification is a piece of pseudocode, there are no execution paths to be found. Therefore, different methods have to be devised to find computationally loosely coupled test cases.

What components can be found in a program specification? In this book we assume that two kinds of language constructs can be found in a program specification: condition clauses and action clauses.[1] Roughly speaking, a *condition clause* is an expression that can be either true or false. It corresponds to a proposition or a predicate in the language of symbolic logic (or first-order predicate calculus, a review of which is included in Appendix A). On the other hand, an *action clause* is an expression that describes an action to be taken by the program during execution. For example, consider the following specification.

Specification 3.1   Write a program that takes three positive integers as input and determine if they represent three sides of a triangle, and if they do, indicate what type of triangle it is. To be more specific, it should read three integers and set a flag as follows:

- If they represent a scalene triangle, set the flag to 1.
- If they represent an isosceles triangle, set the flag to 2.
- If they represent an equilateral triangle, set the flag to 3.
- If they do not represent a triangle, set the flag to 4.

We can see that in this specification there are four condition clauses:

- They represent a scalene triangle.
- They represent an isosceles triangle.
- They represent an equilateral triangle.
- They do not represent a triangle.

and four action clauses:

- Set the flag to 1.
- Set the flag to 2.
- Set the flag to 3.
- Set the flag to 4.

Such clauses can be used to find out how the function implemented by the program can be decomposed into a set of subprograms. We can then choose the subprograms as the components to be exercised during the test.

To see the theoretical significance of this approach, it is useful to view a program as an artifact that embodies a mathematical function $f : X \to Y$, where f is often implemented as a set of n subfunctions [i.e., $f = \{f_1, f_2, \ldots, f_n\}$, $f_i : X_i \to Y$, and $X = X_1 \cup X_2 \cup \cdots \cup X_n$]. Thus, to see if f is implemented correctly, we need to

---

[1]In the method of cause–effect graphing, a condition clause is a *cause* and an action clause is an *effect* [MYER79]; and in the language of decision tables [WELL81, HURL83], a clause is called a *stub*.

exercise every subfunction f_i (for all $1 \leq i \leq n$) at least once during the test. Note that in this way, if two test cases exercise two different subfunctions, they will also be loosely coupled computationally because they will be processed by two different subprograms. Therefore, an effective and efficient way to test the program is to use a test set consisting of one element from each subdomain X_i. In terms of the second principle of test-case selection, we choose subfunctions as the components to be exercised during the test. This is the formal basis for the subfunction test discussed in Section 3.1.

Because of some complicating factors to be discussed later, it is not always easy or possible to identify all subfunctions in the program from the program specification. In Section 3.2 we present a simplified version of subfunction testing that is easier to perform. As discussed in Chapter 2, it is conceivable that the programmer might implement the computation to be performed by each subprogram correctly but might err in partitioning the input domain. The method of subfunction testing and its simplified versions are not developed with such programming faults in mind. To increase the probability of revealing such faults, the test cases will have to be selected in a particular way, as discussed in Section 3.3.

Finally, recall that we depend on finding computationally loosely coupled test cases to achieve a high probability of fault discovery, and we have been using the information on functional decomposition to find such cases. It turns out that such cases can also be found based on other information, such as the nature of computation performed by the program, the programming language used, the personal habit of the program creator, and so on. The general term for that process is *error guessing*, discussed in Section 3.4.

3.1 SUBFUNCTION TESTING

In subfunction testing, the components to be exercised are the subfunctions implemented by the program. To be more precise, if the program specification says that $f : X \rightarrow Y$ is the function to be implemented by the program, and describes f explicitly as a set $\{f_1, f_2, \ldots, f_n\}$ of n subfunctions such that $f_i : X_i \rightarrow Y$ for all $1 \leq i \leq n$ and $X = X_1 \cup X_2 \cup \ldots \cup X_n$, then to do subfunction testing is to test the program with a test set consisting of at least one element from every subdomain X_i. We assume that subfunction f_i will compute its value for every element in X_i by performing the same sequence of operations. Otherwise, f_i has to be further decomposed until this property is satisfied.

When we say "the same sequence of operations" in this chapter, we often require that no branching or looping constructs are used in prescribing the operations involved. The need for such constructs is not intrinsic or absolute. Exactly the same sequence of operations can be prescribed without using any branching or looping constructs on one level of abstraction, while the use of such constructs might become necessary on another level when we move down the levels of abstraction. For examples, in plain English, we can say "reduce every element in the set by 15%," "sort the elements in the set," and "count the number of nonzero elements in the set" without using any branching or looping constructs. That is not so if we move down the level of abstraction and try to say the same in a programming language such as C++. The use of branching and looping constructs becomes necessary. In this chapter, therefore, description of the operations in the specification language is implied whenever we say "the same sequence of operations."

The reason for doing subfunction testing is that any two inputs in the same subdomain will be processed by the same sequence of operations and therefore are computationally tightly coupled. On the other hand, any two inputs in different subdomains will be processed by different sequences of operations and thus are loosely coupled. Hence, a test set consisting of at least one element from each subdomain will have a high probability of revealing faults in the program.

To select test cases for subfunction testing is therefore to identify the input domain X and the subdomains X_i's from the program specification. We first analyze the program specification to identify X, the set of all valid inputs, and Y, the set of all possible outputs. We then identify all subsets of X, each of which contains elements that are to be processed by the program in the same way, and select one element from each subset to form the test set. The subdomains X_i's can be described conveniently in the form $X_i = \{x | x \in X \land C_i(x)\}$, where C_i is called a *domain predicate*, a condition used to define the subdomain X_i. The domain predicates C_i's are to be found or derived from the program specification.

To illustrate, consider Specification 3.1 again. The input domain is the set of all triples of integers; that is, $X = \{<x_1, x_2, x_3> | x_i$ is an integer *and* MININT $\leq x_i$ *and* $x_i \leq$ MAXINT$\}$, where MININT and MAXINT stand for the smallest and the largest allowable integer, respectively, of the machine on which the program will be executed. Out-of-range integers will be treated by the operating system and the compiler as usual, and are not discussed here.

From the specification it is obvious that the input domain X will be partitioned into four subdomains X_1, X_2, X_3, and X_4, such that

$$X = X_1 \cup X_2 \cup X_3 \cup X_4$$

where

$$X_1 = \{<x_1, x_2, x_3> \mid <x_1, x_2, x_3> \in X \land \text{TRIANGLE}(x_1, x_2, x_3)$$
$$\land \text{SCALENE}(x_1, x_2, x_3)\}$$

$$X_2 = \{<x_1, x_2, x_3> \mid <x_1, x_2, x_3> \in X \land \text{TRIANGLE}(x_1, x_2, x_3)$$
$$\land \text{ISOSCELES}(x_1, x_2, x_3)\}$$

$$X_3 = \{<x_1, x_2, x_3> \mid <x_1, x_2, x_3> \in X \land \text{TRIANGLE}(x_1, x_2, x_3)$$
$$\land \text{EQUILATER}(x_1, x_2, x_3)\}$$

$$X_4 = \{<x_1, x_2, x_3> \mid <x_1, x_2, x_3> \in X \land \neg\text{TRIANGLE}(x_1, x_2, x_3)\}$$

where TRIANGLE(x_1, x_2, x_3) stands for the predicate "x_1, x_2, and x_3 form the three sides of a triangle," SCALENE(x_1, x_2, x_3) for the predicate "x_1, x_2, and x_3 form the three sides of a scalene triangle," ISOSCELES(x_1, x_2, x_3) for the predicate "x_1, x_2, and x_3 form the three sides of an isosceles triangle," and EQUILATERAL(x_1, x_2, x_3) for the predicate "x_1, x_2, and x_3 form the three sides of an equilateral triangle." These predicates can be readily translated into a logical expression:

$$\text{TRIANGLE}(x_1, x_2, x_3) \equiv x_1 > 0 \wedge x_2 > 0 \wedge x_3 > 0 \wedge x_1 + x_2 > x_3 \wedge x_2$$

$$+ x_3 > x_1 \wedge x_3 + x_1 > x_2$$

$$\text{SCALENE}(x_1, x_2, x_3) \equiv x_1 \neq x_2 \wedge x_2 \neq x_3 \wedge x_3 \neq x_1$$

$$\text{ISOSCELES}(x_1, x_2, x_3) \equiv x_1 = x_2 \wedge x_2 \neq x_3 \wedge x_3 \neq x_1 \vee x_1 \neq x_2 \wedge x_2 = x_3$$

$$\wedge x_3 \neq x_1 \vee x_1 \neq x_2 \wedge x_2 \neq x_3 \wedge x_3 = x_1$$

$$\text{EQUILATERAL}(x_1, x_2, x_3) \equiv x_1 = x_2 \wedge x_2 = x_3 \wedge x_3 = x_1$$

For this example, to do subfunction testing, therefore, is simply to test-execute the program with a test set consisting of four test cases, one each from subdomains X_1, X_2, X_3, and X_4. A possible test set would be $T = \{<3, 4, 5>, <3, 3, 4>, <7, 7, 7>, <2, 3, 6>\}$. The four subfunctions to be exercised, f_1, f_2, f_3, and f_4, are "set flag to 1," "set flag to 2," "set flag to 3," and "set flag to 4," respectively.

This test set can be considered well chosen only if (the source code of) the program is implemented such that it is composed of only four feasible execution paths, each of which embodies one and only one subfunction prescribed in the specification. So we will have to ask if the program is likely to be so implemented. For a simple program such as this, the answer is most likely to be affirmative. It may not be so, however, if the program is written in a low-level language or if it is composed by an automatic program generator. More will be said about this question later.

Next, we use a slightly more complex example to explain fully the steps involved in identifying and partitioning the input domain, and the alternatives available at each step.

Specification 3.2 Write a program to reformat a text as follows. Given a text terminated by an ENDOFTEXT character and consisting of words separated by BLANK or NEWLINE characters, reformat it to a line-by-line form in accordance with the following rules: (1) line breaks are made only where the given text has BLANK or NEWLINE; (2) each line is filled as far as possible as long as (3) no line will contain more than MAXPOS characters. The resulting text should contain no blank lines. Sound an alarm and terminate the program if the text contains an oversized word.

As before, we first identify the input domain. It is assumed that the input text is read by the program one character at a time. Therefore, the input is the set of all

ASCII characters, assuming that the input is to be provided through a keyboard. We can start by partitioning the input domain into three subdomains, X_{EW}, X_{ET}, and X_{AN}, where:

- X_{EW}: the set of end-of-the-word markers in the input text consisting of BLANK (white space) and NEWLINE characters
- X_{ET}: the set consisting of end-of-the-text markers
- X_{AN}: the set consisting of all alphanumerical characters and punctuation marks that may appear in the input text

We note here that in reality a keyboard can generate nonprintable (or control) characters as well, which are neither of the above. To simplify the discussion here, however, we shall assume that X_{EW}, X_{ET}, and X_{AN} constitute a partition of X (i.e., $X = X_{EW} \cup X_{ET} \cup X_{AN}$, and X_{EW}, X_{ET}, and X_{AN} are mutually exclusive). By assuming that the input domain is partitioned in this way, we are in effect assuming that the function implemented by the program is decomposed into three subfunctions: f_{EW}, f_{ET}, and f_{AN}. This assumption is good enough for subfunction testing purposes if each subfunction can be implemented as a single sequence of operations (i.e., no branch operation is needed in describing each subfunction). Otherwise, further partitioning has to be performed until this requirement is satisfied.

Let us examine what the program needs to do if we partition the input domain into a set of subdomains as shown in Table 3.1. Note that the description of every subfunction in the table contains an "if" statement, indicating that the inputs in the same subdomain may be processed by different sequences of operations. Why is that so? It is due to the fact that what needs to be done for a particular input is depends not only on its membership in a particular subdomain but on the previous inputs as well. In other words, the function to be performed is not only dependent on the membership of the input character but also on the context in which it is read by the program. In this case the context provided by the preceding sequence of inputs is predicated by the branch condition of the conditional statement used to describe the operations to be performed.

For example, if the current character is an end-of-the-text character, the program needs to write the current word and terminate. The current word could be written on the current line or the next line, depending on whether or not there is enough room on the current line to append the word without violating the length restriction. There is enough room if the length of the word plus the length of the line is less than MAXPOS, the maximum length allowable on a line. Therefore, we can partition subdomain X_{ET} further by using the predicate "*wordlength* + *linelength* < *MAXPOS*." In this way, all elements in X_{ET} satisfying this predicate will be processed by the program in the same way (provided that the program is written correctly), as will be those in X_{ET} that do not satisfy this predicate.

By partitioning all three subdomains as described above, we obtain Table 3.2. Note that a conditional statement was used to describe the function to be performed for elements in $X_{1.1}$. The subfunction there will have to write the current word to

TABLE 3.1   Trial Partition of the Input Domain

Subdomain	Domain Predicate	Subfunction
1	$x \in X_{EW}$	[The input character is either a blank or a newline]

if *wordlength* > 0 **then**
    begin
        if *linelength* + *wordlength* $\geq$ MAXPOS **then**
            begin
                write(*newline*);
                linelength := *wordlength*
            end
        else
            begin
                write(*blank*);
                linelength := *linelength* + *wordlength*
            end;
        write(*word*);
        wordlength := 0;
    end;
read(*char*);

| 2 | $x \in X_{ET}$ | [The input character is an end-of-the-text mark] |

if *wordlength* + *linelength* $\geq$ MAXPOS **then**
    write(*newline*);
else
    write(*blank*);
write(*word*);
write(*char*);
exit;

| 3 | $x \in X_{AN}$ | [The input character is alphanumeric] |

append(*char*, *word*);
wordlength := *wordlength* + 1;.
if *wordlength* > MAXPOS **then**
    begin
        write(*alarm*);
        exit
    end
else
    read(*char*);

the current line or the next line, depending on whether there is enough room on the current line. There is not enough room on the current line if the predicate "*wordlength* + *linelength* $\geq$ *MAXPOS*" is true. By using this predicate to partition subdomain 1.1 in Table 3.2 further, we obtain the decomposition listed in Table 3.3, where every subfunction is describable by a straight-line code.

TABLE 3.2   Further Partitioning of the Input Domain

Subdomain	Domain Predicate	Subfunction
1.1	$x \in X_{EW}$ *and* *wordlength* > 0	[The input character is either a blank or a newline that marks the end of the current word]

		if *linelength* $+$ *wordlength* $\geq$ MAXPOS **then**
		   begin
		     write(*newline*);
		     linelength := *wordlength*
		   end
		 else
		   begin
		     write(*blank*);
		     linelength := *linelength* $+$ *wordlength*
		   end;
		 write(*word*);
		 wordlength := 0;
		 read(*char*);

1.2	$x \in X_{EW}$ *and* *wordlength* ≤ 0	[The input character is either a blank or a newline that is redundant]
		read(*char*);
2.1	$x \in X_{ET}$ *and wordlength* $+$ *linelength* $\geq$ MAXPOS	[The input character is an end-of-the-text mark and the current word is too long to be written on the current line]

		write(*newline*);
		 write(*word*);
		 write(*char*);
		 exit

2.2	$x \in X_{ET}$ *and wordlength* $+$ *linelength* $<$ MAXPOS	[The input character is an end-of-the-text mark and the current word can be written on the current line]

		write(*blank*);
		 write(*word*);
		 write(*char*);
		 exit

3.1	$x \in X_{AN}$ *and wordlength* $>$ MAXPOS	[The input character is alphanumeric and the current word is too long]

		append(*char*, *word*);
		 wordlength := *wordlength* $+$ *1*;
		 write(*alarm*);
		 exit;

3.2	$x \in X_{AN}$ *and wordlength* $\leq$ MAXPOS	[The input character is alphanumeric and the current word is not too long]

		append(*char*, *word*);
		 wordlength := *wordlength* $+$ *1*;.
		 read(*char*);

TABLE 3.3   Complete Partitioning of the Input Domain

Subdomain	Domain Predicate	Subfunction
1.1.1	$x \in X_{EW}$ *and* *wordlength* > 0 *and* *linelength* $+$ *wordlength* $\geq$ MAXPOS	[The input character is either a blank or a newline] write(*newline*); *linelength* := *wordlength*; write(*word*); *wordlength* := 0; read(*char*);
1.1.2	$x \in X_{EW}$ *and* *wordlength* > 0 *and* *linelength* $+$ *wordlength* $<$ MAXPOS	[The input character is either a blank or a newline] write(*blank*); *linelength* := *linelength* + *wordlength*; write(*word*); *wordlength* := 0; read(*char*);
1.2	$x \in X_{EW}$ *and* *wordlength* ≤ 0	[The input character is either a blank or a newline that is redundant] read(*char*);
2.1	$x \in X_{ET}$ *and* *wordlength* $+$ *linelength* $\geq$ MAXPOS	[The input character is an end-of-the-text mark and the current word is too long to be written on the current line] write(*newline*); write(*word*); write(*char*); exit
2.2	$x \in X_{ET}$ *and* *wordlength* $+$ *linelength* $<$ MAXPOS	[The input character is an end-of-the-text mark and the current word can be written on the current line] write(*blank*); write(*word*); write(*char*); exit
3.1	$x \in X_{AN}$ *and* *wordlength* $>$ MAXPOS	[The input character is alphanumeric and the current word is too long] append(*char, word*); *wordlength* := *wordlength* + 1; write(*alarm*); exit;
3.2	$x \in X_{AN}$ *and* *wordlength* $\leq$ MAXPOS	[The input character is alphanumeric and the current word is not too long] append(*char, word*); *wordlength* := *wordlength* + 1;. read(*char*);

Necessary context for the program to determine what to do for a particular input character can also be provided by defining the input domain as a set of sequences of two characters instead of single characters. For example, consider Specification 3.2 again. Since X, the set of all possible input characters, can be partitioned into three subdomains, the set of sequences of two characters, XX, can be partitioned into $3 \times 3 = 9$ subdomains as follows:

$$X = X_{AN} \cup X_{ET} \cup X_{EW}$$

$$XX = (X_{AN} \cup X_{ET} \cup X_{EW})(X_{AN} \cup X_{ET} \cup X_{EW})$$

$$= X_{AN}X_{AN} \cup X_{AN}X_{ET} \cup X_{AN}X_{EW} \cup X_{ET}X_{AN} \cup X_{ET}X_{ET} \cup X_{ET}X_{EW}$$

$$\cup X_{EW}X_{AN} \cup X_{EW}X_{ET} \cup X_{EW}X_{EW}$$

In Table 3.4, x_i is the current character and x_{i-1} is the character read just before the current one. The rightmost column indicates what the program should do for the current character x_i in the context of x_{i-1}.

Subdomains 1, 2, and 3 need to be further partitioned to eliminate the need to use conditional statements in describing the subfunctions to be performed. By repeating the partitioning procedure illustrated above, we obtain Table 3.5. Based on the analysis above, to do a subfunction test on the program specified by Specification 3.2, therefore, is to test the program with a set of texts that satisfies all 12 domain predicates in Table 3.5.

Discussion

Suppose that the program implements some function $f : X \to Y$, and suppose that some domain predicates, say C_1, C_2, and C_3, are available to partition the input domain X into subdomains $X_1, X_2, \ldots, X_n$ such that X_1 is the subset of X that makes $C_1(x) \equiv F$, $C_2(x) \equiv F$, and $C_3(x) \equiv F$; X_2 is the subset of X that makes $C_1(x) \equiv F$, $C_2(x) \equiv F$, and $C_3(x) \equiv T$; x_3 is the subset of X that makes $C_1(x) \equiv F$, $C_2(x) \equiv T$, and $C_3(x) \equiv F$; and so on. These three predicates can be used in conjunction to partition the input domain up to eight subdomains, as enumerated in Table 3.6.

Since a program is described by a text of finite length, it can only describe a finite number of actions the program can take to compute a subfunction. Let us suppose that there are five such primitives in the program, A_1, A_2, A_3, A_4, and A_5. Let us further suppose that subfunction f_1 is computed by using actions A_2 and A_3; f_2 is computed by using actions A_1 and A_5, and so on, shown in Table 3.7, where a check mark in the lower part of the table indicates that that action identified on the row head is used in computing the subfunction defined in the subdomain identified at the column head. For example, A_2 and A_3 are used to compute f_1 defined in X_1, and A_2, A_3, and A_4 are the actions used to compute f_8 defined in X_8.

The table constructed as described here is known as a decision table, first developed to describe the design of a program [WELL81]. A decision table can be simplified to reduce the number of columns for subfunctions by combining the subdomains in

TABLE 3.4 Trial Partitioning of the Input Domain as a Set of Pairs

Subdomain	Domain Predicate	Subfunction

1	$x_{i-1}x_i \in X_{AN}X_{AN}$	[The current character is part of a new word]
		
		append(*char*, *word*);
		wordlength := *wordlength* + 1;
		if *wordlength* > *MAXPOS* **then**
		    begin
		        write(*alarm*);
		        exit
		    end
		else
		    read(*char*);

2	$x_{i-1}x_i \in X_{AN}X_{ET}$	[The current character marks the end of the text]
		
		append(*char*, *word*);
		if *linelength* + *wordlength* ≥ *MAXPOS* **then**
		    write(*newline*);
		write(*word*);
		exit;

3	$x_{i-1}x_i \in X_{AN}X_{EW}$	[The current character marks the end of a new word]
		
		if *linelength* + *wordlength* ≥ *MAXPOS* **then**
		    begin
		        write(*newline*);
		        linelength := 0
		    end
		else
		    write(*blank*);
		write(*word*);
		linelength := *linelength* + *wordlength*;
		wordlength := 0;
		read(*char*);

4	$x_{i-1}x_i \in X_{ET}X_{AN}$	[The current character is redundant] No reaction is expected from the program.
5	$x_{i-1}x_i \in X_{ET}X_{ET}$	[The current character is redundant] No reaction is expected from the program.
6	$x_{i-1}x_i \in X_{ET}X_{EW}$	[The current character is redundant] No reaction is expected from the program.

7	$x_{i-1}x_i \in X_{EW}X_{AN}$	[The current character is the beginning of a new word]
		
		append(*char*, *word*);
		wordlength := *wordlength* + 1;
		read(*char*);

(*Continued*)

TABLE 3.4 (*Continued*)

Subdomain	Domain Predicate	Subfunction
8	$x_{i-1}x_i \in X_{EW}X_{ET}$	[The current character marks the end of the input text that has a space or new-line character at the end] write(*char*); exit;
9	$x_{i-1}x_i \in X_{EW}X_{EW}$	[The current character is redundant] read(*char*);

which the same function is defined. For example, the subfunctions f_5 and f_6 appears to be identical because both use A_2 and A_3 to compute the value of the subfunctions. (That needs to be verified by the tester because the same set of actions may be used in different ways.) If f_5 and f_6 are indeed computed in the same way, they can be combined by deleting either column and changing the subdomain description as shown in Table 3.8. The entry "—" means "it does not matter" or "it is irrelevant" to that particular predicate. The columns for X_5 and X_6 have identical entries. Therefore, these two columns can be merged to reduce the table, as shown in Table 3.9.

It should be pointed out at this point that if the decision table is to be used by the programmer for source-code composition, merging of columns will make the resulting source code more compact. On the other hand, if the decision table is to be used by a tester for test-case selection, the merit of merging the columns in the table becomes debatable. The obvious merit is that one fewer test case will be required. But without examining the source code to be tested, there is no way to tell if the programmer implemented these two columns jointly as a single subfunction or separately as two subfunctions. If the merging of the two columns led to the choice of a single test case, one of the two subfunctions will not be exercised during the test.

The point being made here is that if the decision table is to be used for test-case selection, it is not advisable to merge two columns of this nature unless reduction in the number of test cases has a higher priority over the enhancement of probability in fault detection. Next, observe that in general not all domain predicates are totally independent in the sense that assignment of truth value to a domain predicate will affect that of another. Let us suppose that C_2 implies C_3. This means that whenever C_2 is true, C_3 is true also. This is to be indicated by listing the implied truth values in parentheses, as shown in Table 3.10. Because the truth values of domain predicates for X_3 will now become identical to that of X_4, and that of X_7 will become identical to that of X_8, f_3 should be computed in the same way as f_4, and f_7 should be computed in the same way as f_8. Table 3.10 is thus revised to become Table 3.11.

We can now proceed to eliminate the columns for X_4 and X_8. The reason we choose to eliminate X_4 instead of X_3 is that the column for X_3 carries more information. It says that to find an element in X_3 (and X_4), all one has to do is to find an element in the input domain X that satisfies $\neg C_1$ and C_2. Predicate C_3 can be disregarded. The

TABLE 3.5 Complete Partitioning of the Input Pairs

Subdomain	Domain Predicate	Subfunction

1.1	$x_{i-1}x_i \in X_{AN}X_{AN}$ *and* $wordlength >$ *MAXPOS*	[The current character is part of a new word that is too long]
		
		append(*char, word*);
		wordlength := wordlength + 1;
		write(*alarm*);
		exit;

1.2	$x_{i-1}x_i \in X_{AN}X_{AN}$ *and* $wordlength \leq$ *MAXPOS*	[The current character is part of a new word of proper length]
		
		append(*char, word*);
		wordlength := wordlength + 1;
		read(*char*);

2.1	$x_{i-1}x_i \in X_{AN}X_{ET}$ *and* $linelength +$ $wordlength \geq$ *MAXPOS*	[The current character marks the end of the text and the last word has to be written on the next line]
		
		append(*char, word*);
		write(*newline*);
		write(*word*);
		exit;

2.2	$x_{i-1}x_i \in X_{AN}X_{ET}$ *and* $linelength +$ $wordlength <$ *MAXPOS*	[The current character marks the end of the text and there is enough room on the current line to write the last word]
		
		append(*char, word*);
		write(*word*);
		exit;

3.1	$x_{i-1}x_i \in X_{AN}X_{EW}$ *and* $linelength +$ $wordlength \geq$ *MAXPOS*	[The current character marks the end of a new word that has to be written on the next line]
		
		write(*newline*);
		write(*word*);
		linelength := wordlength;
		wordlength := 0;
		read(*char*);

3.2	$x_{i-1}x_i \in X_{AN}X_{EW}$ *and* $linelength +$ $wordlength <$ *MAXPOS*	[The current character marks the end of a new word that can be written on the current line]
		
		write(*blank*);
		write(*word*);
		linelength := linelength + wordlength;
		wordlength := 0;
		read(*char*);

4	$x_{i-1}x_i \in X_{ET}X_{AN}$	[The current character is redundant] No reaction is expected from the program.

(*Continued*)

TABLE 3.5 (*Continued*)

Subdomain	Domain Predicate	Subfunction
5	$x_{i-1}x_i \in X_{ET}X_{ET}$	[The current character is redundant]
		No reaction is expected from the program.
6	$x_{i-1}x_i \in X_{ET}X_{EW}$	[The current character is redundant]
		No reaction is expected from the program.
7	$x_{i-1}x_i \in X_{EW}X_{AN}$	[The current character is the beginning of a new word]

		append(*char*, *word*);
		wordlength := *wordlength* + *1*;
		read(*char*);

8	$x_{i-1}x_i \in X_{EW}X_{ET}$	[The current character marks the end of the input text that has a space or new-line character at the end]
		write(*char*); exit;
9	$x_{i-1}x_i \in X_{EW}X_{EW}$	[The current character is redundant]
		read(*char*);

TABLE 3.6 Partitioning Input Domain X with Three Predicates

Domain Predicate	Subdomain							
	X_1	X_2	X_3	X_4	X_5	X_6	X_7	X_8
C_1	F	F	F	F	T	T	T	T
C_2	F	F	T	T	F	F	T	T
C_3	F	T	F	T	F	T	F	T

TABLE 3.7 Subdomains and Subfunctions

Domain Predicate	Subdomain							
	X_1	X_2	X_3	X_4	X_5	X_6	X_7	X_8
C_1	F	F	F	F	T	T	T	T
C_2	F	F	T	T	F	F	T	T
C_3	F	T	F	T	F	T	F	T
A_1		√	√	√			√	
A_2	√		√	√	√	√	√	√
A_3	√			√	√	√		√
A_4			√					√
A_5		√					√	

TABLE 3.8   Identical Functions Defined in Two Subdomains

Domain Predicate	Subdomain							
	X_1	X_2	X_3	X_4	X_5	X_6	X_7	X_8
C_1	F	F	F	F	T	T	T	T
C_2	F	F	T	T	F	F	T	T
C_3	F	T	F	T	—	—	F	T
A_1		✓	✓	✓			✓	
A_2	✓		✓	✓	✓	✓	✓	✓
A_3	✓			✓	✓	✓		✓
A_4				✓				✓
A_5		✓					✓	

TABLE 3.9   Merger of Two Subfunctions

Domain Predicate	Subdomain						
	X_1	X_2	X_3	X_4	X_{5+6}	X_7	X_8
C_1	F	F	F	F	T	T	T
C_2	F	F	T	T	F	T	T
C_3	F	T	F	T	—	F	T
A_1		✓	✓	✓		✓	
A_2	✓		✓	✓	✓	✓	✓
A_3	✓			✓	✓		✓
A_4				✓			✓
A_5		✓				✓	

TABLE 3.10   Effect on Implied Domain Predicates

Domain Predicate	Subdomain						
	X_1	X_2	X_3	X_4	X_{5+6}	X_7	X_8
C_1	F	F	F	F	T	T	T
C_2	F	F	T	T	F	T	T
C_3	F	T	(T)	T	—	(T)	T
A_1		✓	✓	✓		✓	
A_2	✓		✓	✓	✓	✓	✓
A_3	✓			✓	✓		✓
A_4				✓			✓
A_5		✓				✓	

same argument holds true for columns X_7 and X_8. The result is Table 3.12, which shows that the number of subdomains have been reduced from eight to five.

For those who are familiar with the subject of logic design (see, e.g., [GIVO03]), it is interesting to observe that the domain predicates (in a decision table) are very much like the input variables of a combinational network. Each X_i corresponds to a

TABLE 3.11   Revision of f_3

Domain Predicate	Subdomain						
	X_1	X_2	X_3	X_4	X_{5+6}	X_7	X_8
C_1	F	F	F	F	T	T	T
C_2	F	F	T	T	F	T	T
C_3	F	T	(T)	T	—	(T)	T
A_1		✓	✓	✓			
A_2	✓		✓	✓	✓	✓	✓
A_3	✓		✓	✓	✓	✓	✓
A_4						✓	✓
A_5		✓					

TABLE 3.12   Merger of X_3 and X_4

Domain Predicate	Subdomain				
	X_1	X_2	$X_{3.4}$	X_{5+6}	$X_{7.8}$
C_1	F	F	F	T	T
C_2	F	F	T	F	T
C_3	F	T	(T)	—	(T)
A_1		✓	✓		
A_2	✓		✓	✓	✓
A_3	✓		✓	✓	✓
A_4					✓
A_5		✓			

minterm. Each A_i is a Boolean function expressed in the sum of minterms, and the constituent minterms are marked by a check mark in the table. Some minterms can be combined if they are shared by the Boolean functions in some manner, and render it possible to simplify the Boolean function representation of A_i's. For those who are not conversant with the subject of logic design, the simplification process can be facilitated by using cause–effect graphs [ELME73], described in [MYER79].

3.2   PREDICATE TESTING

In the subfunction testing just described, the components to be exercised are subfunctions of the function implemented by the program. What we do essentially is find domain predicates and the conditions that partition the input domain into a set of subdomains in which those subfunctions are defined. We then select one element from each of these subdomains; for example, if C_1 and C_2 are the domain predicates, there will be four possible combinations of these two domain predicates: $C_1 \wedge C_2$, $C_1 \wedge \neg C_2$, $\neg C_1 \wedge C_2$, and $\neg C_1 \wedge \neg C_2$. To do subfunction testing is to exercise every subfunction at least once during a test: to test the program with one test case from each subdomain defined by $C_1 \wedge C_2$, $C_1 \wedge \neg C_2$, $\neg C_1 \wedge C_2$, and $\neg C_1 \wedge \neg C_2$.

In predicate testing, the components to be exercised are domain predicates. We exercise each domain predicate with two test cases, one that makes the predicate true, and another that makes the predicate false. For instance, if we find two domain predicates C_1 and C_2 in the specification, to do predicate testing is to test the program with four test cases, each individually satisfying C_1, $\neg C_1$, C_2, and $\neg C_2$, respectively. This method can be viewed as an approximation of subfunction testing because its intent is to test the program with at least one element from each subdomain created by the domain predicates C_1 and C_2.

It should be noted that since the selection of test cases is done piecemeal, some combination of C_1 and C_2 may not have a representative element in the resulting set of test cases. For example, we might select x_1 and x_2 to satisfy C_1 and $\neg C_1$, and select x_3 and x_4 to satisfy C_2 and $\neg C_2$, respectively. If it turns out that x_1, x_2, x_3, and x_4 individually satisfy $C_1 \wedge C_2$, $\neg C_1 \wedge \neg C_2$, $\neg C_1 \wedge C_2$, and $C_1 \wedge \neg C_2$, respectively, it would be perfect. It would be just the same as doing a subfunction test. But since the selection of x_1 and x_2 is made independent of the selection of x_3 and x_4, we might end up selecting an x_1 that satisfies $C_1 \wedge C_2$, an x_2 that satisfies $\neg C_1 \wedge \neg C_2$, an x_3 that satisfies $C_1 \wedge C_2$, and an x_4 that satisfies $\neg C_1 \wedge \neg C_2$. The net effect is that the four test cases would come from two of the four subdomains only!

What is wrong with testing the program with four test cases from two of the four subdomains? In terms of the second principle of test-case selection, it can be explained as follows. Selection of x_1 and x_2 to satisfy C_1 and $\neg C_1$ ensures that x_1 and x_2 will be loosely coupled computationally, and selection of x_3 and x_4 to satisfy C_2 and $\neg C_2$ will have the same effect. But there is nothing to guarantee that any of the four pairs (x_1, x_3), (x_1, x_4), (x_2, x_3), and (x_2, x_4) are loosely coupled computationally. The fault-discovery probability of using a test set so constructed would therefore not be as high as that of using a test set constructed for subfunction testing, where all test cases will be loosely coupled. Nevertheless, the analysis needed to select test cases would be considerably simpler, and thus the cost would be lower than the cost of subfunction testing.

To enhance the fault-discovery capability of the method, take all domain predicates into consideration when the test cases are being selected. Every time a test case is selected, make note of the subdomain to which it belongs, and avoid selecting a test case from any subdomain that is already represented, if all possible. Keep in mind that some combinations of domain predicates cannot be satisfied by any element of the input domain because domain predicates may not be totally independent. In that event, multiple representations from a subdomain may be unavoidable.

Those who are familiar with the method of equivalence partitioning (MEP) described by Myers [MYER79] may deem the present method similar, or even identical, to MEP. There are some similarities. For example, both methods require extraction of domain predicates (called *input conditions* in MEP), and both methods select test cases by choosing inputs that satisfy the predicates in certain ways. In general, we can say that the intent of these two methods is the same: to exercise subfunctions during the test. There are some differences in the steps involved, but we shall not dwell on them because they would be of little interest to most readers.

The present method can be viewed as a counterpart of the branch testing presented in Chapter 2 because the domain predicates identified in this method will in one form or another show up as branch predicates in the source code. If the counterpart of any of the domain predicates identified in this method cannot be found in the source code, the cause should be investigated, because the programmer may have neglected to implement some part of the program specification.

3.3   BOUNDARY-VALUE ANALYSIS

In boundary-value analysis, the test cases are selected to exercise the limits or con-straints imposed on the program input/output that can be found in, or derived from, the program specifications. In the abstract, the input (output) domain is an infinite and multiple-dimensional space. In practice, it is partitioned into two major subdomains containing valid and invalid inputs (outputs): *valid* in the sense that it is within the normal range of program operation and the program should produce a correct output for every input in the range, *invalid* in the sense that it is outside the normal range program operation and the program is not expected to produce a correct value of the function implemented by the program. The program is, however, expected to produce a clear indication to the user that the input is invalid and that the user should take a certain action, if appropriate. The valid–invalid subdomain is generally defined by the hardware on which the program is test-executed, the limits imposed by the operating system and the compiler used, or the limits imposed by the application domains. In this method, instead of selecting a test case arbitrarily from a subdomain, a multiple of test cases are to be selected near or on the boundaries of each subdomain.

To select test cases, the specifications are studied to identify the boundaries of all data to be created and used in the program. Test cases are selected that lie directly on, above, and beneath the boundaries of input and output variables to explore program behavior along the border. In particular, a user is directed as follows:

1. If an input variable is defined in a range from the lower bound LB to the upper bound UB, use LB, UB, LB − δ, and UB + δ, where δ stands for the smallest value assumable by the variable, as the test cases.
2. Use rule 1 for every output variable.
3. If the input or output of a program is a sequence (e.g., a sequential file or a linear list), focus attention on the first and last elements of the sequence, the sequence that is of zero to maximum length.
4. Use your ingenuity to search for additional boundary values.

Note that this method differs from domain-predicate testing in three respects: (1) rather than checking to see if the program will execute correctly for a repre-sentative element in a subdomain, it attempts to determine if the program defines the subdomains correctly along the borders between the subdomains; (2) rather than selecting test cases based on input conditions alone, it also requires derivation of test cases based on output conditions; and (3) it requires sufficient knowledge in the programming environment as well as the application domain.

The present method can be viewed as the counterpart of the domain-strategy testing presented in Chapter 2. It is designed to probe program behavior on and near the borders of a domain. Note, however, that instead of probing the program behavior at all subdomain borders in domain-strategy testing, the present method does that only for the borders that demarcate the valid and invalid inputs.

In terms of the second principle of test-case selection, the rationale behind the present method can be explained as follows. If the program is implemented properly and the operating system does what it is supposed to do while the program is being tested, the computational steps taken at LB, LB $-$ δ, UB, and UB $+$ δ of a datum used in the program should be significantly different. This means that the test cases selected at these points will be loosely coupled computationally. Hence, the test cases so chosen will have an enhanced capacity for fault discovery.

3.4   ERROR GUESSING

Recall that we have been using the strategy of building an effective test set by adding to the set being constructed a new element that is loosely coupled to any other element already in the set. A new element is loosely coupled to other elements if it is to be processed by a different sequence of operations, or if it is located on, or near, the border of a domain, as discussed in earlier sections.

We avoid choosing two elements from the same subdomain because in general they are computationally tightly coupled because they will be processed by the program with the same sequence of operations. But if we know a subfunction well, we may be able to find two inputs that are not tightly coupled even if they belong to the same subdomain. For example, if we know that the program input is a file and that the file could be empty, that empty-file input will be loosely coupled to other nonempty inputs. If we know that the arithmetic operation of division is included in computing a subfunction, we know that input that causes the divisor to become zero will be loosely coupled to other elements in the same subdomain. If we know that the author of the program has the tendency to commit missed-by-one error in composing a loop construct, the input that causes a loop to iterate zero or one time will be loosely coupled to the others. If we know that one of the subfunctions specified in the program specification has a mathematical pole at a certain point in the input domain, that input will be coupled loosely to others. There are others that can be found based on the knowledge of the skill or habit of the programmer, the programming language used, the programming environment in which the program will be developed and deployed, the intricacies in the application domain, and common sense about computer programming. We call that *error guessing* if new test cases are found in the ways just mentioned.

Test-case selection in this method is carried out mostly in an intuitive and ad hoc manner. It is done based not only on the program specification but also on the tester's intuition and knowledge in all related fields. The tester uses his or her knowledge to compile a list of possible errors or error-prone situations, and then selects test cases based on that list.

For example, consider Specification 3.2. After reading the specification the tester may wonder if the program is written correctly for the following situations:

- An input text of length zero
- A text containing no ENDOFTEXT character
- A text containing a word of length MAXPOS
- A text containing a very long word (of length greater than MAXPOS)
- A text containing nothing but BLANKs and NEWLINEs
- A text with an empty line
- Words separated by two or more consecutive BLANKs or NEWLINEs
- A line with BLANK as the first or last character
- A text containing digits or special characters
- A text containing nonprintable characters
- MAXPOS set to a number greater than the system default line length

In addition to experience in the problem domain and software construction, testing, and debugging, study of work on programming style (e.g., [KEPI99]) may help one to cultivate skill in error guessing.

The method of error guessing is probably most useful to expert users who have the need to do testing but have no access to the source code or program specification. For those who have access to the source code or program specification, the same knowledge can be used more effectively in the process of code or specification inspection (walkthrough) described in Section 6.4. It is in general easier to use that knowledge to locate a suspected fault through inspection than to use it to find an appropriate input that will reveal the fault in the test result. Besides, for the purpose of detecting and removing faults in the program, the method of inspection has the advantage that when a fault is detected, the nature of the fault and its location also become known. When a fault is revealed in a test, often a considerable amount of effort will be needed to identify and locate the source of the problem.

3.5   DISCUSSION

To build a software tool to automate the process of test-case selection based on program specification, the tool must have the capability to process the language in which the design or specification is written. Since such documents are usually written in a natural language, the capability for natural language processing required would be costly to acquire. Furthermore, the specification of a program usually does not contain all information needed to complete the test-case selection process. Some of that has to be derived from the documents by inference or from the facts available from other sources. For example, the information contained in Tables 3.3 and 3.5 cannot be derived mechanically from Specification 3.2. From the discussion in Sections 3.1 and 3.2, we can see that the analysis required is similar to what is done in the process of detailed program design. The cost of building such a tool is prohibitively high. Instead of building tools to extract the information from program specification automatically, it is more practical to require the program designer to provide the information which he or she might already have produced in the process of program design.

To be more specific, if subfunction (or predicate) testing is prescribed in a software development plan, the plan should also require the development team to provide all information needed for test-case selection. For each program unit, it must be clearly indicated how the function implemented by that unit is to be decomposed: that is, how the input domain is to be partitioned into subdomains, and the precise definition of each subfunction. Such information can be used directly to select test cases as described in Sections 3.1 and 3.2.

Although the method of boundary-value analysis is traditionally classified as a specification-based method, the information needed to select test cases can actually be obtained more readily from the source code. Construct a list of input/output variables based on the source code and then construct another based on the program specifications. There should be a one-to-one correspondence between the entries in these two lists. Otherwise, the discrepancies must be resolved before the lists can be used to select test cases as described in Section 3.3. Boundary-value analysis is largely a manual method.

Error guessing is also a manual method, but a computerized database can be built to facilitate its applications. The database may include generic information such as common mistakes committed by all programmers, and pitfalls associated with the programming language used. It may also include information peculiar to the project or the programmer. For example, some projects were known to suffer from frequent changes in requirements. The database may include items that have been subjected to frequent change. Some companies track all mistakes made by their programmers. The statistics compiled through such practice may be included in the database to help the tester to make the right guesses.

In short, automation is difficult and is not the most effective way to reduce the cost of specification-based test-case selection. It is the software engineering practice of building test cases whenever possible, especially at the detail program design stage, that will lead to a significant reduction in cost.

EXERCISES

3.1 Consider the following program specification: GW Ice-Cream Warehouse receives and distributes ice cream in 1-gallon cans. Information about each shipment received or distributed is entered by a clerk into a computerized database system.

A program is written to produce a weekly management report showing the net change in inventory of each item during the week. As depicted below, the report begins with a heading, which is followed by the report body. The report concludes with a line indicating the number of items that have a net change in inventory. Note that each item is identified by a string of no more than 16 characters.

GW Ice-Cream Co. Weekly Management Report	
Item	Net Change (gal)
BingCherry	−33
ChocolateMint	+46
FrenchVanilla	−77
LemonLime	−46
NuttyCocktail	+33
Sundae	+125
Number of items changed =	6

In practice, this program is to obtain all needed data from the database system. It is assumed that with an appropriate retrieval command, this database system is capable of producing all pertinent data as a stream of records, each of which contains three fields: the item name (a string), the type of shipment (R for received, D for distributed), and the quantity of that shipment (a nonnegative integer). The fields in a record are separated by a single blank character. The records in a stream are in alphabetical order by item names. A record is terminated by a carriage return, and a stream is terminated by a record with a single period as the item name.

Use the error-guessing method to find a set of test cases for the program.

3.2 Use the predicate testing method to find a set of test cases for the following program specification: Write a program that takes three positive integers as input and determine if they represent three sides of a triangle, and if they do, indicate what type of triangle it is. To be more specific, it should read three integers and set a flag as follows:

- If they represent a scalene triangle, set it to 1.
- If they represent an isosceles triangle, set it to 2.
- If they represent an equilateral triangle, set it to 3.
- If they do not represent a triangle, set it to 4.

3.3 Use the boundary-value analysis method to find a set of test cases for the following program specification: Write a program to compute the cubic root of a real number using Newton's method. Set q to 1.0 initially and compute the value of the expression $(2.0 * q + r/(q * q))/3.0$, where r is a given real number. If the value of this expression is almost the same as that of q (i.e., if the difference is less than or equal to d, where d is a given constant considerably smaller than q), return this value as the cube root of r. Otherwise, assign the value of this expression as the next value of q and repeat the computation.

3.4 Apply the subfunction testing method to find a set of test cases for the program specified in Exercise 3.2.

3.5 The method of predicate testing can be thought of as the counterpart of branch testing among the code-based test-case selection methods. What are the counterparts of boundary-value analysis and subfunction testing?

3.6 Critics of code-based test-case selection methods often argue that if a programmer failed to implement a certain part of a specification, no test cases would be selected to exercise that part of the program if the test cases are selected based on the source code. Refute or support that argument.

4 Software Testing Roundup

The code- and specification-based methods presented in earlier chapters are suitable primarily for use by the software developers in unit and integration testing, where the primary goal is to find faults in the program and have them removed. In practice, the need to test may arise in a user organization as well. The main purpose there is to assess the reliability of a software system in hand so that proper actions can be taken to deal with procurement or deployment issues. In that case, the code- and specification-based methods may become difficult to use because (1) the source code is generally not available to users, (2) users may not have access to information needed to apply code- or specification-based methods; and (3) a finished software product is usually so complex that users would not be in a position to test the system in parts even if the source code and specifications are both available.

A possible alternative is to test the software system as a whole and select test cases based on the operational characteristics of the software. For example, test cases can be selected based on an operational profile (i.e., a probability distribution of possible inputs in production runs). What can be revealed by a test case with a high probability in input distribution is important to the user because if the program works incorrectly for that test case, it will have a greater impact on the reliability of that program than in those with a low probability. On the other hand, what can be discovered through a low-probability test case is of much less value to the user unless the application has an unusually high reliability requirement.

Parenthetically, we would also like to point out that a faulty program may produce erroneous outputs that are inconsequential to the user, such as an extra nonprintable character at the end of a text line, or a missing pixel at the very end of each high-resolution 5- by 7-in. photographic print processed by the program. Unfortunately, we have no way of determining the possible consequence of a fault in a program until it is discovered somehow.

Using the operational scenarios of a software system, we may also be able to assess the economical impact of a failure. The ability to make this assessment is of practical importance because it will allow us to estimate the benefit of a test in economic terms. Interested readers may wish to refer to a method for estimating the cost of testing developed by Sherer [SHER92a]. The result of applying the method to a real-world job may be found in LeBlanc's thesis [LEBL99].

If we can assess the economical impact of a failure, we can assess the benefit of a test. When we start testing a software system, the cost and benefit of the test will increase with time. At some point, however, the benefit will start to level off because latent faults become fewer and farther apart, whereas the rate of increase in cost will remain about the same throughout. Hence, there will be a point in time at which the net benefit (i.e., the benefit minus the cost) peaks, and farther down the time line there will be another point at which it diminishes completely. Depending on the goal to be achieved, either of these can be chosen as the time to stop testing. If the cost-effectiveness is of primary importance, stop the test when the net benefit starts to decline. On the other hand, if reliability is more important, continue the test until the net benefit crosses into negative territory.

4.1   IDEAL TEST SETS

At present, there is no known test method that allows us to conclude from a successful test that a program is completely fault-free. If such a method exists, what properties should it have? In this chapter we present a theoretical result in this regard due to Goodenough and Gerhart [GOGE77]. First, we introduce the concept of an *ideal test set*, which is defined to be a set of test cases (selected from the input domain) such that a successful test of the program with this test set implies that the program will execute correctly with any input from the input domain.

To be more precise, let:

- S be a program
- D be the input domain of S
- T be a subset of D, called a test set
- $S(d)$ denote the result of executing program S with input d, where d is an element of D
- $OK(d)$ be a predicate that becomes true if and only if program S terminates cleanly for an execution with input d, and $S(d)$ is an acceptable result

Elements of T are called *test cases*. Set T constitutes an *ideal test set*, or an *ideal set of test cases*, if the fact that the program executes correctly with every element in T implies that it will execute correctly with any element of D. In theoretical computer science, we simply say that T is an ideal test set if $(\forall t)_T (OK(t)) \supset (\forall d)_D (OK(d))$ is a theorem. If we can find an ideal set of test cases for a given program, we can conclude from a success test that the program is completely error-free.

A test of the program using test set T is said to be *successful* if the program executes correctly with every element of T. Formally,

$$SUCCESSFUL(T) \equiv (\forall t)_T (OK(t))$$

In other words, SUCCESSFUL(T) is a shorthand for the statement "the program executes correctly with every element of T." A successful test of the program with a test case from T does not make this statement true. This statement is true only when it executes correctly with every element in T.

A set of subsets of D is called a *power set* of D, denoted 2^D. For example, if $D = \{a, b\}$, then $2^D = \{\{\ \}, \{a\}, \{b\}, \{a, b\}\}$, where $\{\ \}$ denotes an empty set. A test set is specified by using a condition called a *test-case selection criterion*. Let C be the test-case selection criterion. Then any subset of D (i.e., any element of the power set of D) satisfying C is a test set prescribed by C. For example, C could be something like "a set consisting of one element only." In that case, either $\{a\}$ or $\{b\}$ can be used as the test set.

A test-case selection criterion, C, is said to be *reliable* if and only if programs succeed or fail consistently when executing a set of test cases satisfying C. To be more precise,

$$\text{RELIABLE}(C) \equiv (\forall T_1)_{2^D}(\forall T_2)_{2^D}(C(T_1) \wedge C(T_2) \supset (\text{SUCCESSFUL}(T_1)$$
$$\equiv \text{SUCCESSFUL}(T_2)))$$

A test-case selection criterion, C, is said to be *valid* for a particular program if and only if there exists a set of test cases satisfying C that will cause the program to fail the test if the program is incorrect. To be more precise,

$$\text{VALID}(C) \equiv (\exists d)_D(\neg \text{OK}(d)) \supset (\exists T)_{2^D}(C(T) \wedge \neg \text{SUCCESSFUL}(T))$$

Note that validity does not imply that every set of test cases selected with C will cause the program to fail the test if the program is incorrect. It requires only that there exists at least one such set.

To clarify these concepts, let us consider a program with a single integer input. The program is intended to compute the remainder of $d \div 5$, but instead, it computes the remainder of $d \div 3$, where "$\div$" denotes integer division. To express it in the formalism introduced above, $S(d) = (d \bmod 3)$ for all $d \in D$ and $\text{OK}(d) \equiv S(d) = (d \bmod 5)$.

Observe that the program works correctly for all integers $15k + 0$, $15k + 1$, and $15k + 2$; that is, $\text{OK}(15k + 0)$, $\text{OK}(15k + 1)$, and $\text{OK}(15k + 2)$, for all nonnegative integers k, but it works incorrectly otherwise. Listed below are a few possible test-case selection criteria:

- $C_1(T) \equiv (T = \{1\}) \vee (T = \{2\})$ (reliable but not valid). Criterion C_1 says that the test set must consist of one and only one element, and the element has to be either 1 or 2. The program will produce 1 as the output for test case 1 and will produce 2 as the output for input 2. That is, $S(1) = (1 \bmod 3) = 1$ and $S(2) = (2 \bmod 3) = 2$. Since $\text{OK}(1) \equiv (1 \bmod 5) = (1 \bmod 3) \equiv T$ and $\text{OK}(2) \equiv (2 \bmod 5) = (2 \bmod 3) \equiv T$, the criterion is reliable. It is not valid because by using this test-case selection criterion the test will always be successful.

- $C_2(T) \equiv (T = \{t\}) \wedge (t \in \{0, 1, 2, 3, 4\})$ (not reliable but valid). Criterion C_2 says that the test set must contain one and only one element, and the element has to be 0, 1, 2, 3, or 4. Since $S(1) = \bmod(1, 3) = \bmod(1, 5) \equiv \text{OK}(1)$,

$S(4) = \text{mod}(4, 3) = 1 \neq \text{mod}(4, 5) = 4 \equiv \neg\text{OK}(4)$, it is not reliable, but it is valid because the program would not execute correctly with input 3 or 4.

- $C_3(T) \equiv (T = \{t\}) \wedge (t \in \{3, 4, 5, 6\})$ (reliable and valid). Criterion C_3 says that the test set should consist of only one integer in the range 3 to 6 inclusive. It is reliable because the test will fail consistently. It is valid because there is a test set that causes the test to fail.

- $C_4(T) \equiv (T = \{t, t + 1, t + 2, t + 3\}) \wedge (t \in D)$ (reliable and valid). C_4 requires the test set to contain four consecutive integers. It is valid because at least one of any four consecutive integers will cause the program to produce an incorrect result (i.e., will cause the test to fail). It is reliable because the program will fail with every test set if this criterion is used.

Goodenough and Gerhart [GOGE77] have shown that a successful test constitutes a direct proof of program correctness if it is done with a set of test cases selected by a test criterion that is both reliable and valid. This can be formally stated as a theorem as follows.

Theorem 4.1

$$(\exists C)(\text{VALID}(C) \wedge \text{RELIABLE}(C) \wedge (\exists T)_{2^D}(C(T) \wedge \text{SUCCESSFUL}(T)))$$
$$\supset \text{SUCCESSFUL}(D)$$

In general, it is difficult to prove the validity and reliability of a test-case selection criterion. In some cases, however, it may become trivial. For example, the proof of validity becomes trivial if C, the test-case selection criterion, does not exclude any member of D, the input domain, from being selected as a test case. If C does not allow any member of D to be selected, C can be valid only if the program is correct. In that case, it is required to prove the program's correctness in order to prove the validity of C. The proof of reliability becomes trivial if C requires selection of all elements in D because in that case there will only be one set of test cases. The proof of reliability also becomes trivial if C does not allow any element from D to be selected.

Before leaving the subject, we would like to present another important result obtained on this subject [HOWD75]. Essentially, it says that an ideal test set discussed above is not computable (i.e., an algorithm for finding ideal test sets for all programs does not exist).

Theorem 4.2   There exists no computable procedure H which given an arbitrary program S with domain D can be used to generate a nonempty proper subset $T \subset D$ such that

$$(\forall t)_T(\text{OK}(t)) \supset (\forall d)_D(\text{OK}(d))$$

This is a rather disappointing result, but it is useful to know the existence of this result so that no one will waste time searching for an algorithm to find ideal test sets.

4.2   OPERATIONAL TESTING

In this section we present a test-case selection method that is drastically different from those described in Chapters 2 and 3. Instead of choosing inputs that have high probabilities of revealing faults in the program, we could choose inputs that have high probabilities of being used in production runs as the test cases. To that end, the test cases are to be selected based on an operational profile. Let $USE(d)$ be the predicate that input $d \in D$ will be used in a production run of the program, and let $p(USE(d))$ be the probability that d will be used in a production run. A distribution of $p(USE(d))$ over the elements of D is called an *operational profile*.

We can use the operational profile to select a test set T_0 consisting of all elements in the input domain whose probability of being used in production runs is greater than or equal to some threshold value μ. That is,

$$T_0 = \{t | t \in D \land p(USE(t)) \geq \mu\}$$

Here μ is to be selected in such a way that $\Sigma p(USE(t))$ over all $t \in T_0$ is greater than or equal to a predetermined value, say γ. A test of a program using a test set so constructed is called an *operational* (or *use-based*) *test*.

What can be accomplished by performing an operational test on a given program? If we test the program with T_0, and if the test is successful, we can claim that γ is the probability that the program will work correctly in production runs. In other words, if γ is represented as a percentage, the program is γ percent reliable from the end user's point of view. Therefore, we can use an operational test to assess the reliability of a program (in production runs). Note that elements of T_0 are those inputs that have high probabilities of being used in a production run. Therefore, if a fault is revealed in an operational test, removal of that fault will contribute significantly to enhancing program reliability. This is in contrast to a debug test, in which a test case t with a very high $p(\neg OK(t))$ but very low $p(USE(t))$ might be used. If it reveals a fault, and if that fault is removed, it would have a small impact on program reliability.

It must be pointed out that the importance of a test case t is not determined exclusively by $p(USE(t))$ but also by the nature and severity of damage that the program failure may cause by running the program with that input. We discuss this subject in more detail at a more appropriate point later.

Procedurally, we make use of an operational profile to select test cases for operational testing. The operational profile of a software system is a probability distribution Q over its input domain D (i.e., an assignment to each element of D a probability of use in production runs). These probabilities sum to 1 over the elements of the input domain [i.e., $\Sigma_{d \in D} Q(d) = 1$]. To perform an operational test of a program is to test the program with a subset of n inputs with the highest probability of use.

In most applications, an element−by−element operational profile is far too detailed to obtain, and even a crude approximation requires considerable effort from the tester [MUSA93]. A practical way to construct an operational profile is to make use of the knowledge that the program will treat a certain subset of inputs, say X, in the same way. We then select a representative element χ from X and assign to it the use probability $\Sigma_{d \in X} Q(d)$. In words, we construct an approximated operational profile by partitioning the input domain into a set of "functionally equivalent" subdomains, and assign to each subdomain a use probability that is equal to the sum of that of its constituent elements. An operational test is to be performed by randomly selecting an element from each such subdomain.

For example, consider a payroll program used by a particular company. If we know that that program will process in exactly the same way the payroll information for any employee who earns a gross pay ranging from $4000 to $4999, and if 5% of the employees are in that category, we can define a subdomain consisting of input data for such employees and assign to it a use probability of 5%. To test the program operationally, only one test case needs to be selected randomly from that subdomain.

It should be clear by now that both debug and operational testing can be used to improve the reliability of a software product by detecting and subsequently removing latent faults. The question now is: Which is better? Frankl et al. have attempted to answer this question, but unfortunately, no simple and clear-cut answer was provided in their report [FHLS98]. Nevertheless, we believe that the following relevant comments can be made based on their findings.

Debug testing is commonly believed to be more effective than operational testing in revealing latent faults in a program. It should be noted, however, that the probability of failures caused by faults so discovered during production runs will be lower than that caused by faults discovered in operational testing. This is so because the test cases used in operational testing are those inputs most likely to be used in production runs, whereas the test cases used in debug testing can be anywhere on the probability distribution curve, including those used rarely, if ever. To put it in another way, the faults discovered in operational testing generally will lead to a shorter mean time between failures in production runs than those faults discovered in debug testing. Mean time between failures is an effective measure of reliability. If we have the faults discovered in operational testing removed, it will improve the mean time between failures more significantly than if we have the faults discovered in debug testing removed. That is, as far as the reliability is concerned, removal of faults discovered in operational testing will have a greater impact than removal of the faults discovered in debug testing.

Next, it should be remembered that the merit of operational testing mentioned above holds true only if the operational profile used to select test cases matches the one in reality. Otherwise, an operational test will become a debug test of arbitrary design. It should also be remembered that the operational profile of a software system often changes with time. Operational testing is attractive because it is easy to understand and easy to perform. If a test is successful, we will be able to assess the reliability achieved. On the other hand, if a test fails, we will be able to improve the reliability significantly by removing the fault revealed. Furthermore, it is applicable to any software system, large or small, regardless of the language and paradigm used in building the system. That is definitely problematic for debug testing.

Debug testing is clearly better if the probability that a failure point (i.e., an element of input domain that will cause the program to fail) will be selected in debug testing is greater than the probability that that point will be used in production runs. On the other hand, operational testing is clearly better if the probability that a failure point will be selected in debug testing is less than the probability that a point will be used in production runs. This could happen, for example, if only one test case is to be selected from each subdomain in debug testing, and failure points concentrate in one subdomain. In that case all test cases except one will be useless, and operational testing will become superior. This point would not be helpful in practice, however, because the whereabouts of failure points are unknown.

Some program failures may be more important than the others, depending on the cost incurred by, or damages inflicted on, the user. Thus, we cannot compare the effectiveness based on the number of failures detected alone. Debug testing may consistently reveal faults that lead to failures of little consequence. In that case, removal of those faults would have very little value to the end user.

A failure point in a safety-critical program may have an extremely low probability of being used in production runs but produce catastrophic results. Such a failure point will never be selected as a test case in operational testing. In that case, debug testing is clearly better. It should be remembered, however, that there is no guarantee that the fault will be discovered through debug testing, nor can we use debug testing to assert the absence of such a failure point in the input domain or to assess the level of reliability achieved.

Finally, it should be remembered that the reliability achieved through debug testing remains valid unless the program is modified in some way. The same cannot be said, however, about the reliability achieved through operational testing. In general, operational profiles change in time and with application environments. Consequently, it is entirely possible that in another time or place, the same software system may, in fact, not be as reliable as it is claimed to be.

4.3 INTEGRATION TESTING

Integration testing is a process in which the components of a software system are integrated into a functioning whole. After we have all components completed and thoroughly tested, we have to put them together to form an executable image of the entire system. Unless the system is very small, consisting of just a few components, we cannot accomplish this simply by compiling each component and then linking them together. The reason for this is that there will be problems: One cannot expect a program to work flawlessly the first time around. With all components integrated at the same time, it would be very difficult to isolate the problems and locate the sources of the problems. Even if we can find and remove the faults that way, it would be tedious and time consuming to recompile and relink all components whenever a change is made to a component.

A better way is to integrate the components incrementally. We start by putting two components together to form a subsystem, and test it thoroughly. We then proceed to integrate one component at a time into the subsystem so formed until the entire system is completed. Location and removal of the source of the problem become more manageable. Furthermore, there is no need to recompile and relink all components every time when a change is made to a component. There are two major approaches to this task: bottom-up and top-down. Each has advantages and disadvantages, and they can be combined to chart a hybrid approach that is deemed better in some cases.

Bottom-Up Integration   This approach begins with unit testing, followed by subsystem testing, followed by testing of the entire system. Unit testing has the goal of discovering faults in the individual system modules. The modules are tested in isolation from one another in an artificial environment known as a *test harness*, which consists of the driver programs and data necessary to exercise the modules. Modules are combined to form subsystems, and subsystems are then integrated to form the system as a whole. This approach is particularly appropriate for programs such as operating systems, in which the lowest-level modules are device drivers and service routines. Without those modules in place, it would be difficult to tell if a program is working correctly.

Advantages:
1. Unit testing is eased by a system structure that is composed of small, loosely coupled modules.
2. Since most input/output operations are done by the lower-level modules, how to feed test cases to the program is less of a problem.

Disadvantages:
1. The necessity to write and debug test harness for modules and subsystems. Test harness preparation can amount to 50% or more of the coding and debugging effort.
2. The necessity to deal with the complexity resulting from combining modules and subsystems into larger and larger units.

Top-Down Integration   This approach starts with the main routine and one or two immediately subordinate routines in the system structure. After this top-level skeleton has been thoroughly tested, it becomes the test harness for its immediately subordinate routines. Top-down integration requires the use of program stubs to simulate the effect of lower-level routines that are called by those being tested.

Advantages:
1. System integration is distributed throughout the implementation phase; modules are integrated as they are developed.
2. Top-level interfaces are tested first and most often.
3. The top-level routines provide a natural test harness for lower-level routines.
4. Faults are localized to the new modules and interfaces that are being added.

Disadvantages:
1. Sometimes it may be difficult to find top-level input data that will exercise a lower-level module in a particular manner.

2. The evolving system may be very expensive to run as a test harness for new routines on a lower level.

3. It may be costly to relink and reexecute a system each time a new routine is added.

4. It may not be possible to use program stubs to simulate modules below the current level.

Sandwich Integration   This approach is predominantly top-down, but bottom-up techniques are used on some modules and subsystems. This mix alleviates many of the problems encountered in pure top-down testing and retains the advantages of top-down integration at the subsystem and system level. Typically, the tester will start by finding a way to form a small subsystem consisting of modules on all levels to minimize the need of test drivers and stubs, and then proceed to add one module at a time to complete the integration. Sandwich integration also makes it easier to determine what the test cases should be and the corresponding outputs that should be expected. This approach will lead to the production of a functioning subsystem sooner than can be achieved using other methods.

Phased Integration   In the phased approach, units at the next level are integrated all at once, and the system is tested before integrating all modules at the next level.

Unit testing is a point of contention often raised in debates over the strategies to be used in integration testing. Poston and Bruen [POBR87] state that unit tests "let the engineers locate the problem areas and causes within minutes." Beizer [BEIZ84] and Hetzel [HETZ88] also advocate unit testing. On the other hand, Mills [MILL86], Yourdon [YOUR89], and Collins and Blay [COBL83] recommended integration strategies in which units are not tested in isolation but are tested only after integration into a system.

Experiments conducted by Solheim and Rowland [SORO93] indicated that top-down strategies generally produce the most reliable systems and are most effective in terms of fault detection. They conjectured that the higher reliability is related to the fact that the higher-level modules have a relatively high probability of being exercised by any given test case and are hence are more important than lower-level modules. The higher fault detection rate appeared to be caused by the fact that the top-down strategy exercises more modules per test case than do the other strategies. The experiments did not indicate a clear preference for either phased or incremental strategies.

Note that the approaches described in this section cannot be applied to object-oriented programs because there is no obvious top or bottom in the control structures of such programs.

4.4   TESTING OBJECT-ORIENTED PROGRAMS

All test methods discussed in earlier chapters were developed for programs written in a procedural language. Those test methods should, in principle at least, remain applicable to object-oriented programs because an object-oriented language is a pro-cedural language as well. Nevertheless, there are complicating factors idiosyncratic to the use of an object-oriented language or paradigm that require certain changes in the ways those methods are to be applied.

The common practice in debug testing a large software system is that we do unit testing first, followed by integration testing. What we do in unit testing is to test-execute a part of the program in isolation. It should be small so that if the test fails, the source of the failure can be readily located and removed. On the other hand, because it has to be test-executed in isolation, it must be large enough to constitute a complete syntactic unit that can be compiled separately. For a traditional software system written in C, it is commonly taken as a function or a set of related functions.

A method in an object-oriented program has the form of, and works like, a function in C. Nevertheless, it cannot be treated as a unit in unit testing because it does not constitute a syntactic unit that can be compiled separately. It is encapsulated in a larger program unit called a *class*, and may make use of other methods in the same class in its operation. Therefore, a *unit* in unit testing of an object-oriented program should be a class or a set of related classes.

Second, a class usually contains a storage unit that is implemented as some data structure in the private part that is not visible (i.e., not directly accessible to the test harness). Thus if we test-execute the unit with an input that causes changes in the content of the storage, the tester will have no way to determine if the correct changes have been made. For example, if the unit being tested is a class that implements a stack, there is no way to determine if an appropriate element has been added to the top of that stack after a PUSH operation has been performed.

A possible solution to this problem is to require the designer to make the class testable by including additional methods in the class that can be invoked to inspect the internal state of the class. Such methods are basically the software instruments permanently inserted in the program for testing and debugging purposes. Of course, the tester has to find some way to establish the correctness of the instruments before they can be used for their intended purposes.

Third, the internal storage of a class makes it a program unit with memory. This means that if the class is to be invoked with a sequence of inputs, the ordering of the inputs is important. For example, if we somehow determined that a stack class has to be tested with a PUSH and a POP, sending the class a sequence of messages "PUSH, POP" may produce a test result different from that of sending "POP, PUSH." The former will cause no net change to the stack content, whereas the latter may cause an error or exception if the initial stack content is empty.

Of course, this problem is not unique to an object-oriented program. A traditional program unit may have memory and thus the same problem as well. But the problem of having to deal with a unit with memory is far more common in testing object-oriented programs because of the way the units (i.e., classes) are organized. Recall that in an object-oriented program, direct access to the implementation of a method or data structure is not allowed. Whatever that we wish to do with an object has to be accomplished by invoking its methods in sequence and thus can be specified by a sequence of identities of methods. In the language of object-oriented technology, such a sequence is called a *message*. When a program unit in an object-oriented program needs to do something by making use of methods (in the same class or in other classes), it passes messages to invoke those methods.

A message is said to be *valid* if it is a sequence of invocations of methods in the class that will cause the methods to be executed with inputs from their intended input domains. To see what constitutes a *valid message* in unit-testing a class, it is useful to construct a directed graph as follows. There will be as many nodes as the number of methods in the class, each of which is associated uniquely with a method. An edge will emanate from node *A* and terminate at node *B* if it is permissible to send message *A* followed by message *B*. For the sake of argument we shall call such a graph a *message graph*. (It is called a *flow graph* by Zweben et al. [ZWHK92].)

Figure 4.1 shows a sample message graph for a stack class. With this class one can create a new stack, push an element on the stack, pop an element from the top, or examine the top element by using the methods NEW, PUSH, POP, and TOP, respectively. This graph shows that the message NEW cannot be followed by the message POP or TOP because the stack is empty immediately after the message NEW.

Note that a message is valid if and only if it forms a path in the message graph. Thus, in accordance with Figure 4.1, the message (NEW PUSH POP NEW PUSH POP) is valid, whereas (NEW PUSH POP NEW POP PUSH) is not. An invalid message will cause the program to fail or an exception to be raised. Obviously, we need to choose a valid message as a test case if the goal is to cause a certain program component to be exercised during the test. On the other hand, we should choose invalid messages as test cases if the purpose is to determine if appropriate exceptions would be raised.

It should be obvious that the test-case selection methods discussed in preceding chapters can be applied to unit-test a class as usual. A possible complicating factor is that the methods are invoked by messages. That is, the test cases are now messages instead of mere input data. If a message is chosen to cause a particular component

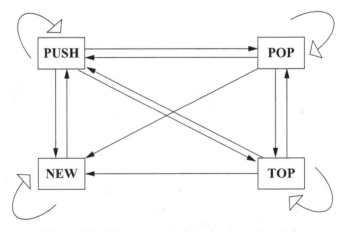

Figure 4.1   Message graph for a simple stack module.

in a method to be exercised, and if that message turns out to be invalid, it has to be replaced by a valid message that will serve the same purpose.

Because some classes in an object-oriented program may be created by making use of inheritance, a question may arise as to the extent to which a class has to be unit-tested if it is similar in some way to another class that has been completely unit-tested. Frankl and Weyuker have proposed 11 axioms for checking the completeness of a test [FRWE88], some of which, noted below, may be useful in answering that type of questions. For example, if we replace an inherited method with a locally defined method that performs the same function, will the test set for the inherited method be adequate for the locally defined method? According to Frankl and Weyuker's fifth axiom, the answer is negative. It says that an adequate test set for one algorithm is not necessarily an adequate test set for another even though they compute the same function. We can answer the same question based on the second principle of test-case selection. A test set that exercises every component in a program does not necessarily exercise every component in another, even though they compute the same function.

We can ask the same question about two programs of the same shape: that is, if one can be transformed into another through simple replacement of one or more relational operators with another, one or more arithmetic operators with another, or one or more constants with another. This type of situation occurs when the same items are inherited along different ancestor paths (i.e., via changes in the precedence ordering in a multiple inheritance scheme). Is the same test set adequate for both? The answer is negative according to Frankl and Weyker's sixth axiom on general multiple change. We can also see this based on the second principle of test-case selection because the changes may alter the control flow and thus the components exercised during the test.

Frankl and Weyuker's seventh axiom, called the *antidecomposition axiom*, states that something tested in one context will have to be retested if the context changes. For example, suppose that a given method has been thoroughly tested within the context of a given class. Further suppose that a specialization (i.e., a subclass or a derived class) is created based on this class and that the specialization inherits the tested method from the generalization (i.e., a superclass or base class). Even though a method has been tested thoroughly within the context of the generalization, it may not be so in the context of the specialization unless it is retested in a different context.

Frankl and Weyuker's eighth axiom, called the *anticomposition axiom*, states that adequate testing of each unit in isolation usually cannot be considered the same as adequate testing of the entire (integrated) program. According to this axiom, if we change the underlying implementation of an object and keep the interface intact, it is insufficient to test the modified object in isolation. We will have to retest all dependent units (e.g., specializations and units that directly reference the modified object) as well.

Finally, the guidelines for integration testing discussed in the preceding section remain applicable primarily to an object-oriented software system. Classes will be unit-tested in isolation and then integrated into the system incrementally for integration testing.

Recall that for traditional programs, integration testing can be done in either top-down or bottom-up manner. Unfortunately, there is no clear top or bottom in the organization of an object-oriented program (i.e., no invocation hierarchy). A class performs its function by invoking methods in the class or in other classes in such a way that the invocation graph has the structure of a graph instead of a (hierarchical) tree structure. Therefore, it is difficult to develop a general rule. In general, one may start with a small set of classes that can be used to produce an executable image and then expand it by adding one class at a time. The order in which the classes are integrated into the system will affect both the amount of test harness required and the number of new and useful test cases that we can find. Therefore, it should be chosen accordingly to optimize test efficiency.

4.5   REGRESSION TESTING

A program should be regression tested after it is modified to remove a fault or to add a function. The process is to rerun all or some of the previous tests, and introduce new test cases if necessary, to assure that no errors have been introduced through the changes or to verify that the software still performs the same functions in the same manner as did its older version. Testing is done in the same sequence of stages as it is done during development: unit testing, integration testing, system testing, and acceptance testing.

In performing a regression test for the unit changed, the program is instrumented to generate symbolic traces and the new traces are compared with those generated prior to the change. The effects of the change will become more obvious and readily understood from the symbolic traces.

A library of test cases is needed to make this test possible. It should be built and maintained such that past test cases and corresponding symbolic traces can be stored and retrieved efficiently.

4.6   CRITERIA FOR STOPPING A TEST

So far we have assumed that the test-case selection method we choose will produce a manageably small test set and that we will have enough time and resources to test every element in the test set so there is no need to worry about when to stop testing. But there are situations under which that assumption does not hold: for example, if we select test cases based on the operational profile, as discussed in Section 4.2, or if the test cases are chosen randomly from the input domain. New elements can be added endlessly to the test set being constructed. Under such circumstances the question of when to stop testing becomes germane. An obvious answer to this question is to dilute the test requirement by reducing the number of test cases to be used. For example, in software development contracts it is often stipulated that only some (say, 60%), rather than all, statements in the source code be exercised at least once during the test.

There is, however, a more elegant way to determine when to stop a test. Sherer has shown that it is possible to estimate the cost and benefit of doing program testing systematically, and it is therefore possible to find the optimal time to stop [SHER91]. She started by identifying potential faults in the program, assessing the possible economical impacts of failures that may be caused by those faults, and estimating the probabilities of such failures during a predetermined operation period to compute R, the risk.

The theory provides a formula to compute ΔR, the amount of reduction in R resulting from detection followed by removal of faults in the program through debug testing. It is assumed that no new fault is introduced in the debugging process. The theory also provides a way to estimate C, the cost of testing, which is essentially the sum of the cost of machine time and the labor required to do testing and debugging. The net benefit (NB) of doing the debug testing is therefore equal to the reduction in risk minus the cost of testing (i.e., NB $= \Delta R - C$). According to Sherer's theory, the cost of testing increases almost linearly with the time required to do the test. Initially, the latent faults in the program are more numerous and thus easier to find. Thus, ΔR, the reduction in risk, tends to increase exponentially with time. Gradually, the latent faults become fewer and harder to find, and the magnitude of ΔR starts to level off. The net benefit, NB, therefore increases exponentially at the beginning, then starts to level off, and reaches its maximum at t_γ^*. If further testing is done beyond that point, the increase in cost starts to outpace the increase in benefit, and the net benefit decreases, eventually becoming zero and then negative. The relationship among risk, cost, and benefit is depicted by the curves shown in Figure 4.2. The obvious time to stop the testing is t_γ^*, when the net benefit becomes maximal, or if ultrareliability is required, the point at which the net benefit becomes zero.

The method outlined above is conceptually enlightening. To use it in practice, however, is not easy because it involves estimation of several statistical parameters that require historical data and good knowledge of statistics [LEBL99].

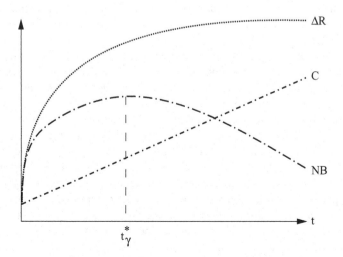

Figure 4.2   General plot of cost versus benefit in doing debug testing.

4.7   CHOOSING A TEST-CASE SELECTION CRITERION

Having been presented with a plethora of test-case selection criteria, the reader may wonder which criterion to use in practice. We address this question in the remainder of the chapter. The answer would be obvious if for a given program we knew how to formulate a criterion that is both reliable and valid, as discussed in Section 4.1. Unfortunately, we do not know how to do that in practice.

If an accurate and up-to-date operational profile is available, and if the required reliability of the program to be tested is not ultrahigh, probably the best choice is to perform an operational test. Select as the initial element of the test set the input that has the highest probability of being used in a production run. Then add to the set the input with the same or the next-highest probability. Keep adding elements to the test set until the sum of probabilities of elements in the set becomes equal to or greater than the reliability required. For example, if the reliability required is 99.9% of the time without failure, the probabilities of elements in the test set should add up to 0.999 or greater.

How high must the required reliability be to be ultrahigh? By *ultrahigh* here we mean that validation of the reliability requirement necessitates detection of faults that rarely cause the program to fail in production runs—so rare that the mean time between failures is longer than the time span in which the operational profile is compiled. In that event the test case needed to reveal the fault would not be included in the operational profile. Therefore, the test set constructed based on that profile will never reveal the fault. The only alternative is to perform debug testing.

In this book we argue that the best way to do debug testing is to apply the first principle of test-case selection repeatedly to add new test cases to the test set being constructed, and to use the second principle to determine when to stop the process. The first principle, as the reader may recall, says that in choosing an additional element for a test set, preference should be given to those that are computationally as loosely coupled to the existing elements as possible. The second principle says that there should be enough elements in the test set to exercise every component at least once during the test.

The first principle guides us to construct an *efficient test set*, efficient in the sense that the same fault-discovery probability can be achieved with as few test cases as possible. The second principle guides us to build an *effective test set*, effective in the sense that as many latent faults as possible will be revealed by the test. The second principle requires us to choose a certain type of component to be exercised during the test. That in effect is the same as choosing one of the test-case selection criteria discussed in earlier chapters. For example, if we choose the program statement as the component to be exercised, it is the same as choosing the statement test described in Chapter 2 as the test-case selection criterion; and if we choose the segment of an execution path that begins with a definition of some datum and ends with a use of that definition, it is the same as choosing a criterion for data-flow testing.

Why do we wish to speak of choosing a type of component instead of choosing a test-case selection criterion? There are at least three advantages in doing so. First, it tells us what needs to be done instead of how to do it, thus leaving more room for process innovation and optimization. Second, because the relationship among methods becomes more obvious, it gives us a better sense of their relative fault-discovery capabilities. Third, it allows a test-case selection criterion to be adapted for programs of different sizes, written in different languages, and constructed using different paradigms. More will be said on this point later.

For unit testing in a software development effort, the most popular choice of component appears to be the program statement. Commonly known as *statement testing* this requires that every statement in a program be exercised at least once during a test (see Chapter 2). Statement testing is often criticized as being overly simplistic and inadequate. So what are the possible reasons that this choice is so popular? First, the rationale behind this criterion is easy to understand; second, satisfaction of the criterion can easily be verified; third, the program analysis required is relatively minimal; and fourth, the processes of test-case selection and coverage verification can be automated to a great extent.

The choice of component to be exercised can be "upgraded" from program statement to branch in the control flow if the statement test is deemed inadequate. Generally speaking, there will be a minor increase in the number of test cases but not in the complexity of the analysis required.

If the fault-discovery capability needs to be strengthened further, the coverage tree depicted in Figure 2.5 is used as a guide to select a criterion that has a higher coverage. Generally speaking, the higher the coverage of a criterion, the greater the fault-discovery capability of the test set chosen using that criterion. The fault-discovery capability can also be strengthened by choosing an additional type of component to be exercised from the detailed design or program specification as described in Chapter 3. For example, if time and resources permit, add subfunction testing to boost the fault detection capability. It is arguably the most potent among all methods of test-case selection based on program specifications. If a lesser method is desired due to time or resource constraints, add predicate testing instead, which is effective in discovering faults related to the decomposition of the function specified, or add boundary-value analysis instead, which is effective in discovering faults related to a program's ability to handle correctly the input and output values on, and in the vicinity of, the upper and lower bounds. Use error guessing to choose additional test cases whenever possible because it is relatively easy to do and many programmers do it reasonably well.

In theory, the mutation method appears to be a good testing method if we know for sure that a programmer is competent and if the types of mistakes that he or she tends to make can be expressed in terms of a set of mutation rules. In practice, however, its practical value is limited by the large number of test cases it requires. As exemplified in Section 2.7, the number of test cases needed for a mutation test is usually many times that for a statement test. Judging from the fact that most software developers find it too costly to do a full statement test, it is doubtful that any developers could afford to do a mutation test in practice.

Before proceeding further, we digress momentarily to address the question of how to choose the initial elements of a test set. The following observations should be useful in that connection. The significance of a test result would be greater if the test cases used are the inputs frequently used in production runs as well. The cost of testing would be lower if the correct outputs corresponding to the test cases used are known or readily determinable. Experience shows that expert users or designers of a program often have their own favorite test cases. Such test cases are important in that their owners know exactly what the program is supposed to produce as the test results.

Thus, we can choose the initial elements of the test set as follows. If the designers or expert users of the program have test cases to offer, use them as the initial elements. Otherwise, if the most frequently used inputs (for production runs) are known, use them as the initial elements; otherwise, if the required outputs of some inputs are known or readily determinable, choose them as the initial elements; otherwise, choose as the initial element an input for which the program has to perform some nontrivial computation. The choice of the initial element(s) may not be unique. Different choices of initial element(s) would result in the formation of different test sets. That should be of no concern, however, because most test-case selection criteria can be satisfied by more than one subset of the input domain.

Those who are more theoretically oriented may have noticed that the way we construct a test set follows roughly the way a set is defined recursively in modern mathematics. We have just explained how to find the initial element(s) of the set being defined recursively. The first principle of test-case selection is designed to construct a new element from the existing elements, and the second principle is designed to determine when to terminate the process. This conceptual framework provides a uniform way to specify how a test set is to be built.

Thus, to decide how to select test cases in a particular circumstance, all we need is to choose a type of component to be exercised. For a developer to perform unit testing, the choice of program statement as the component to be exercised has proven to be quite appropriate. Because the developer of a program always has access to the source code as well as the program specifications, the developer has the greatest freedom to choose one or more types of components to be exercised. For integration testing, the component to be exercised may be a function in C++ if it is a traditional program, or a class or method if it is an object-oriented program. For system testing, the component to be tested can be a functional subsystem. In applying the first principle to choose an input that is computationally as loosely coupled as possible to the existing elements, choose one that will cause a different sequence of components to be executed or if not possible, choose one that will cause some components to perform different functions.

User organizations may also have the need to test a program systematically. The purpose is to find as many faults as possible so that an accurate assessment of program reliability can be made. Ordinarily, the user organization has no access to the source code and design documentation. Therefore, the only choice is to test the entire software system as a whole. To perform a reasonably complete test, and to apply the two principles properly, the tester must study the system to identify all the major functional subsystems and learn how they interact. Choose functional subsystems as the type of component to be exercised. In applying the first principle, choose an input that will cause a different sequence of subsystems to be executed or one that will cause at least one subsystem to perform a different function.

EXERCISES

4.1 A program was written to determine if a given year in the Gregorian calendar is a leap year. The well-known part of the rule, stipulating that it is a leap year if it is divisible by 4, is implemented correctly in the program. The programmer, however, is unaware of the exceptions: A centenary year, although divisible by 4, is not a leap year unless it is also divisible by 400. Thus, while year 2000 was a leap year, the years 1800 and 1900 were not. Determine if the following test-case selection criteria are reliable or valid.

(a) $C_1(T) \equiv (T = \{1, 101, 1001, 10001\})$

(b) $C_2(T) \equiv (T = \{t | 1995 \leq t \leq 2005\})$

(c) $C_3(T) \equiv (T = \{t | 1895 \leq t \leq 1905\})$

(d) $C_4(T) \equiv (T = \{t\} \wedge t \in \{400, 800, 1200, 1600, 2000, 2400\})$

(e) $C_5(T) \equiv (T = \{t, t+1, t+2, t+3, t+4\} \wedge t \in \{100, 200, 300, 400, 500\})$

(f) $C_6(T) \equiv (T = \{t, t+1, t+2, \ldots, t+399\} \wedge t \in D)$

(g) $C_7(T) \equiv (T = \{t_1, t_2, t_3\} \wedge t_1, t_2, t_3 \in D)$

4.2 If the second principle of test-case selection (see Chapter 1) is used to develop a test-case selection method, the answer to the question of when to stop testing is obvious: Stop testing when all components have been exercised at least once during the test. Identify all the methods to which this answer is not applicable.

4.3 What are the similarities and differences between traditional programs and object-oriented programs as far as applications of the first and second principles of test-case selection are concerned?

4.4 Enumerate the factors you must consider in choosing between code inspection and testing, and between debug and operational testing.

4.5 Identify tasks that are common in all the methods for test-case selection, and discuss the degree of difficulty in automating each.

5 Analysis of Symbolic Traces

Previously we pointed out that a negative test result is in general more significant than a positive one. If we test-execute a program with a test case, and if the program produced an incorrect result, we can definitely conclude that the program is faulty. If the program produced a correct result, however, all we can say is that the program is correct for that particular input. That is not statistically significant considering the fact that all nontrivial programs have a vast number of possible inputs. The significance of a correct test result can, however, be enhanced by analyzing the execution path to determine the condition under which it will be traversed and the nature of computation to be performed in the process. In this chapter we show how an execution path can be analyzed for this purpose.[1]

5.1 SYMBOLIC TRACE AND PROGRAM GRAPH

As explained briefly earlier, we describe an execution path by using a *symbolic trace*, which is essentially a list of statements and branch predicates that occur on the path. To fix the idea, consider the C++ program below.

Program 5.1

```
#include <iostream>
#include <string>
using namespace std

int atoi(string& s)
{
    int i, n, sign;

    i = 0;
    while (isspace(s[i]))
```

---

[1]Portions of this chapter were adapted, with permission, from "State Constraints and Pathwise Decomposition of Programs," *IEEE Transactions on Software Engineering*, vol. 16, no. 8, Aug. 1990, pp. 880–896.

```
    i = i + 1;
 if (s[i] == '-')
   sign = -1;
 else
   sign = 1;
 if (s[i] == '+' || s[i] == '-')
   i = i + 1;
 n = 0;
 while (isdigit(s[i])) {
   n = 10 * n + (s[i] - '0');
   i = i + 1;
 }
 return sign * n;
}
```

Potentially, this program can be executed along the path described by the following symbolic trace.

Trace 5.2

```
i = 0;
/\ !(isspace(s[i]));
/\ !(s[i] == '-');
sign = 1;
/\ !(s[i] == '+' || s[i] == '-');
n = 0;
/\ (isdigit(s[i]));
n = 10 * n + (s[i] - '0');
i = i + 1;
/\ !(isdigit(s[i]));
return sign * n;
```

In the above, each expression prefixed with a digraph "/\" denotes a predicate that must be evaluated true at that point in the control flow. The reason for choosing this special symbol will be given later. We say "potentially" because this list is constructed based on the syntax of the program. This path may turn out to be an infeasible path if no input can make all the predicates true.

We present another symbolic trace to illustrate the idea further.

Trace 5.3

```
#include <iostream>
#include <string>
using namespace std
```

```
int atoi(string& s)
{
    i = 0;
    /\ (isspace(s[i]));
    i = i + 1;
    /\ !(isspace(s[i]));
    /\ (s[i] == '-');
    sign = -1;
    /\ !(s[i] == '+' || s[i] == '-');
    n = 0;
    /\ (isdigit(s[i]));
    n = 10 * n + (s[i] - '0');
    i = i + 1;
    /\ (isdigit(s[i]));
    n = 10 * n + (s[i] - '0');
    i = i + 1;
    /\ !(isdigit(s[i]));
    return sign * n;
}
```

This trace is obtained by iterating each loop one more time and redirecting the execution at the first "if" statement. We also show that the declarative part of the program can be included if the information included therein is needed to understand the trace better.

Next, to help envisage the structure of an execution path, we introduce a graphic representation of a program called a *program graph*. We use a directed graph to represent the control-flow structure of a program. Each edge in the graph is associated with a pair of the form $</\backslash C, S>$, where C is the condition that must be true for that edge to be traversed, and S is a description of the computation to be performed when that edge is traversed. Program 5.1 can thus be represented by the program graph shown in Figure 5.1 and Trace 5.2 can be represented by the program graph depicted in Figure 5.2.

5.2   THE CONCEPT OF A STATE CONSTRAINT

Before we can proceed to develop rules for simplifying a symbolic trace, we need to clarify the semantics of a pair of the form $</\backslash C, S>$, which, in the abstract, is the basic element of any symbolic trace. One may be tempted to say that it is equivalent to a conditional statement of the form "if C, then S." A closer look at what is represented by a symbolic trace will show that it is not. If C is true, $</\backslash C, S>$ and "if C, then S" will do the same. If C is false, however, "if C, then S" will do nothing [i.e., will not change the value of any variables (data structures) involved]. Given $</\backslash C, S>$,

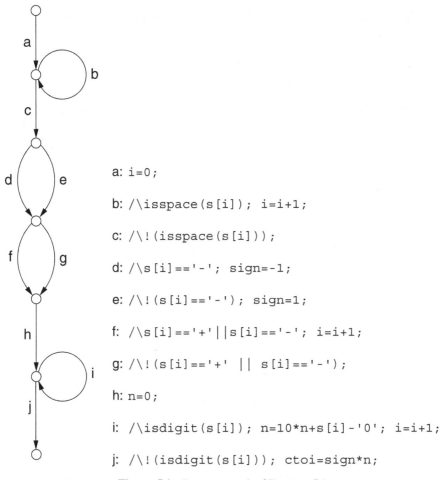

a: `i=0;`

b: `/\isspace(s[i]); i=i+1;`

c: `/\!(isspace(s[i]));`

d: `/\s[i]=='-'; sign=-1;`

e: `/\!(s[i]=='-'); sign=1;`

f: `/\s[i]=='+'||s[i]=='-'; i=i+1;`

g: `/\!(s[i]=='+' || s[i]=='-');`

h: `n=0;`

i: `/\isdigit(s[i]); n=10*n+s[i]-'0'; i=i+1;`

j: `/\!(isdigit(s[i])); ctoi=sign*n;`

Figure 5.1   Program graph of Program 5.1.

however, we know only that the path associated with that pair will not be traversed. From this pair we cannot derive any information about what the program is going to do if C is false. Therefore, it is more appropriate to say that the meaning of $</\backslash C, S>$ becomes undefined if C is false.

For that reason we call $/\backslash C$ a constraint instead of a path or branch predicate. To be more specific, we shall use $/\backslash C$ as a shorthand notation for the restrictive clause [HUAN08]: *The program state at this point must satisfy predicate C, or else the program becomes undefined.* By *program state* here we mean the aggregate of values assumed by all variables involved. Since this clause constrains the states assumable by the program, it is called a *state constraint*, or simply a *constraint*, and is denoted $/\backslash C$.

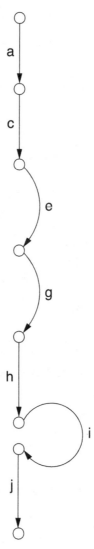

Figure 5.2 Execution path in Program 5.1.

State constraints are designed to be inserted into a program to create another program. For example, given a program of the form S_1; S_2, a new program can be created by inserting the constraint $/\backslash C$ between the two statements to form a new program: S_1; $/\backslash C$; S_2. This new program is said to be created from the original by constraining the program states to C prior to execution of S_2. Intuitively, this new program is a subprogram of the original because its definition is that of the original program restricted to C. Within that restriction, this new program performs the same computation as the original.

A state constraint is a semantic modifier. The meaning of a program modified by a state constraint can be defined formally in terms of Dijkstra's *weakest precondition*[2] [DIJK76] as follows. Let S be a programming construct and C be a predicate; then for any postcondition R:

Axiom 5.4 $\text{wp}(/\backslash C; S, R) \equiv C \wedge \text{wp}(S, R)$.

To better explain how a constraint modifies the semantics of a program, we now define two possible relations among programs. The first is the logical equivalence of two programs, which can be defined precisely as follows.

Definition 5.5   Program S_1 is said to be *equivalent* to S_2 if $\text{wp}(S_1, R) \equiv \text{wp}(S_2, R)$ for any postcondition R. This relation is denoted by $S_1 \Leftrightarrow S_2$.

The second is a weaker relation, called the *subprogram relation*.

Definition 5.6   Program S_2 is said to be a *subprogram* of program S_1 if $\text{wp}(S_2, R) \supset \text{wp}(S_1, R)$ for any postcondition R. This relation is denoted by $S_1 \Rightarrow S_2$.

With these definitions, one can now determine the relationship between any programs, with or without state constraints. For example, consider again the programs $S_1; S_2$ and $S_1; /\backslash C; S_2$ mentioned previously. Since $\text{wp}(S_1; /\backslash C; S_2, R) \equiv \text{wp}(S_1, \text{wp}(/\backslash C; S_2, R)) \equiv \text{wp}(S_1, C \wedge \text{wp}(S_2, R)) \equiv \text{wp}(S_1, C) \wedge \text{wp}(S_1, \text{wp}(S_2, R)) \equiv \text{wp}(S_1, C) \wedge \text{wp}(S_1; S_2, R)$, it follows that $\text{wp}(S_1; /\backslash C; S_2, R) \supset \text{wp}(S_1; S_2, R)$. Thus, by Definition 5.6, program $S_1; /\backslash C; S_2$ is a subprogram of program $S_1; S_2$. In general, a symbolic trace of a program constitutes a subprogram of the original as defined by Definition 5.6.

We can trivially constrain a program with a condition C that is always true (i.e., $C \equiv T$). In that case $\text{wp}(/\backslash T; S, R) \equiv T \wedge \text{wp}(S, R) \equiv \text{wp}(S, R)$, and therefore, by Definition 5.5, $/\backslash T; S \Leftrightarrow S$. That is, a state constraint will have no effect on a program if it is always true. On the other hand, if $C \equiv F$ (i.e., if C is always false), $\text{wp}(/\backslash F; S, R) \equiv F \wedge \text{wp}(S, R) \equiv F \equiv \text{wp}(/\backslash F; S', R)$ for any S, S', and R, and therefore $/\backslash F; S \Leftrightarrow /\backslash F; S'$. In words, any two programs are (trivially) equivalent if both are constrained by a predicate that can never be true.

5.3   RULES FOR MOVING AND SIMPLIFYING CONSTRAINTS

A state constraint not only constrains the program state directly at the point where it is placed, but also indirectly at other points upstream and downstream in control flow as well. Note that in program $S_1; /\backslash C; S_2$, the predicate C is true if and only if $\text{wp}(S_1, C)$ is true before execution of S_1. Thus, by constraining the program state

---

[2]The weakest precondition of program S with respect to postcondition Q, commonly denoted by $\text{wp}(S, Q)$, is defined as the weakest condition for the initial state of S such that activation of S will certainly result in a properly terminating happening, leaving S in a final state satisfying Q.

between S_1 and S_2 to C, it also constrains the program state indirectly before S_1 to $\text{wp}(S_1, C)$, and the program state after S_2 to R, where $\text{wp}(S_2, R) \equiv C$.

The *scope* of a state constraint, which is defined to be the range of control flow within which the constraint has an effect, may or may not span the entire program. A state constraint will have no effect beyond a statement that undefines, or assigns a constant value to, the variables involved. For example, a state constraint such as $x > 0$ will have no effect on the program states beyond the statement `read(x)` upstream, the statement `return` downstream if x is a local variable, or the statement $x := 4$ upstream or downstream.

Another view of this property is that exactly the same constraint on the program states in $S_1; S_2$ can be affected by placing constraint $/\backslash\text{wp}(S_1, C)$ before S_1 or constraint $/\backslash C$ before S_2. To be more precise, $S_1; /\backslash C; S_2 \Leftrightarrow /\backslash\text{wp}(S_1, C); S_1; S_2$ if the scope of $/\backslash C$ is not terminated by S_1. In general, this relationship can be stated as follows.

Theorem 5.7 $S; /\backslash R \Leftrightarrow /\backslash\text{wp}(S, R); S$.

This relation can be used repeatedly to move a constraint upstream: that is, to constrain the program equivalently at a different point upstream. We shall use Trace 5.2 to demonstrate how it works.

```
        i = 0;
        /\ !(isspace(s[i]));
        /\ !(s[i] == '-');
        sign = 1;
        /\ !(s[i] == '+' || s[i] == '-');
        n = 0;
        /\ (isdigit(s[i]));
        n = 10 * n + (s[i] - '0');
        i = i + 1;
        /\ !(isdigit(s[i]));
        return sign * n;

⇔      /\ !(isspace(s[0]));
        i = 0;
        /\ !(s[i] == '-');
        sign = 1;
        /\ !(s[i] == '+' || s[i] == '-');
        n = 0;
        /\ (isdigit(s[i]));
        n = 10 * n + (s[i] - '0');
        i = i + 1;
        /\ !(isdigit(s[i]));
        return sign * n;
```

⇔
```
/\ !(isspace(s[0]));
/\ !(s[0] == '-');
/\ !(s[0] == '+' || s[0] == '-');
i = 0;
sign = 1;
n = 0;
/\ (isdigit(s[i]));
n = 10 * n + (s[i] - '0');
i = i + 1;
/\ !(isdigit(s[i]));
return sign * n;
```

⇔
```
/\ !(isspace(s[0]));
/\ !(s[0] == '-');
/\ !(s[0] == '+' || s[0] == '-');
/\ (isdigit(s[0]));
i = 0;
sign = 1;
n = 0;
n = 10 * n + (s[i] - '0');
i = i + 1;
/\ !(isdigit(s[i]));
return sign * n;
```

⇔
```
/\ !(isspace(s[0]));
/\ !(s[0] == '-');
/\ !(s[0] == '+' || s[0] == '-');
/\ (isdigit(s[0]));
i = 0;
sign = 1;
n = 0;
n = 10 * n + (s[i] - '0');
/\ !(isdigit(s[i+1]));
i = i + 1;
return sign * n;
```

⇔
```
/\ !(isspace(s[0]));
/\ !(s[0] == '-');
/\ !(s[0] == '+' || s[0] == '-');
/\ (isdigit(s[0]));
/\ !(isdigit(s[1]));
i = 0;
sign = 1;
n = 0;
n = 10 * n + (s[i] - '0');
i = i + 1;
return sign * n;
```

The basic step of source-code transformation made possible by virtue of Theorem 5.7 is also known as *backward substitution* [DIJK90], so called because the theorem is usually applied to an assignment statement of the form "$x := e$" and $\mathrm{wp}(x := e, R)$ is computed by substituting e at every occurrence of x in R.

In an attempt to find an appropriate test case, it is usually only apparent that a certain condition must be true at some point in the control flow so that a certain branch will be traversed when the control reaches that point, but it is often difficult to tell what has to be true at the input to make that condition true at that point. We can find the answer systematically by performing backward substitution repeatedly along the symbolic trace.

On other occasions it may become necessary to determine if a given (syntactic) path in the program (graph) is feasible, and if so, what inputs would cause that path to be traversed. We could find the answer systematically by constructing the symbolic trace of the path and then performing backward substitution repeatedly until all path constraints are located on top of the trace. Any input that satisfies all the constraints on the top simultaneously will cause the trace to be traversed. On the other hand, if no input can satisfy all constraints in aggregate (i.e., if the conjunction of all constraints is a contradiction), that path is an infeasible path. We saw the need to make this determination in Chapter 2 when finding test cases for data-flow testing.

To illustrate, let us reconsider Program 2.2, which is repeated below together with its program graph (Figure 5.3) for convenience.

```
main()
{
    int x, y, z;
    cin >> x >> y;
    z = 1;
    while (y != 0) {
        if (y % 2 == 1)
            z = z * x;
        y = y / 2;
        x = x * x;
    }
    cout << z << endl;
}
```

By studying the path segments in Figure 5.3 that have to be exercised during a du-path test, we see that the loop in Program 2.2 may have to be iterated zero, one, or two times to traverse the paths described by αη, αβδεη, αβγεη, αβδεβδεη, αβδεβγεη, αβγεβδεη, and αβδεβγεη. Using the rules developed above, we see the shortest execution path,

αη: cin >> x >> y;
       z = 1;

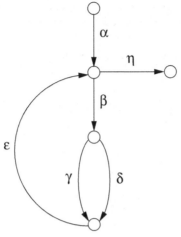

where   α: cin >> x >> y;
         z = 1;

         β: /\ y != 0;

         γ: /\ !(y % 2 == 1);

         δ: /\ y % 2 == 1;
            z = z * x;

         ε: y = y / 2;
            x = x * x;

         η: /\ !(y != 0);
               cout << Z << endl;

Figure 5.3   Program graph of Program 2.2.

         /\ !(y != 0);
         cout << z << endl;

⇔   cin >> x >> y;
         /\ y == 0;
         z = 1;
         cout << z << endl

which can be traversed by letting y == 0. Observe that the direction of execution in this program would not be influenced by the value of variable *x* and thus is not mentioned in the remainder of this discussion.

Next, the paths generated by iterating the loop once include the following:

αβδεη:
```
cin >> x >> y;
z = 1;
/\ y != 0;
/\ y % 2 == 1;
z = z * x;
y = y / 2;
x = x * x;
/\ !(y != 0);
cout << z << endl;
```

⟺
```
cin >> x >> y;
/\ y != 0;
/\ y % 2 == 1;
/\ (y / 2 == 0);
z = 1;
z = z * x;
y = y / 2;
x = x * x;
cout << z << endl;
```

Path αβδεη can be traversed by letting y == 1. On the other hand, we see that the next path,

αβγεη:
```
cin >> x >> y;
z = 1;
/\ y != 0;
/\ !(y % 2 == 1);
y = y / 2;
x = x * x;
/\ !(y != 0);
cout << z << endl;
```

⟺
```
cin >> x >> y;
/\ y != 0;
/\ !(y % 2 == 1);
/\ (y / 2 == 0);
z = 1;
y = y / 2;
x = x * x;
cout << z << endl;
```

cannot be traversed, and thus cannot be used as a candidate path in selecting test cases. Next we analyze the four paths obtained by iterating the loop twice.

αβδεβδεη:
```
cin >> x >> y;
z = 1;
/\ y != 0;
/\ y % 2 == 1;
z = z * x;
y = y / 2;
x = x * x;
/\ y != 0;
/\ y % 2 == 1;
z = z * x;
y = y / 2;
x = x * x;
/\ !(y != 0);
cout << z << endl;
```

⇔
```
cin >> x >> y;
/\ y != 0;
/\ y % 2 == 1;
/\ y / 2 != 0;
/\ (y / 2) % 2 == 1;
/\ ((y / 2) / 2) == 0);
z = 1;
z = z * x;
y = y / 2;
x = x * x;
z = z * x;
y = y / 2;
x = x * x;
cout << z << endl;
```

which can be traversed by letting y == 3. The other path, obtained similarly by iterating the loop once, is

αβδεβγεη:
```
cin >> x >> y;
z = 1;
/\ y != 0;
/\ y % 2 == 1;
z = z * x;
y = y / 2;
x = x * x;
```

```
/\ y != 0;
/\ !(y % 2 == 1);
y = y / 2;
x = x * x;
/\ !(y != 0);
cout << z << endl;
```

⇔
```
cin >> x >> y;
/\ y != 0;
/\ y % 2 == 1;
/\ y / 2 != 0;
/\ !((y / 2) % 2 == 1);
/\ ((y / 2) / 2) == 0);
z = 1;
z = z * x;
y = y / 2;
x = x * x;
y = y / 2;
x = x * x;
cout << z << endl;
```

which cannot be traversed by any y. The five constraints listed on top of the symbolic trace cannot be satisfied simultaneously by any integer y.

Next, consider the four potential execution paths obtained by iterating the loop twice.

αβγεβδεη:
```
cin >> x >> y;
z = 1;
/\ y != 0;
/\ !(y % 2 == 1);
y = y / 2;
x = x * x;
/\ y != 0;
/\ y % 2 == 1;
z = z * x;
y = y / 2;
x = x * x;
/\ !(y != 0);
cout << z << endl;
```

⇔
```
cin >> x >> y;
/\ y != 0;
/\ !(y % 2 == 1);
/\ y / 2 != 0;
```

```
/\ (y / 2) % 2 == 1;
/\ (y / 2) / 2 == 0);
z = 1;
y = y / 2;
x = x * x;
z = z * x;
y = y / 2;
x = x * x;
cout << z << endl;
```

This symbolic trace represents a feasible execution path that can be traversed by letting y == 2.

```
αβγεβγεη:    cin >> x >> y;
             z = 1;
             /\ y != 0;
             /\ !(y % 2 == 1);
             y = y / 2;
             x = x * x;
             /\ y != 0;
             /\ !(y % 2 == 1);
             y = y / 2;
             x = x * x;
             /\ !(y != 0);
             cout << z << endl;
```

```
⇔            cin >> x >> y;
             /\ y != 0;
             /\ !(y % 2 == 1);
             /\ y / 2 != 0;
             /\ !(y / 2) % 2 == 1;
             /\ (y / 2) / 2 == 0);
             z = 1;
             y = y / 2;
             x = x * x;
             y = y / 2;
             x = x * x;
             cout << z << endl;
```

This symbolic trace represents an infeasible path because its constraints cannot be satisfied simultaneously by any y.

As explained in Section 2.5, checking the path segments that have to be exercised during an all-du-path test against the set of all feasible paths that iterate the loop up to towfold, reveals that we need one more execution path that contains εβγε as a subpath. Some reflection will show that path αβδεβγεβδεη is a possibility. We check next to see if it is feasible.

```
αβδεβγεβδεη:    cin >> x >> y;
                z = 1;
                /\ y != 0;
                /\ y % 2 == 1;
                z = z * x;
                y = y / 2;
                x = x * x;
                /\ y != 0;
                /\ !(y % 2 == 1);
                y = y / 2;
                x = x * x;
                /\ y != 0;
                /\ y % 2 == 1;
                z = z * x;
                y = y / 2;
                x = x * x;
                /\ !(y != 0);
                cout << z << endl;

    ⇔           cin >> x >> y;
                /\ y != 0;
                /\ y % 2 == 1;
                /\ y / 2 != 0;
                /\ !((y / 2) % 2 == 1);
                /\ (y / 2) / 2 != 0;
                /\ ((y / 2) / 2) % 2 == 1;
                /\ (((y / 2) / 2) / 2) == 0;
                z = 1;
                z = z * x;
                y = y / 2;
                x = x * x;
                y = y / 2;
                x = x * x;
                z = z * x;
                y = y / 2;
                x = x * x;
                cout << z << endl;
```

This path can be traversed by letting $y == 5$. It is indeed a candidate path.

To summarize, there are only four feasible execution paths generated by iterating the loop in Program 2.2 at most twice, although syntactically it appears to have seven:

αη, αβδεη, αβγεη, αβδεβδεη, αβδεβγεη, αβγεβδεη, and αβδεβγεη. It turns out that αβγεη, αβγεβγεη, and αβδεβγεη are infeasible paths. Only αη, αβδεη, αβδεβδεη, and αβγεβδεη are feasible paths and thus can be used as candidate paths in the data-flow test-case selection process discussed in Section 2.5.

Now we know how to move all the constraints to the top of the trace. The next question is: What is signified by a concatenation of two or more constraints? It can be shown, as the direct consequence of Axiom 5.4, that concatenation means logical conjunction semantically. Formally,

Corollary 5.8 $/\backslash C_1; /\backslash C_2; S \Leftrightarrow /\backslash C_1 \wedge C_2; S.$

By applying this relation to the trace immediately above, we obtain

```
⇔    /\ !(isspace(s[0])) && !(s[0] == ' ') && !(s[0] == '+'
||   s[0] == '-') && (isdigit(s[0])) && !(isdigit(s[1])));
     i = 0;
     sign = 1;
     n = 0;
     n = 10 * n + (s[i] - '0');
     i = i + 1;
     return sign * n;
```

One reason why the state constraints in a program can be simplified is that some state constraints are implied by the others and thus can be eliminated. To be more specific, if two state constraints C_1 and C_2 are such that $C_1 \supset C_2$, then C_2 can be discarded because $C_1 \wedge C_2 \equiv C_1$. For example, in the symbolic trace shown above, (isdigit(s[0])) implies that !(isspace(s[0]))&&!(s[0]== '-')&&!(s[0]=='+'||s[0]=='-'). Therefore, the constraint on top, and hence the entire trace, can be simplified to:

Trace 5.9

```
⇔    /\ (isdigit(s[0]))&&!(isdigit(s[1])));
     i = 0;
     sign = 1;
     n = 0;
     n = 10 * n + (s[i] - '0');
     i = i + 1;
     return sign * n;
```

Some state constraints may be eliminated in the simplification process because it is always true due to computation performed by the program. For example, the following program contains such a constraint:

$$x := 0;$$
$$y := x + 1;$$
$$/\backslash y \neq 0;$$

$\Leftrightarrow$ $x := 0;$
$$/\backslash x + 1 \neq 0;$$
$$y : x + 1;$$

$\Leftrightarrow$ $/\backslash 0 + 1 \neq 0;$
$$x := 0;$$
$$y := x + 1;$$

$\Leftrightarrow$ $/\backslash T;$
$$x := 0;$$
$$y := x + 1;$$

$\Leftrightarrow$ $x := 0;$
$$y := x + 1;$$

Definition 5.10   A state constraint is said to be *tautological* if it can be eliminated without changing the function implemented by the program. To be more precise, the constraint $/\backslash C$ in the program $S_1; /\backslash C; S_2$ is tautological if and only if $S_1; /\backslash C; S_2 \Leftrightarrow S_1; S_2$.

5.4 RULES FOR MOVING AND SIMPLIFYING STATEMENTS

As one might have observed in previous examples, moving state constraints interspersed in the statements to the same point in control flow often leaves a long sequence of assignment statements in the program. These assignment statements may be combined and simplified by using the three equivalence relations presented in the following.

Corollary 5.11 $x := E_1; x := E_2 \Leftrightarrow x := (E_2)_{E_1 \to x}.$
    Here $(E_2)_{E_1 \to x}$ denotes the expression obtained from E_2 by substituting E_1 for every occurrence of x in E_2. For example, an application of this corollary to the third and fourth assignment statements of Trace 5.9 yields

```
/\ (isdigit(s[0]))&&!(isdigit(s[1]));
i = 0;
sign = 1;
n = 0;
n = 10 * n + (s[i] - '0');
i = i + 1;
return sign * n;
```

```
⇔      /\ (isdigit(s[0])) && !(isdigit(s[1]));
       i = 0;
       sign = 1;
       n = s[i] - '0';
       i = i + 1;
       return sign * n;
```

Although in general two assignment statements cannot be interchanged, an assignment statement may be moved downstream under certain circumstances. In particular,

Corollary 5.12 If x_2 does not occur in E_1, then

$$x_1 := E_1; x_2 := E_2 \Leftrightarrow x_2 := (E_2)_{E_1 \to x_1}; x_1 := E_1$$

By applying this rule to the last symbolic trace to move the statement sign $= 1$ downstream, we obtain the following:

```
⇔      /\ (isdigit(s[0])) && !(isdigit(s[1]));
       i = 0;
       sign = 1;
       n = s[i] - '0';
       i = i + 1;
       return sign * n;
⇔      /\ (isdigit(s[0])) && !(isdigit(s[1]));
       i = 0;
       n = s[i] - '0';
       sign = 1;
       i = i + 1;
       return sign * n;
⇔      /\ (isdigit(s[0])) && !(isdigit(s[1]));
       i = 0;
       n = s[i] - '0';
       i = i + 1;
       sign = 1;
       return sign * n;
```

The purpose of an assignment statement is to assign a value to a variable so that it can be used in some statements downstream. Now if the rule above is used to move an assignment statement downstream past all statements in which the assigned value is used, the statement becomes redundant and thus can be deleted.

Definition 5.13 A statement in a program is said to be *redundant* if its sole purpose is to define the value of a data structure and this particular value is not used anywhere in the program.

Obviously, a redundant statement can be removed without changing the computation performed by the program.

Corollary 5.14 If $x_1 := E_1; x_2 := E_2$ is a sequence of two assignment statements such that by interchanging these two statements, $x_1 := E_1$ becomes redundant, then $(x_1 := E_1; x_2 := E_2) \Leftrightarrow x_2 := (E_2)_{E_1 \rightarrow x_1}$.

For example, let's interchange the last two statements in the last trace, which is repeated below for convenience.

```
⇔      /\ (isdigit(s[0])) && !(isdigit(s[1]));
       i = 0;
       n = s[i] - '0';
       i = i + 1;
       sign = 1;
       return sign * n;

⇔      /\ (isdigit(s[0])) && !(isdigit(s[1]));
       i = 0;
       n = s[i] - '0';
       i = i + 1;
       return 1 * n;
       sign = 1;

⇔      /\ (isdigit(s[0])) && !(isdigit(s[1]));
       i = 0;
       n = s[i] - '0';
       i = i + 1;
       return n;
```

In general, Corollary 5.14 becomes applicable when $x_2 := E_2$ is the last statement to make use of the definition provided by $x_1 := E_1$. Corollaries 5.12 and 5.14 can be used to reduce the number of assignment statements in a program and thus the number of steps involved in computation. The end result is often a simpler and more understandable program. For example, the trace above can be further simplified as demonstrated below.

```
⇔      /\ (isdigit(s[0])) && !(isdigit(s[1]));
       n = s[0] - '0';
       i = 0;
       i = i + 1;
       return n;

⇔      /\ (isdigit(s[0])) && !(isdigit(s[1]));
       n = s[0] - '0';
       i = 0 + 1;
       i = 0;
       return n;
```

```
⇔      /\ (isdigit(s[0])) && !(isdigit(s[1]));
       n = s[0] - '0';
       i = 1;
       return n;
⇔      /\ (isdigit(s[0])) && !(isdigit(s[1]));
       n = s[0] - '0';
       return n;
⇔      /\ (isdigit(s[0])) && !(isdigit(s[1]));
       return s[0] - '0';
       n = s[0] - '0';
⇔      /\ (isdigit(s[0])) && !(isdigit(s[1]));
       return s[0] - '0';
```

Recall that program `atoi` is a program that takes a string of digits as input and returns the integer value it represents. The simplified symbolic trace obtained above clearly shows that this execution path will be traversed if the first character is a digit and the second is not (it is supposed to be a null character used to indicate the end of an input). In that case the value returned by the function `atoi` is set equal to the ASCII representation of digit $s[0]$ minus that of digit 0. That is precisely the integer value assumed by the single digit read. From this analysis we can definitely conclude, without further testing, that function `atoi` will work correctly if the input is a single digit.

In summary we have presented three rules, Corollaries 5.11, 5.12, and 5.14, for simplifying a sequence of assignment statements based on their syntax. Needless to say, there are cases in which simplification can be done based on the semantics rather than on the syntax of the statements involved. For example, consider the following sequence of assignment statements in C++:

```
r = a % b;
a = b;
b = r;
r = a % b;
a = b;
b = r;
```

The three corollaries just mentioned are not applicable. Yet this sequence can be simplified to

```
a = a % b;
b = b % a;
r = b;
```

The possibility of making this simplification is made obvious through the use of a technique called *symbolic execution*, discussed in Section 6.2. Mechanization of this process, however, would be considerably more difficult than mechanization of the three corollaries presented in this section.

5.5 DISCUSSION

The analysis method described above is useful for some programs but not for others. In this section we explain why that is so and discuss the problems involved in automating the analysis process. As mentioned previously, most real-world programs contain loop constructs, and a loop construct expands potentially into a very large, if not infinite number of execution paths. What would the value of the analysis method be if we had to apply it to so many paths in a program?

It is possible to take another view of the execution paths in a program and, on a conceptual level, claim that the number of feasible execution paths in a program should be finite and manageably small, for the following reason. Suppose that the program embodies a function f that is defined on a set D. Usually, a program p is designed to implement f by decomposing f into a set of n subfunctions, that is, $f = \{f_1, f_2, \ldots, f_n\}$ such that $D = D_1 \cup D_2 \cup \cdots \cup D_n$ and f_i is f restricted to D_i, for all $1 \leq i \leq n$. If the program is constructed correctly, it must be composed of n execution paths or n symbolic traces such that $p = \{p_1, p_2, \ldots, p_n\}$, where each p_i implements subfunction f_i. The constraints in p_i jointly define the input subdomain D_i, and the statements in p_i describe how f_i is to be computed. Since a human designer generally can handle confidently only a finite and manageably small number of different objects, it is difficult to imagine that he or she would complicate the problem by decomposing a function into an unwieldy large number of subfunctions, hence creating that many execution paths in the resulting program! At a certain level of abstraction, therefore, one can argue that a properly designed program would consist of only a manageably small number of feasible execution paths.

The usefulness of the present analysis method is neither universal nor trivial. It is relatively easy for a skeptic to produce a counterexample to prove the former. What we would like to do in the following is to prove the latter by using examples to show that contrary to statements commonly found in the literature, the increase in feasible execution paths due to conditional statements in the program is exponential in syntax but not necessarily so in the number of feasible execution paths. Furthermore, the total number of feasible execution paths in a program with loop constructs is often manageably small.

First, consider the following C++ program.

Program 5.15

```
main ()
{
    int   i, j, k, match;
        cin >> i >> j >> k;
```

```
        cout << i << j << k << endl;
        if (i <= 0 || j <= 0 || k <= 0) goto L500;
        match = 0;
        if (i != j) goto L10;
        match = match + 1;
  L10:  if (i != k) goto L20;
        match = match + 2;
  L20:  if (j != k) goto L30;
        match = match + 3;
  L30:  if (match != 0) goto L100;
        if (i+j  <= k) goto L500;
        if (j+k  <= i) goto L500;
        if (i+k  <= j) goto L500;
        match = 1;
        goto L999;
  L100: if (match != 1) goto L200;
        if (i+j  <= k) goto L500;
  L110: match = 2;
        goto L999;
  L200: if (match != 2) goto L300;
        if (i+k  <= j) goto L500;
        goto L110;
  L300: if (match != 3) goto L400;
        if (j+k  <= i) goto L500;
        goto L110;
  L400: match = 3;
        goto L999;
  L500: match = 4;
  L999: cout << match << endl;
}
```

There are 14 "if" statements in this program. Any attempt to understand this program through symbolic-trace analysis would appear futile because common wisdom has it that 14 "if" statements will create as many as $2^{14} \approx 16,000$ execution paths in the program, a number that is far greater than any human brain can handle. Fortunately, a great majority of those paths are infeasible. In fact, only 12 of them are feasible and are described by the simplified symbolic traces shown below.

```
t1:   cin >> i >> j >> k;
      cout << i << j << k << endl;
      /\ (i <= 0) || (j <= 0) || (k <= 0);
      match = 4;
      cout << match << endl;
t2:   cin >> i >> j >> k;
      cout << i << j << k << endl;
```

```
       /\ (i > 0) && (j > 0) && (k > 0)
       /\ (i + j > k) && (j + k > i) && (i + k <= j)
       /\ (i != j) && (i != k) && (j != k)
       match = 4;
       cout << match << endl;
t3:    cin >> i >> j >> k;
       cout << i << j << k << endl;
       /\ (i > 0) && (j > 0) && (k > 0)
       /\ (i + j > k) && (j + k <= i)
       /\ (i != j) && (i != k) && (j != k)
       match = 4;
       cout << match << endl;
t4:    cin >> i >> j >> k;
       cout << i << j << k << endl;
       /\ (i > 0) && (j > 0) && (k > 0)
       /\ (i + j <= k)
       /\ (i != j) && (i != k) && (j != k)
       match = 4;
       cout << match << endl;
t5:    cin >> i >> j >> k;
       cout << i << j << k << endl;
       /\ (i > 0) && (j > 0) && (k > 0)
       /\ (j + k <= i)
       /\ (i != j) && (j == k)
       match = 4;
       cout << match << endl;
t6:    cin >> i >> j >> k;
       cout << i << j << k << endl;
       /\ (i > 0) && (j > 0) && (k > 0)
       /\ (i + k <= j)
       /\ (i != j) && (i == k)
       match = 4;
       cout << match << endl;
t7:    cin >> i >> j >> k;
       cout << i << j << k << endl;
       /\ (i > 0) && (j > 0) && (k > 0)
       /\ (i + j <= k)
       /\ (i == j) && (i != k)
       match = 4;
       cout << match << endl;
t8:    cin >> i >> j >> k;
       cout << i << j << k << endl;
       /\ (i > 0) && (j > 0) && (k > 0)
```

```
      /\ (i == j) && (i == k) && (j == k)
      match = 3;
      cout << match << endl;
t9:   cin >> i >> j >> k;
      cout << i << j << k << endl;
      /\ (i > 0) && (j > 0) && (k > 0)
      /\ (i + j > k)
      /\ (i == j) && (i != k)
      match = 2;
      cout << match << endl;
t10:  cin >> i >> j >> k;
      cout << i << j << k << endl;
      /\ (i > 0) && (j > 0) && (k > 0)
      /\ (j + k > i)
      /\ (i != j) && (j == k)
      match = 2;
      cout << match << endl;
t11:  cin >> i >> j >> k;
      cout << i << j << k << endl;
      /\ (i > 0) && (j > 0) && (k > 0)
      /\ (i + k > j)
      /\ (i != j) && (i == k)
      match = 2;
      cout << match << endl;
t12:  cin >> i >> j >> k;
      cout << i << j << k << endl;
      /\ (i > 0) && (j > 0) && (k > 0)
      /\ (i != j)&& (i != k) && (j != k)
      /\ (i + j > k) && (j + k > i) && (i + k > j)
      match = 1;
      cout << match << endl;
```

Next, consider the following example program (adapted from [HUAN08]) in C++.

Program 5.16

```
#include <iostream>
#include <string>
using namespace std;

string getstring();

int main()
```

```
{
  string rfilename;

  rfilename = getstring();
  cout << rfilename << endl;
}

string getstring()
{
  string buf, buf1;
  int  c1, c2, c3, j, k, k1, k2, n1, n2, testflag;
  char ch;

  c << "Enter the file name to be recoded:" << endl
  cin >> buf;
  buf.replace(0, buf.find(';')+1, buf);

  if (buf.find(']') == npos)
    buf1 = "";
  else
    buf1 = buf.substr(0, buf.find(']')+1);
  buf.erase(0, buf.find(']'));
  if (buf.find('.') != npos)
    buf = buf.substr(0, buf.find('.'));
  c1 = buf.length();

  if (c1 < 9) {
    c2 = 9 - c1;
    n1 = 9;
    n2 = c1;
    if (c1 < c2)
      testflag = 1;
    else {
      j = c1;
      c1 = c2;
      c2 = j;
      testflag = 0;
    }
    if (c1 == 0) {
      k1 = c2;
      k2 = c2;
    }
    else {
      k1 = c2 / c1;
      k2 = c2 % c1;
```

```
    }
    buf[n1] = '\0';
    for (k = 0; k < c1; ++k) {
      if (k2 == 0)
        c2 = k1;
      else {
        c2 = k1 + 1;
        --k2;
      }
      if (testflag)
      c3 = 1;
      else {
      c3 = c2;
      c2 = 1;
      }
      for (j = 0; j < c2; ++j) {
        buf[n1-1] = '9';
        --n1;
      }
      if (n1 != n2)
        for (j = 0; j < c3; ++j) {
          buf[n1-1] = buf[n2-1];
          --n1;
          --n2;
        }
    }
  }
buf.insert(9, ".ABC");
buf.insert(0, buf1);
return buf;
}
```

The reader may wish to determine what this program does without reading the helpful information given below. Tests in the past indicated that very few people could answer this question completely and correctly in half an hour or less.

The first part of the program is relatively easy to understand. The second part (printed in boldface) is not. The following symbolic trace describes one of the execution paths in the highlighted part of the program.

```
/\ c1 < 9;
c2 = 9 - c1;
n1 = 9;
n2 = c1;
/\ c1 < c2;
testflag = 1;
```

```
/\ !(c1 == 0);
k1 = c2 / c1;
k2 = c2 % c1;
buf[n1] = '\0'

k = 0;
/\ k < c1;
/\ k2 == 0;
c2 = k1;
/\ testflag;
c3 = 1;
j = 0;
/\ j < c2;
buf[n1-1] = '9';
n1 = n1 - 1;
j = j + 1;
/\ j < c2;
buf[n1-1] = '9';
n1 = n1 - 1;
j = j + 1;
/\ !(j < c2);
/\ n1 != n2;
j = 0;
/\j < c3
buf[n1-1] = buf[n2-1];
n1 = n1 - 1;
n2 = n2 - 1;
j = j + 1;
/\ !(j < c3);

k = k + 1;
/\ k < c1;
/\ k2 == 0;
c2 = k1;
/\ testflag;
c3 = 1;
j = 0;
/\ j < c2;
buf[n1-1] = '9';
n1 = n1 - 1;
j = j + 1;
/\ j < c2;
buf[n1-1] = '9';
n1 = n1 - 1;
j = j + 1;
/\ !(j < c2);
```

```
/\ n1 != n2;
j = 0;
/\j < c3
buf[n1-1] = buf[n2-1];
n1 = n1 - 1;
n2 = n2 - 1;
j = j + 1;
/\ !(j < c3);

k = k + 1;
/\ k < c1;
/\ k2 == 0;
c2 = k1;
/\ testflag;
c3 = 1;
j = 0;
/\ j < c2;
buf[n1-1] = '9';
n1 = n1 - 1;
j = j + 1;
/\ j < c2;
buf[n1-1] = '9';
n1 = n1 - 1;
j = j + 1;
/\ !(j < c2);
/\ !(n1 != n2);
```

Using the method described in this chapter, this symbolic trace can readily be simplified to

```
⇔      /\ c1 == 3;
       buf[9] = '\0';
       buf[8] = '9';
       buf[7] = '9';
       buf[6] = buf[2];
       buf[5] = '9';
       buf[4] = '9';
       buf[3] = buf[1];
       buf[2] = '9';
       buf[1] = '9';
```

It turns out that the second part of the program consists of only 10 feasible execution paths, despite the fact that it contains six "if" statements and three "for" loops! Furthermore, each symbolic trace can be greatly simplified, as exemplified above.

Program 5.16 is adapted from a legacy software tool designed to reconstruct file descriptors. An input file descriptor for this program may consist of four fields:

[<drive name>]<file name>.<file type>; <version number>

All fields except the file name are optional. The program reads a file descriptor in this format, truncates the file name to the length 9 if it is longer, and pads it with 9's if it is shorter, so that the length of the resulting file name is exactly 9. The padding must be done such that the 9's are distributed as evenly as possible. The program then changes the file type to "ABC" and discards the version number. The drive name, if any, remains unchanged. The simplified symbolic trace clearly shows how the padding process is carried out if the input file name is of length 3.

There are 10 feasible execution paths in Program 5.16: one for each length of the file name ranging from 1 to 9, and one for all other lengths. All 10 simplified symbolic traces are shown below to demonstrate to what extent the process of file-name reformatting performed by the program can be explicated by this method (the variable $c1$ represents the length of the input file name).

```
/\ c1 >= 9;

/\ c1 == 0;
buf[9] = '\0';

/\ c1 == 1;
buf[9] = '\0';
buf[8] = '9';
buf[7] = '9';
buf[6] = '9';
buf[5] = '9';
buf[4] = '9';
buf[3] = '9';
buf[2] = '9';
buf[1] = '9';

/\ c1 == 2;
buf[9] = '\0';
buf[8] = '9';
buf[7] = '9';
buf[6] = '9';
buf[5] = '9';
buf[4] = buf[1];
buf[3] = '9';
buf[2] = '9';
buf[1] = '9';
```

```
/\ c1 == 3;
buf[9] = '\0';
buf[8] = '9';
buf[7] = '9';
buf[6] = buf[2];
buf[5] = '9';
buf[4] = '9';
buf[3] = buf[1];
buf[2] = '9';
buf[1] = '9';

/\ c1 == 4;
buf[9] = '\0';
buf[8] = '9';
buf[7] = '9';
buf[6] = buf[3];
buf[5] = '9';
buf[4] = buf[2];
buf[3] = '9';
buf[2] = buf[1];
buf[1] = '9';

/\ c1 == 5;
buf[9] = '\0';
buf[8] = '9';
buf[7] = buf[4];
buf[6] = buf[3];
buf[5] = '9';
buf[4] = buf[2];
buf[3] = '9';
buf[2] = buf[1];
buf[1] = '9';

/\ c1 == 6;
buf[9] = '\0';
buf[8] = '9';
buf[7] = buf[5];
buf[6] = buf[4];
buf[5] = '9';
buf[4] = buf[3];
buf[3] = buf[2];
buf[2] = '9';

/\ c1 == 7;
buf[9] = '\0';
```

```
buf[8]  =  '9';
buf[7]  =  buf[6];
buf[6]  =  buf[5];
buf[5]  =  buf[4];
buf[4]  =  buf[3];
buf[3]  =  '9';

/\ c1 ==  8;
buf[9]  =  '\0';
buf[8]  =  '9';
```

As expected, the present analysis method is not as useful as demonstrated above for all programs. For example, there is a class of loop constructs that expand into a large number of execution paths, each of which is defined for only one element in the input domain. The following C++ program exemplifies such a program (adapted from [MANN74]).

Program 5.17

```
cin >> x;
y = 1;
while (x <= 100) {
   x = x + 11;
   y = y + 1;
}
while (y != 1) {
   x = x - 10;
   y = y - 1;
   while (x <= 100) {
      x = x + 11;
      y = y + 1;
   }
}
z = x - 10;
cout << "z = " << z << endl;
```

If we execute this program with $x = 97$, the execution will proceed along the path described by the following symbolic trace [HUAN08]:

```
cin >> x;
y = 1;
/\ x <= 100;
x = x + 11;
y = y + 1;
```

```
/\ !(x <= 100);
/\ y != 1;
x = x - 10;
y = y - 1;
/\ x <= 100;
x = x + 11;
y = y + 1;
/\ !(x <= 100);
/\ y != 1;
x = x - 10;
y = y - 1;
/\ x <= 100;
x = x + 11;
y = y + 1;
/\ !(x <= 100);
/\ y != 1;
x = x - 10;
y = y - 1;
/\ x <= 100
x = x + 11;
y = y + 1;
/\ !(x <= 100);
/\ y != 1;
x = x - 10;
y = y - 1;
/\ !(x <= 100);
/\ !(y != 1);
z = x - 10;
cout << "z = " << z;
```

By using the method presented earlier in the chapter, we can simplify this trace to

```
cin >> x;
/\ x == 97;
z = 91;
cout << "z = " << z << endl;
```

This result simply says that this execution path is defined for only one input, $x = 97$, and it does nothing but assign 91 to output variable z. In fact, Program 5.16 will expand into a distinct execution path for any input (x) less than or equal to 100, each of which is defined for one and only one value of x.

In general, it becomes pointless to use the present analysis method if an execution path is defined for a single element in the input domain as exemplified here, because the same result can be obtained much more readily through a test execution. The usefulness of the present analysis method is, to a great extent, determined by the degree to which we can simplify the symbolic trace.

5.6   SUPPORTING SOFTWARE TOOL

We can build two software tools to support the analysis method: an instrumentor and a trace analyzer. The *instrumentor* inserts necessary software instruments into a program to generate symbolic trace automatically during program execution. The *trace analyzer*, on the other hand, helps the user to rewrite a given symbolic trace into another that is logically equivalent but different in form. Neither of these tools is available on the market. For the benefit of those who may wish to automate the method, we discuss the instrumentor in Chapter 7 and the analyzer below.

We can build an analyzer to mimic the way we analyze a symbolic trace manually as explained earlier in the chapter. To do so, the analyzer needs to provide the basic functional capabilities of a modern interactive screen-oriented text editor so that the user can view a reasonably large segment of the trace being analyzed, scroll it up and down, select a portion of text for cut and paste, do searching and replacement, and undo previous operations to a certain extent. On top of these, the analyzer needs to provide two transformation functions. The first is to move a constraint upstream in accord with Theorem 5.7 and Corollary 5.8, and the second is to move a statement downstream in accord with Corollaries 5.11, 5.12, and 5.14.

Since the usefulness of the present method hinges largely on our ability to simplify the symbolic trace being analyzed, it is important that the analyzer include the capability to help the user carry out expression simplification. A software tool for simplification is difficult to build and computationally expensive to deploy, but it would enhance the usefulness of the present method substantially.

Neither transformation nor simplification can be automated completely; they have to be carried out interactively. Therefore, the effectiveness of a specific implementation is largely dependent on how its user interface is designed. In the remainder of this section we describe a user interface scheme that has proved to be effective through experimentation.

Let us consider Trace 5.2 again. The analysis tool is to display the trace on the screen as depicted below. Needless to say, a scroll bar is provided if the trace is too long to be displayed in its entirety.

C-up	S-down	Simplify	Validate	Undo

```
i = 0;
/\ !(isspace(s[i]));
/\ !(s[i] == '-');
sign = 1;
/\ !(s[i] == '+' || s[i] == '-');
n = 0;
/\ (isdigit(s[i]));
```

```
n = 10 * n + (s[i] - '0');
i = i + 1;
/\ !(isdigit(s[i]));
return sign * n;
```

The analyzer accepts the command described in the postfix notation; that is, the user has to specify the operand first and then the operation to be performed. Using the interface described here, the user selects the operand by using the selection feature of the text editor, and then clicks one of the function buttons on the top to perform the operation.

To make it easy to use, it is proposed that the user be provided with two alternative ways to select the operand. The default operand is the first, and only the first, syntactically complete constraint or statement following the current cursor position. Thus, if the cursor is placed in the middle of the first assignment statement as shown below, what is selected is the first constraint: /\ !(isspace(s[i])).

| C-up | S-down | Simplify | Validate | Undo |

```
i =◊0;
/\ !(isspace(s[i]));
/\ !(s[i] == '-');
sign = 1;
/\ !(s[i] == '+' || s[i] == '-');
n = 0;
/\ (isdigit(s[i]));
n = 10 * n + (s[i] - '0');
i = i + 1;
/\ !(isdigit(s[i]));
return sign * n;
```

Alternatively, the user can use the mouse to select the operand by clicking and dragging over the text just as is done in text editing. For example, the selection made above can be done alternatively as depicted below. Note that the first method can only be used to select a single constraint or statement, while the second can be used to select multiple constraints or statements or a portion of a constraint or statement.

| C-up | S-down | Simplify | Validate | Undo |

```
i =0;
◊      /\ !(isspace(s[i]));
       /\ !(s[i] == '-');
       sign = 1;
       /\ !(s[i] == '+' || s[i] == '-');
```

```
n = 0;
/\ (isdigit(s[i]));
n = 10 * n + (s[i] - '0');
i = i + 1;
/\ !(isdigit(s[i]));
return sign * n;
```

What we have just selected is a constraint. To simplify this symbolic trace, the user needs to move this constraint upstream as far as possible. This tool allows the user to do this by clicking the C-up (stands for "constraint up") button to move the constraint over any constraint or statement, immediately preceding it in accordance with Theorem 5.7. For this particular example, this operation should result in the following display:

| C-up | S-down | Simplify | Validate | Undo |

```
◊      /\ !(isspace(s[0]));
       i =0;
       /\ !(s[i] == '-');
       sign = 1;
       /\ !(s[i] == '+' || s[i] == '-');
       n = 0;
       /\ (isdigit(s[i]));
       n = 10 * n + (s[i] - '0');
       i = i + 1;
       /\ !(isdigit(s[i]));
       return sign * n;
```

By performing this operation repeatedly to every constraint in the trace, the analyzer should eventually produce the result depicted below.

| C-up | S-down | Simplify | Validate | Undo |

```
/\ !(isspace(s[0]));
/\ !(s[0] == '-');
/\ !(s[0] == '+' || s[0] == '-');
/\ (isdigit(s[0]));
/\ !(isdigit(s[1]));
i = 0;
sign = 1;
n = 0;
```

```
n = 10 * n + (s[i] - '0');
i = i + 1;
return sign * n;
```

Note that the operation of C-up can be applied to the constraints in any order. As the results, the constraints may appear on the top in a different order, but the order in which the constraints are listed is immaterial. This is so because by Corollary 5.8, a concatenation of constraints is logically equivalent to a conjunction of the same, and the logical operation of conjunction is commutative.

Having all the constraints located on the top, the user can now proceed to simplify the assignment statements on the bottom. Like the process of simplifying constraints, that of simplifying the assignment statements may be performed in any order. To illustrate, suppose that the user wish's to proceed by moving the assignment statement n = 0 next. By moving the cursor to the head of this statement:

| C-up | S-down | Simplify | Validate | Undo |

```
   /\ !(isspace(s[0]));
   /\ !(s[0] == '-');
   /\ !(s[0] == '+' || s[0] == '-');
   /\ (isdigit(s[0]));
   /\ !(isdigit(s[1]));
   i = 0;
   sign = 1;
◇  n = 0;
   n = 10 * n + (s[i] - '0');
   i = i + 1;
   return sign * n;
```

and clicking the S-down button, the display should be changed to.

| C-up | S-down | Simplify | Validate | Undo |

```
   /\ !(isspace(s[0]));
   /\ !(s[0] == '-');
   /\ !(s[0] == '+' || s[0] == '-');
   /\ (isdigit(s[0]));
   /\ !(isdigit(s[1]));
   i = 0;
   sign = 1;
◇  n = 10 * 0 + (s[i] - '0');
   i = i + 1;
   return sign * n;
```

The transformed assignment statement can now be simplified by clicking the simplify button. The analyzer should produce the following display of the trace:

| C-up | S-down | Simplify | Validate | Undo |

```
      /\  !(isspace(s[0]));
      /\  !(s[0]  ==  '-');
      /\  !(s[0]  ==  '+'  ||  s[0]  ==  '-');
      /\  (isdigit(s[0]));
      /\  !(isdigit(s[1]));
      i = 0;
      sign = 1;
◊     n = s[i]  -  '0';
      i = i + 1;
      return sign * n;
```

By applying similar operations repeatedly in accordance with Corollaries 5.11, 5.12, and 5.14 to move all the assignment statements downstream, the analyzer should eventually produce the following result:

| C-up | S-down | Simplify | Validate | Undo |

```
/\  !(isspace(s[0]));
/\  !(s[0]  ==  '-');
/\  !(s[0]  ==  '+'  ||  s[0]  ==  '-');
/\  (isdigit(s[0]));
/\  !(isdigit(s[1]));
return s[0]  -  '0';
```

Up to this point, all operations performed can be carried out with relative ease. The information needed to do so can be obtained by parsing the symbolic trace and performing a data-flow analysis for all the variables involved. Simplification of frequently encountered expressions, such as reducing x+0 to x, x*1 to x, or x+1+1+1 to x+3, can be done using a rule-based rewriting system.

Simplification of a concatenation of constraints is to be done based on Corollary 5.8, which says that $/\backslash C_1; /\backslash C_2; S$ is logically equivalent to $/\backslash C_1 \wedge C_2; S$. It is also known that if C_1 implies ($\supset$) C_2, then $C_1 \wedge C_2$ can be reduced to C_1. The problem is to find pairs of constraints that can be simplified using this fact.

A simple approach to simplification of a conjunction of n predicates $C_1 \wedge C_2 \wedge \cdots \wedge C_n$ is to use a mechanical theorem prover to prove that $C_i \supset C_j$ for all $1 \leq i, j \leq n$ and $i \neq j$. If successful, it means that C_i implies C_j, and therefore C_j can be discarded. Otherwise, C_j remains.

If the analyzer has this theorem-proving capability, all we need to do is to select all the constraints on the top of the trace and click the simplify button. The analyzer should display the following as the result.

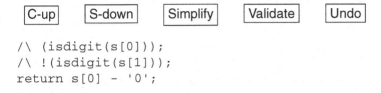

```
/\ (isdigit(s[0]));
/\ !(isdigit(s[1]));
return s[0] - '0';
```

Finally, there are times when the user may wish to restate the constraints to suit the analysis need, but cannot be sure if the restated constraints are logically equivalent to the original. In that case, the user can make use of the function provided by the validate button. By selecting a sequence of constraints and clicking the validate button, the analyzer will store the constraints selected and check to see if it is logically equivalent to the one stored previously. To use this function, the user should select the constraints to be altered, click the validate button, make the alteration, and then click the validate button again. The analyzer will produce an appropriate message to indicate whether or not the alteration made is an equivalence transformation.

EXERCISES

5.1 Identify three feasible execution paths in Program 5.1 and determine for each (**a**) the condition under which it will be traversed, and (**b**) the computation it performs in the process. Simplify your answers to the extent possible.

5.2 Draw the program graph for each of the following programming constructs:
  (a) **if** B **then** S_1 **else** S_2
  (b) **if** B_1 **then** S_1 **else if** B_2 **then** S_2 **else** S_3
  (c) **while** B **do** S
  (d) **do** S **until**–neg B

5.3 How does a program graph differ from a traditional flowchart? What are the advantages and disadvantages of representing a program with a program graph?

5.4 Program 1.1 is logically equivalent to Program 5.15. What additional theorems are needed to show that rigorously?

6 Static Analysis

By *static analysis* here we mean a process by which we attempt to find symptoms of programming faults or to explicate the computation performed by the program by scrutinizing the source code without test-executing it on a computer. Sometimes a part of a program may be formed abnormally. We call that an *anomaly* instead of a fault because it may or may not cause the program to fail. It is nevertheless a symptom of possible programming error. Examples of anomalies include structural flaws in a program module, flaws in module interface, and errors in event sequencing. Such anomalies can be found by examining the source code systematically.

Types of structural flaw detectable by static analysis include:

- *Extraneous entities.* An extraneous semicolon at the end of a "for" statement like the one shown below, its body will never be executed until the empty "for" statement is terminated.

$$\begin{aligned}
&\text{for } (i = 0, \ j = n - 1; \ i < j; \ i\texttt{++}, \ j\texttt{--});\\
&\qquad \{\text{char temp} = a[i];\\
&\qquad\quad\ a[i] = a[j];\\
&\qquad\quad\ a[j] = \text{temp};\\
&\qquad \}
\end{aligned}$$

- *Improper loop nesting.* This could happen if a "goto" statement is used in the nested loops.
- *Unreferenced labels.* They do not necessarily lead to any failures, but they definitely indicate that the programmer has overlooked something.
- *Unreachable statements.* Improper placement of a "return" statement or incorrect formulation of a branch predicate which becomes always true (i.e., a tautology) or always false (i.e., a contradiction) may cause a segment of code to become unreachable.
- *Transfer of control into a loop.* This could happen if the use of a "goto" statement is allowed.

Types of interface flaw detectable:

- Inconsistencies in the declaration of data structures
- Improper linkage among modules (e.g., discrepancy in the number and types of parameters)
- Flaws in another interprogram communication mechanism, such as the common blocks used in FORTRAN programs

Types of event-sequencing errors detectable include:

- Priority-interrupt handling conflict
- Error in file handling
- Data-flow anomaly
- Anomaly in concurrent programs

The best known examples of event-sequencing error are data-flow anomalies and extension of that in concurrent programs. We discuss that in the following section.

Needless to say, programs may contain faults that are semantic in nature and cannot be detected through syntactic analysis of the source code. For example, in C++, a beginner may write

```
char* p;
strcpy(p, "Houston");
```

which is syntactically correct but semantically wrong. It should be written as

```
char* p;
p = buffer;             //p points to buffer
strcpy(p, "Houston")    //place a copy of "Houston" in buffer
```

Understanding the program is required to detect semantic errors. Program understanding can be facilitated by using the techniques of symbolic execution (or analysis) discussed in Section 6.2 and program slicing discussed in Section 6.3.

The method of code inspection (walkthrough) should be a part of any discussion on error detection through static analysis. It is a process in which the source code of a program is scrutinized by a team of programmers, including the author of the program, in a concerted manner. Its effectiveness derives from the use of collective wisdom and the fact that a programming error is often more obvious to someone other than its creator. The roles played by the participants and the procedures they followed are discussed in Section 6.4.

Finally, we discuss methods for proving program correctness. Admittedly, the methods are impractical. Nevertheless, it is important for an advanced program tester to become familiar with the subject because some techniques developed in proof construction are useful in program testing. Besides, the tester may find the concepts and languages used in proving program correctness useful in communicating correctness problems and in making related technical decisions.

6.1 DATA-FLOW ANOMALY DETECTION

In executing a program, a program component, such as a statement, may act on a variable (datum) in three different ways: *define, reference,* and *undefine*. For example, in executing the statement "$x := x + y - z$," it will reference x, y, and z first, and then define x. When a "return" statement is executed, it will undefine all the variables declared to be local in that part of the program. In some languages or programming environments, a program also undefines the control variable of a loop upon termination of the loop.

Normally, a variable comes into existence in a program and assumes the state of being undefined via a declarative statement, and the actions applied to this variable should be in the order "define," followed by "reference" one or more times, and then "undefine" or "define." For example, consider the data flow in Program 2.2 along path $\alpha\beta\delta\epsilon\eta$, the symbolic trace of which is listed in Table 6.1 together with the actions taken on the variables involved. From this table we can see that when the program is being executed along the path, the sequences of actions taken on variables x, y, and z are drrdu, drrrdru, and drdru, respectively.

The data flow with respect to that variable is said to be anomalous if the program does not act on that variable in that order. There are three types of data-flow anomaly: ur type for undefine and reference, du type for define and undefine, and dd type for define and define again [FOOS76]. Since no subsequences of actions ur, du, or dd

TABLE 6.1   Data Flow Along Path $\alpha\beta\delta\epsilon\eta$ in Program 2.2

	Actions Taken on Variables:[a]		
Statements on the Execution Path $\alpha\beta\delta\epsilon\eta$	x	y	z
cin >> x >> y;	d	d	
z = 1;			d
/\ y != 0;		r	
/\ y % 2 == 1;		r	
z = z * x;	r		r, d
y = y / 2;		r, d	
x = x * x;	r, d		
/\ !(y != 0);		r	
cout << z << endl;			r
return (implicit)	u	u	u

[a]d, define; r, reference; u, undefine.

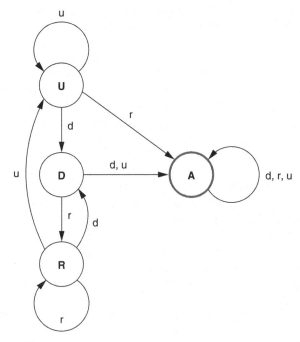

Figure 6.1   State-transition graph of the states assumable by a variable.

occur in the sequences of actions taken on variables x, y, and z, it means that no data-flow anomaly occurred along the path in Program 2.2.

To facilitate discussion, we consider a variable as being in one of four possible states: undefined (U), defined (D) (but not referenced), referenced (R), and abnormal (A). When the program acts on it during execution, it will change its states as illustrated in Figure 6.1. [*Remark*: The reason that we made a variable to stay in the state of anomaly (A) will be explained later when we discuss detection of data-flow anomaly through program instrumentation.]

It should be noted that the presence of a data-flow anomaly does not necessarily cause the program to produce an incorrect output. Nevertheless, it is a symptom of possible programming error and requires the attention of the analyzer. For example, some programmers have the habit of initializing a flag to either true or false at the beginning of the program, and set it to a proper value subsequently at an appropriate point. That constitutes a dd type of data-flow anomaly but not a programming fault. On the other hand, when a variable is found to be defined and defined again without an intervening use (i.e., the presence of a dd-type anomaly) in a program that has a long history of maintenance, it is probably a symptom of a programming fault. That dd-type anomaly is created by two different statements, one of which has to be deleted. The programmer either forgot to do that, or was unaware of its existence!

The same idea can be applied to concurrent programs consisting of tasks (or concurrent processes) that run in concurrency asynchronously. A concurrent program may act on its tasks as follows. S*chedule* a task (i.e., place its control block in the running queue of the operating system), make it *wait* for a task or resource (i.e., place its control block in a waiting queue), or *unschedule* it (i.e., remove its control black from any queue). The following types of anomaly may therefore be found in a concurrent program: A task is (1) made to wait for another task not scheduled or guaranteed to have terminated previously, or (2) scheduled to run in parallel with itself.

Of course, a concurrent process also may define, reference, and undefine its variables, and therefore may induce data-flow anomalies as described previously. In addition, due to the fact that concurrent processes may cooperate or communicate by making use of data defined by other processes, and the fact that they will run at their own speed once spawned, they may induce data-flow anomalies in different ways. For example, a process may reference a variable that is yet to be defined by another process, reference a variable that is defined by a wrong process, or define a variable whose value ends up being unused, and so on.

In general, anomalies due to event sequencing in a program can be found by (1) identifying all feasible execution paths in the program, (2) finding the sequences of actions taken by the program on a particular variable or task of interest on those paths, and (3) examining each sequence to see if any subsequence representing an anomaly occur therein. For example, to find data-flow anomalies in a program with respect to a variable, say x, we analyze each statement in the program to determine its actions on x. Analyze the program to find all possible execution paths and the sequences of actions taken on x. There is a data-flow anomaly if any of those sequences contains ur, du, or dd as a subsequence.

Although the idea is very simple, in practice, detection of a data-flow anomaly is complicated by, among others, the following factors:

1. Most, if not all, programs contain loop constructs. A loop construct expands into a prohibitively large number of execution paths.
2. A path found on the control-flow graph may turn out to be infeasible. An anomaly occurring on an infeasible path will be of no interest to us.
3. To determine the actions taken by a statement, we need to know the exact identity of every variable that occurs in the statement. That is difficult, if not impossible, if the variable is an array element.

These problems can be overcome through dynamic analysis (the technique of program instrumentation), discussed in Chapter 7.

Finding a sequence of actions taken by the program on a variable is a problem in data-flow analysis that is important in compiler object-code optimization. Information about the actions taken on a variable can be used by an optimizing compiler to decide whether to keep the value of that variable in the register for impending use. Interested readers may find a more complete treatment of this subject in a compiler-construction book (e.g., [AHSU86]).

6.2   SYMBOLIC EVALUATION (EXECUTION)

If we test a program for an input, and if the result produced is incorrect, it is of great significance in that it indicates the existence of a fault in the program. On the other hand, if the result is correct, that result allows us only to conclude that the program will work correctly for that particular input. We will be able to instill more confidence in that program if, in addition to that test result, we understand how the program arrives at that result. This understanding often can be achieved by reading the code. Nevertheless, not every piece of code can be readily understood, and any method that can be used to facilitate this process is of practical importance.

In this section we describe a method called *symbolic execution* that is helpful primarily in visualizing what is accomplished by a sequence of assignment statements. In the next section we describe a method called *program slicing* that facilitates program understanding by allowing us to identify and drop statements that are irrelevant to the computation of values of certain variables at some point in the program. The basic idea of symbolic execution can be explained as follows. If we trace the values assumed by variables by executing the program for a particular point in the input domain, we see only how the program works for that particular input. Now if we can find some way to execute the program such that it can accept symbolic inputs and produce symbolic formulas as outputs, we should be able to determine the correctness of the program for a more general case. This argument led to the development of symbolic execution [KING75, KING76].

To fix the idea, let us consider the following example program (in pseudocode):

```
read(x, y);
z := x + y;
x := x - y;
z := x * z;
write(z);
```

This program should produce the following value trace if it is executed in an ordinary manner with $x = 2$ and $y = 4$.

	x	y	z
read(x, y);	2	4	undefined
z := x + y;	2	4	6
x := x - y;	-2	4	6
z := x * z;	-2	4	-12
write(z);	-2	4	-12

Now if we execute this program symbolically with $x = a$ and $y = b$, it will produce the following value trace, which clearly indicates that it is designed to compute $x^2 - y^2$.

	x	y	z
read(x, y);	a	b	undefined
$z := x + y$;	a	b	$a + b$
$x := x - y$;	$a - b$	b	$a + b$
$z := x * z$;	$a - b$	b	$a * a - b * b$
write(z);	$a - b$	b	$a * a - b * b$

Shown below is another example: a loop body iterated twice.

$$r := a \% b;$$
$$a := b;$$
$$b := r;$$
$$r := a \% b;$$
$$a := b;$$
$$b := r;$$

It is not immediately clear what this segment of code does. We can perform a symbolic execution by letting $a := A, b := B$, and $r := R$, to yield

$$r := A \% B;$$
$$a := B;$$
$$b := A \% B;$$
$$r := B \% (A \% B);$$
$$a := A \% B;$$
$$b := B \% (A \% B);$$

The last three lines listed above clearly suggest that the original segment of code can be simplified to

$$a := a \% b;$$
$$b := b \% a;$$
$$r := b;$$

As one can see from the example above, when an expression is evaluated symbolically, the symbolic values of the variables in the expression are substituted into the expression. If the expression constitutes the right part of an assignment statement, the resulting symbolic value becomes the new symbolic value of the variable on the left of the assignment operator.

If the program consists of more than one execution path, it is necessary to choose a path through the program to be followed. The path can be represented conveniently by the associated trace subprogram defined elsewhere. To illustrate, consider the following FORTRAN program designed to solve quadratic equations by using the formula

$$x = \frac{-b \pm \sqrt{b^2 - 4ac}}{2a}$$

Program 6.1

```
C OBTAINS SOLUTIONS OF THE EQUATION A*X**2 + B*X + C = 0
C
   10 READ (5, 11) A, B, C
   11 FORMAT (3F10, 0)
      WRITE (6, 12) A, B, C
   12 FORMAT (' 0A =', 1PE16.6, ', B =', 1PE16.6, ',
       C =', 1PE16.6)
      IF (A .EQ. 0.0 .AND. B .EQ. 0.0 .AND. C .EQ. 0.0) STOP
      IF (A .NE. 0.0 .OR. B .NE. 0.0) GOTO 20
      WRITE (6, 13) C
   13 FORMAT (' EQUATION SAYS', 1PE16.6, ' = 0')
      GOTO 90
   20 IF (A .NE. 0.0) GOTO 30
      R1 = -C/B
      WRITE (6, 21) R1
   21 FORMAT (' ONE ROOT. R = ', 1PE16.6)
      GOTO 90
C     A IS NOT ZERO
   30 IF (C .NE. 0.0) GOTO 40
      R1 = -B/A
      R2 = 0.0
      WRITE (6, 31) R1, R2
   31 FORMAT (' R1 =', 1PE16.6, ', R2 =', 1PE16.6)
      GOTO 90
C     GENERAL CASE: A, C NON-ZERO
   40 RREAL = -B/(2.0*A)
      DISC = B**2 - 4.0*A*C
      RIMAG = SQRT(ABS(DISC))/(2.0*A)
      IF (DISC .LT. 0.0) GOTO 50
      R1 = RREAL + RIMAG
      R2 = RREAL - RIMAG
      WRITE (6, 31) R1, R2
      GOTO 90
   50 R1 = -RIMAG
      WRITE (6, 51) RREAL, RIMAG, RREAL, R1
   51 FORMAT (' R1 = (', 1PE16.6, ', ', 1PE16.6, ')',
   $     ', R2 = (', 1PE16.6, ', ', 1PE16.6, ')')
   90 GOTO 10
      END
```

Listed below is a symbolic trace (see Chapter 5) representing a possible execution path in the program.

```
READ (5, 11) A, B, C
/\.NOT. (A .EQ. 0.0 .AND. B .EQ. 0.0 .AND. C .EQ. 0.0)
/\ (A .NE. 0.0 .OR. B .NE. 0.0)
/\ (A .NE. 0.0)
/\ (C .NE. 0.0)
RREAL = -B/(2.0*A)
DISC = B**2 - 4.0*A*C
RIMAG = SQRT(ABS(DISC))/(2.0*A)
/\.NOT. (DISC .LT. 0.0)
R1 = RREAL + RIMAG
R2 = RREAL - RIMAG
WRITE (6, 31) R1, R2
```

We can move all of the constraints to the top as described in Chapter 5 first:

```
READ (5, 11) A, B, C
/\ (A .NE. 0.0 .OR. B .NE. 0.0 .OR. C .NE. 0.0)
/\ (A .NE. 0.0 .OR. B .NE. 0.0)
/\ (A .NE. 0.0)
/\ (C .NE. 0.0)
/\ (B**2 - 4.0*A*C .GE. 0.0)
RREAL = -B/(2.0*A)
DISC = B**2 - 4.0*A*C
RIMAG = SQRT(ABS(DISC))/(2.0*A)
R1 = RREAL + RIMAG
R2 = RREAL - RIMAG
WRITE (6, 31) R1, R2
```

and then perform a symbolic execution (using the name of each variable as its symbolic value) along the path to yield

```
R1 = -B/(2.0*A) + SQRT(ABS(B**2 - 4.0*A*C))/(2.0*A)
R2 = -B/(2.0*A) - SQRT(ABS(B**2 - 4.0*A*C))/(2.0*A)
```

This demonstrates the usefulness of a symbolic execution because it clearly indicates what the program will do with respect to R1 and R2 if the program is executed along this path.

In general, the result of a symbolic execution is a set of strings (symbols) representing the values of the program variables. These strings often grow uncontrollably during symbolic execution. Thus, the results may not be of much use unless the symbolic execution system is capable of simplifying these strings automatically. Such a simplifier basically requires the power of a mechanical theorem prover. Therefore, a symbolic execution system is a computation-intensive software system, and is relatively difficult to build.

6.3 PROGRAM SLICING

A program written in a procedural language performs its intended function in steps, and the result of each step is stored in a variable (or more complex data structure) for subsequent use. Therefore, understanding, and hence determination, of the correctness of a program can be facilitated by any method that explicates how the value of a variable at a particular point in the control flow is computed. *Program slicing* [WEIS84] is a method developed for that purpose. Given a variable and its location in the control flow in the program, this method can be used to build an executable subprogram from the original program by identifying and discarding the statements irrelevant to the computation of the value to be assumed by that variable at that point.

To illustrate, let us consider the following program:

```
P:   1       begin
     2           read(x, y);
     3           total := 0.0;
     4           sum := 0.0;
     5           if x <= 1
     6               then sum := y
     7               else begin
     8                   read(z);
     9                   total := x * y
     10              end;
     11          write(total, sum)
     12      end.
```

Slice on the value of z at statement 12:

```
S₁:  1       begin
     2           read(x, y);
     5           if x <= 1
     6               then
     7               else begin
     8                   read(z);
     10              end;
     12      end.
```

Slice on the value of total at statement 12:

```
S₂:   1      begin
      2          read(x, y);
      3          total := 0.0;
      5          if x <= 1
      6              then
      7              else begin
      9                  total := x * y
     10              end;
     12      end.
```

Slice on the value of x at statement 9:

```
S₃:   1      begin
      2          read(x, y);
     12      end.
```

Since the purpose of a slice is to perform the same computation for a chosen set of variables at a certain point in the control flow, the desired slice can be specified by a pair where the left component of the pair is a point in the control flow, and the right component is a set of interested variables. Such a pair is called a *slicing criterion*. We assume that the statements in the source code of the program are numbered. Therefore, we use a statement number to specify a point in the control flow. That is, the left component of a slicing criterion is a statement number.

Formally, a slicing criterion of program P is an ordered pair of the form (i, V), where i is a statement number and V is a subset of variables in P. For example, three slicing criteria were used to construct three example slices at the beginning of this section. By the definition above, they can be expressed as

- C_1: $(12, \{z\})$
- C_2: $(12, \{total\})$
- C_3: $(9, \{x\})$

Given a slice criterion (n, V) of program P, a slice can be obtained by deleting all statements that are irrelevant to computation of the value of any variable in V at statement n.

Which statement is relevant, and which is not? Let statement m be the immediate predecessor of statement n in P. Let (n, V) be the slicing criterion. Statement m is relevant with respect to (n, V) if some variables in V are referenced in statement n and defined in statement m. For example, consider the slicing criterion $(12, \{total\})$. Statement 11 is the only predecessor. Since the variable "total" is not defined in statement 11, statement 11 is irrelevant and thus can be excluded. With statement 11 excluded, statement 5 (a compound conditional statement that includes lines 5 through 10) now becomes the immediate processor. Since the variable "total" is defined in this compound statement, statement 5 is relevant and should be included in the slice.

Although the idea of a program slice is intuitively clear, it is difficult to define
it precisely and concisely. The original work on the program slice [WEIS84] did
not provide a method to construct a slice. It only defined a slice as an executable
subprogram having a certain property. In the conceptual framework of this book, that
property can be described as follows. Let P be a program and (i, V) be a slicing
criterion. Let P' be a subprogram of P constructed by deleting some parts of P. P' is
a slice of P with respect to (i, V) if every symbolic trace from the entry to statement
i in P has a corresponding symbolic trace in P', and they compute the same values
for variables in V at statement i.

In the original work [WEIS84], a trace is represented by a sequence of statement
numbers, and the computation performed by the trace is described by a sequence of
expressions obtained by symbolically executing the symbolic trace of the execution
path involved. For comparison purposes, we use examples to show how all these were
done in the original work. Weiss used a value trace to describe an execution path,
and what computation would be performed on the path, using a value trace. A *value
trace* of program P is a list of ordered pairs

$$(n_1, v_1)(n_2, v_2)\cdots(n_k, v_k)$$

where each n_i denotes a statement in P, and each v_i is a vector of values of all
variables in P immediately before the execution of n_i.

For example, the program given earlier in this section makes use of a vector of
variables: $<x, y, z, \text{sum}, \text{total}>$. A possible value trace would be

$$
\begin{aligned}
T_1: \quad & (1, <?, ?, ?, ?, ?>) \\
& (2, <?, ?, ?, ?, ?>) \\
& (3, <X, Y, ?, ?, ?>) \\
& (4, <X, Y, ?, ?, 0.0>) \\
& (5, <X, Y, ?, 0.0, 0.0>) \\
& (6, <X, Y, ?, 0.0, 0.0>) \\
& (11, <X, Y, ?, Y, 0.0>) \\
& (12, <X, Y, ?, Y, 0.0>)
\end{aligned}
$$

and another possible value trace would be

$$
\begin{aligned}
T_2: \quad & (1, <?, ?, ?, ?, ?>) \\
& (2, <?, ?, ?, ?, ?>) \\
& (3, <X, Y, ?, ?, ?>) \\
& (4, <X, Y, ?, ?, 0.0>) \\
& (7, <X, Y, ?, 0.0, 0.0>) \\
& (8, <X, Y, ?, 0.0, 0.0>) \\
& (9, <X, Y, Z, 0.0, 0.0>) \\
& (10, <X, Y, Z, 0.0, X * Y>) \\
& (11, <X, Y, Z, 0.0, X * Y>) \\
& (12, <X, Y, Z, 0.0, X * Y>)
\end{aligned}
$$

In the above we use a question mark (?) to denote an undefined value and use an upper case variable name to denote the value of that variable obtained through an input statement in the program.

Next, given a slicing criterion $C = (i, V)$ and a value trace T, we can define a projection function $\text{Proj}(C, T)$ that deletes from a value trace all ordered pairs except those with i as the left component, and that deletes from the right components of the remaining pairs all values except those of variables in V. Thus

$$\text{Proj}(C_1, T_1) = \text{Proj}((12, \{z\}), T_1)$$

$$= ~~(1, <?, ?, ?, ?, ?>)~~$$
$$~~(2, <?, ?, ?, ?, ?>)~~$$
$$~~(3, <X, Y, ?, ?, ?>)~~$$
$$~~(4, <X, Y, ?, ?, 0.0>)~~$$
$$~~(5, <X, Y, ?, 0.0, 0.0>)~~$$
$$~~(6, <X, Y, ?, 0.0, 0.0>)~~$$
$$~~(11, <X, Y, ?, Y, 0.0>)~~$$
$$(12, <~~X, Y,~~ ?, ~~Y, 0.0~~>)$$
$$= (12, <?>)$$

$$\text{Proj}(C_2, T_1) = \text{Proj}((12, \{\text{total}\}), T_1)$$

$$= ~~(1, <?, ?, ?, ?, ?>)~~$$
$$~~(2, <?, ?, ?, ?, ?>)~~$$
$$~~(3, <X, Y, ?, ?, ?>)~~$$
$$~~(4, <X, Y, ?, ?, 0.0>)~~$$
$$~~(5, <X, Y, ?, 0.0, 0.0>)~~$$
$$~~(6, <X, Y, ?, 0.0, 0.0>)~~$$
$$~~(11, <X, Y, ?, Y, 0.0>)~~$$
$$(12, <~~X, Y, ?, Y,~~ 0.0>)$$
$$= (12, <0.0>)$$

and

$$\text{Proj}(C_3, T_2) = \text{Proj}((9, \{x\}), T_2)$$

$$= ~~(1, <?, ?, ?, ?, ?>)~~$$
$$~~(2, <?, ?, ?, ?, ?>)~~$$
$$~~(3, <X, Y, ?, ?, ?>)~~$$
$$~~(4, <X, Y, ?, ?, 0.0>)~~$$
$$~~(7, <X, Y, ?, 0.0, 0.0>)~~$$
$$~~(8, <X, Y, ?, 0.0, 0.0>)~~$$
$$(9, <X, ~~Y, Z, 0.0, 0.0~~>)$$
$$~~(10, <X, Y, Z, 0.0, X * Y>)~~$$
$$~~(11, <X, Y, Z, 0.0, X * Y>)~~$$
$$~~(12, <X, Y, Z, 0.0, X * Y>)~~$$
$$= (9, <X>)$$

In essence, a projection of a value trace is what is computed by the symbolic trace for that execution path.

Now we are ready to give Weiss's definition [WEIS84]: A slice S of a program P on a slicing criterion $C = (i, V)$ is any executable program satisfying the following two properties:

1. S can be obtained from P by deleting zero or more statements from P.
2. Whenever P halts on an input I with value trace T, S also halts on an input I with value trace T', and $\text{Proj}(C, T) = \text{Proj}(C', T')$, where $C' = (i', V)$, and $i' = i$ if statement i is in the slice, or i' is the nearest successor to i otherwise.

For example, consider P, the example program listed at the beginning of this section and the slicing criterion $C_1 = (12, \{z\})$. According to the definition above, S_1 is a slice because if we execute P with any input $x = X$ such that $X \leq 1$, it will produce the value trace T_1, and as given previously, $\text{Proj}(C_1, T_1) = (12, <?>)$. Now if we execute S_1 with the same input, it should yield the following value trace:

$$T'_1: \quad \begin{aligned} &(1, <?, ?, ?, ?, ?>) \\ &(2, <?, ?, ?, ?, ?>) \\ &(5, <X, Y, ?, ?, ?>) \\ &(6, <X, Y, ?, ?, ?>) \\ &(12, <X, Y, ?, ?>) \end{aligned}$$

Since statement 12 exists in P as well as S_1, $C_1 = C'_1$, and

$$\begin{aligned} \text{Proj}(C'_1, T'_1) &= ((12, \{z\}), T'_1) \\ &= \cancel{(1, <?, ?, ?, ?, ?>)} \\ & \cancel{(2, <?, ?, ?, ?, ?>)} \\ & \cancel{(5, <X, Y, ?, ?, ?>)} \\ & \cancel{(6, <X, Y, ?, ?, ?>)} \\ & (12, <\cancel{X, Y}, ?, \cancel{?, ?}>) \\ &= (12, <?>) \\ &= \text{Proj}(C_1, T_1) \end{aligned}$$

As an example in which $C \neq C'$, consider $C = (11, \{z\})$. Since statement 11 is not in S_1, C' will have to be set to $(12, \{z\})$ instead because statement 12 is the nearest successor of 11. There can be many different slices for a given program and slicing criterion. There is always at least one slice for a given slicing criterion—the program itself. The definition of a slice above is not constructive in that it does not say how to find one. A constructive definition of slice can be found in an article by Lanubile and Visaggio [LAVI97], where the technique of program slicing is exploited to extract functional components automatically from existing software systems for reuse.

The smaller the slice, the easier it is to understand. Hence, it is of practical value to be able to find the minimum slice of a program, minimum in the sense that every part of the slice is absolutely necessary in order to satisfy the slicing criterion. It has been shown, however, that finding minimal slices of a program is equivalent to solving the halting problem—an unsolvable problem in the sense that no single algorithm can be found for this purpose [WEIS84].

6.4   CODE INSPECTION

Code inspection (walkthrough) is a process in which a piece of source code is examined systematically by a group of the program creator's colleagues. The basic idea is that faults in a program often become more obvious to programmers other than the original author. Whatever the reason, the fact is that people read programs written by others more critically and can spot a fault more readily than can its creator. That is the rationale behind the process of code inspection. The inspection should be carried out after the first clean compilation of the code to be inspected and before any formal testing is done on that code.

Objectives

The main objectives of code inspection are:

1. To find logic errors
2. To verify the technical accuracy and completeness of the code
3. To verify that the programming language definition used conforms to that of the compiler to be used by the customer
4. To ensure that no conflicting assumptions or design decisions have been made in different parts of the code
5. To ensure that good coding practices and standards are used and that the code is easily understandable

The style of the code should not be discussed unless it prevents the code from meeting the objectives of the code inspection. This is so because the style is a rather subjective matter, and it is likely that the participants' preferences for programming styles differ significantly and that the difference would not prevent the inspection objectives from being met. In that event, a great deal of time may be wasted in discussing matters of no consequence.

Although an inspection meeting would provide managers with a good opportunity to evaluate the capability of the program creator, they should not be allowed to attend the meeting for that purpose. Otherwise, participants friendly to the creator are likely to refrain from pointing out problems. On the other hand, if the program creator has any adversaries among the participants, it is possible that undue criticisms will be aired at the meeting. The standard of performance will become skewed in either case.

Procedure

A code inspection should involve at least three persons. The inspection team should include:

- The designer, who will answer any questions
- The moderator, who ensures that any discussion is topical and productive
- The paraphraser, who steps through the code and paraphrases it in a natural language such as English

The material needed for inspection includes:

- Program listings and design documents
- A list of assumptions and decisions made in coding
- A participant-prepared list of problems and minor errors

These should ideally be distributed well before the inspection so that each participant has a good understanding of the purpose of the code and how that purpose is served.

In a code inspection the paraphraser walks through the code, paraphrasing or enunciating it in a natural language such as English, with the other participants following along with him or her. The main function of the paraphraser is to make sure that all the code is covered and that every participant is focused on the same part of the code at the same time. The moderator leads the discussion to ensure that the objectives of the code inspection are met effectively and efficiently.

Major problems should not be resolved during the code inspection. Points should be brought up, clarified, and noted, and that is all. Afterward, the designer, with any required consultation, can resolve the problems without burdening the participants unnecessarily. A participant, who can be anyone other than the paraphraser, should be assigned to take notes to record required changes. A copy of these notes or a list of changes that resolve the points raised should be made available to each participant soon after the meeting.

The following types of report should be prepared as the result of a code inspection:

1. A summary report, which briefly describes the problems found during the inspection
2. A form for listing each problem found so that its disposition or resolution can be recorded
3. A list of updates made to the specifications and changes made to the code

Sample forms for these reports are shown in Figures 6.2, 6.3, and 6.4.

Any problem raised in the inspection meeting should be treated like those discovered in a program test. It should be properly identified, recorded, tracked, resolved, and disposed of officially. In practice, developers of reliability-critical software systems are generally required to file a report, commonly known as a *program-trouble*

CODE INSPECTION SUMMARY REPORT

Project: _____   Moderator: _____

Subproject: _____   Inspection date: _____

Module: _____   Check if   new _____   modified _____

Record the number of nontrivial problems found in each of the categories listed.

type of problems	missing	wrong	extra	total
(1) Logic				
(2) Structure and Interface				
(3) Assumption and Design Decision				
(4) Usability and Performance				
(5) Format and Understandability				
(6) Others (specify:)				
TOTAL				

Need to reinspect :   Yes _____   No _____

Designer: _____   Paraphraser: _____   Recorded by: _____

Resources used (in person-hours): Preparation _____   Inspection _____   Total _____

Figure 6.2   Code inspection summary report.

INSPECTION PROBLEM LOG

Project: _____   Moderator: _____

Subproject: _____   Designer: _____

Module: _____   Date of inspection: _____

Intended function: _____

no.	description of problem	moderator sign-off	resolution description and date

Estimated rework(in person-hours): _____

Figure 6.3 Inspection problem log.

RECORD OF CHANGES MADE AS THE RESULT OF CODE INSPECTION/TESTING

Project: _____ Designer: _____

Subproject: _____ Date: _____

no.	date	module	description of changes made to the code or its specification

Figure 6.4 Record of changes made as the result of code inspection.

report (PTR), for every problem identified. Each such report has to be tracked carefully until the problem is finally resolved to the satisfaction of all parties concerned. The code should be reinspected if:

- A nontrivial change to the code was required
- The rate of problems found in the program exceeded a certain limit prescribed by the organization: say, one for every 25 noncommentary lines of the code

A code inspection should be terminated and rescheduled if:

- Any mandatory participant cannot be in attendance
- The material needed for inspection is not made available to the participants in time for preparation
- There is a strong evidence to indicate that the participants are not properly prepared
- The moderator cannot function effectively for some reason
- Material given to the participants is found not to be up to date

The process described above is to be carried out manually, but some part of it could, can be done more readily if proper tools were available. For example, in preparation for a code inspection, if the programmer found it difficult to understand certain parts of the source code, software tools could be used to facilitate understanding. Such tools can be built based on the path-oriented program analysis method [HUAN08] and the technique of program slicing discussed in Section 6.3.

The following points should be noted:

1. Code inspection has been found to be effective in discovering programming faults. It has been reported that more than 75% of programming faults were discovered in experiments.
2. Code inspection is expensive because it is labor intensive. It requires a group of at least four programmers, and to be effective, the group should not work more than 2 hours a day. Experience shows that only about 200 lines of code can be inspected during that period of time.
3. It is difficult to find a programmer who can serve well as a moderator, and a good programmer is not necessarily an effective inspection-team member.
4. Compared to the use of software testing, the use of code inspection does not necessarily lead to a higher overall development cost. This is so because when a fault is discovered in an inspection, its location and nature also become known. An extensive effort is often required to locate the source of a fault discovered through testing.

Despite many published positive assessments of this method in the literature, one should understand that its effectiveness is highly dependent on the quality and skill of the participants involved. In general, we can only say that it is known to be highly effective when the inspection is carried out by qualified personnel in a well-managed organization.

There is a similar process known as *software audition*. In that process the software product is similarly scrutinized by a group of software professionals to ensure that all the standards imposed by the contracting agency are met. Examples of such standards include the way the source code is formatted, absence of "goto" statements and other problematic constructs, inclusion of proper in-line documentation (comments), and compliance to the standards imposed by the intended host operating systems.

6.5 PROVING PROGRAMS CORRECT

In this section we explain how to construct the correctness proof for a program in two distinctly different ways: bottom-up and top-down. The reader should pay special attention to the following: (1) the way the intended function of a program is specified, (2) the concept of the weakest precondition, and (3) the roll of assertions and loop invariants in constructing a correctness proof.

A common task in program verification is to show that for a given program S, if a certain *precondition* Q is true before the execution of S, then a certain *postcondition* R is true after the execution, provided that S terminates. This logical proposition is commonly denoted $Q\{S\}R$ (a notation due to Hoare [HOAR69]). If we succeeded in showing that $Q\{S\}R$ is a theorem (i.e., always true), then to show that S is *partially correct* [LOND77] with respect to some input predicate I and output predicate $\emptyset$ is to show that $I \supset Q$ and $R \supset \emptyset$ (see, e.g., [MANN74, ANDE79]). The correctness proof is partial because termination is not included.

In this conceptual framework, verification of partial correctness can be carried out in two ways. Given program S, input condition I, and output condition $\emptyset$, we may first let postcondition $R \equiv \emptyset$ and show that $Q\{S\}\emptyset$ for some predicate Q and then show that $I \supset Q$. Alternatively, we may let input condition $I \equiv Q$ and show that $Q\{S\}R$ for some predicate R, and then show that $R \supset \emptyset$. In the first approach the basic problem is to find as weak as possible a condition Q such that $Q\{S\}\emptyset$ and $I \supset Q$. A possible solution is to use the method of predicate transformation due to Basu and Yeh [BAYE75] and Dijkstra [DIJK76] to find the weakest precondition. In the second approach the problem is to find as strong as possible a condition R so that $I\{S\}R$ and $R \supset \emptyset$. This problem is fundamental to the method of inductive assertions (see, e.g., [MANN74, LOND77]).

To fix the idea, we first assume that programs are written in a structured language that includes the following constructs:

1. *Assignment statements*: $x := e$
2. *Conditional statements*: **if** B **then** S **else** S'; (*Note*: S and S' are statements and B is a predicate; the **else** clause may be omitted)
3. *Repetitive statements*: **while** B **do** S; or, **repeat** S **until** B

and a program is constructed by concatenating such statements.

As a concrete example, consider the following program for performing integer division:

INTDIV: **begin**
        $q := 0; r := x;$
        while $r \geq y$ **do begin** $r := r - y; q := q + 1$ **end**
    end.

In words, this program divides x by y and stores the quotient and the remainder in q and r, respectively. Suppose we wish to verify that program INTDIV is partially correct with respect to input predicate $x \geq 0 \wedge y > 0$ and output predicate $x = r + q \times y \wedge r < y \wedge r \geq 0$: that is, to prove that

$$(x \geq 0 \wedge y > 0)\{\text{INTDIV}\}(x = r + q \times y \wedge r < y \wedge r \geq 0)$$

is a theorem.

The Predicate Transformation Method: Bottom-Up Approach

We now show how to construct a correctness proof by working from the bottom of the program to the top. Given program S, precondition I, and postcondition $\emptyset$, the proof is to be constructed by finding as weak as possible a condition Q such that $Q\{S\}\emptyset$, and then showing that $I \supset Q$. We make use of the predicate wp(S, R) introduced in Section 5.2. When used in construction of correctness proofs, it is useful to consider this entity as a function of R or a predicate transformer [BAYE75]. It has the following properties:

1. For any S, wp$(S, F) \equiv F$.
2. For any programming construct S and any predicates Q and R, if $Q \supset R$, then wp$(S, Q) \supset$ wp(S, R).
3. For any programming construct S and any predicates Q and R, (wp$(S, Q) \wedge$ wp$(S, R)) \equiv$ wp$(S, Q \wedge R)$.
4. For any deterministic programming construct S and any predicates Q and R, (wp$(S, Q) \vee$ wp$(S, R)) \equiv$ wp$(S, Q \vee R)$.

We define two special statements: skip and abort. The statement skip is the same as the null statement in a high-level language or the "no-op" instruction in an assembly language. Its meaning can be given as wp(skip, $R) \equiv R$ for any predicate R. The statement abort, when executed, will not lead to a final state. Its meaning is defined as wp(abort, $R) \equiv F$ for any predicate R.

In terms of the predicate transformer, the meaning of an assignment statement can be given as wp$(x := E, R) \equiv R_{E \to x}$, where $R_{E \to x}$ is a predicate obtained from R

by substituting E for every occurrence of x in R. The examples listed below should clarify the meaning of this notation.

R	$x := E$	$R_{E \to x}$	Which can be simplified to:
$x = 0$	$x := 0$	$0 = 0$	T
$a > 1$	$x := 10$	$a > 1$	$a > 1$
$x < 10$	$x := x + 1$	$x + 1 < 10$	$x < 9$
$x \neq y$	$x := x - y$	$x - y \neq y$	$x \neq 2y$

For a sequence of two programming constructs S_1 and S_2,

$$\text{wp}(S_1; S_2, R) \equiv \text{wp}(S_1, \text{wp}(S_2, R))$$

The weakest precondition of an if–then–else statement is defined to be

$$\text{wp}(\textbf{if } B \textbf{ then } S_1 \textbf{ else } S_2, R) \equiv B \wedge \text{wp}(S_1, R) \vee \neg B \wedge \text{wp}(S_2, R)$$

For the iterative statement, Basu and Yeh [BAYE75] have shown that

$$\text{wp}(\textbf{while } B \textbf{ do } S, R) \equiv (\exists j)_{j \geq 0}(A_j(R))$$

where $A_0(R) \equiv \neg B \wedge R$ and $A_{j+1}(R) \equiv B \wedge \text{wp}(S, A_j(R))$ for all $j \geq 0$. In practice, the task of finding the weakest precondition of an iterative statement is often hopelessly complex. This difficulty constitutes a major hurdle in proving programs correct using the predicate transformation method.

To illustrate, consider the example program given previously.

INTDIV: **begin**
          $q := 0; r := x;$
          while $r \geq y$ **do begin** $r := r - y; q := q + 1$ **end**
          end.

We can prove the correctness of this program by first computing

$$\textbf{wp}(\textbf{while } r \geq y \textbf{ do begin } r := r - y; q := q + 1 \textbf{ end}, x = r + q \times y \wedge r < y \wedge$$
$$r \geq 0)$$

where $B \equiv r \geq y$

$R \equiv x = r + q \times y \wedge r < y \wedge r \geq 0$

$S: r := r - y; q := q + 1;$

$$A_0(R) \equiv \neg B \wedge R$$

$$\equiv r < y \wedge x = r + q \times y \wedge r < y \wedge r \geq 0$$

$$\equiv x = r + q \times y \wedge r < y \wedge r \geq 0$$

$$A_1(R) \equiv B \wedge \text{wp}(S, A_0(R))$$

$$\equiv r \geq y \wedge \text{wp}(r := r - y; q := q + 1, x = r + q$$

$$\times y \wedge r < y \wedge r \geq 0)$$

$$\equiv r \geq y \wedge x = r - y + (q + 1) \times y \wedge r - y < y \wedge r - y \geq 0$$

$$\equiv x = r + q \times y \wedge r < 2 \times y \wedge r \geq y$$

$$A_2(R) \equiv B \wedge \text{wp}(S, A_1(R))$$

$$\equiv x = r + q \times y \wedge r < 3 \times y \wedge r \geq 2 \times y$$

$$A_3(R) \equiv B \wedge \text{wp}(S, A_2(R))$$

$$\equiv x = r + q \times y \wedge r < 4 \times y \wedge r \geq 3 \times y$$

From these we may guess that

$$A_j(R) \equiv B \wedge \text{wp}(S, A_{j-1}(R))$$

$$\equiv x = r + q \times y \wedge r < (j + 1) \times y \wedge r \geq j \times y$$

and we have to prove that our guess is correct by mathematical induction. Assume that $A_j(R)$ is as given above; then

$$A_0(R) \equiv x = r + q \times y \wedge r < (0 + 1) \times y \wedge r \geq 0 \times y$$

$$\equiv x = r + q \times y \wedge r < y \wedge r \geq 0$$

$$A_{j+1}(R) \equiv B \wedge \text{wp}(S, A_j(R))$$

$$\equiv r \geq y \wedge \text{wp}(r := r - y; q := q + 1, x = r + q$$

$$\times y \wedge r < (j + 1) \times y \wedge r \geq j \times y)$$

$$\equiv r \geq y \wedge x = r - y + (q + 1) \times y \wedge r - y < (j + 1)$$

$$\times y \wedge r - y \geq j \times y$$

$$\equiv x = r + q \times y \wedge r < ((j + 1) + 1) \times y \wedge r \geq (j + 1) \times y$$

These two instances of $A_j(R)$ show that if $A_j(R)$ is correct, then $A_{j+1}(R)$ is also correct, as given above. Hence,

$$\text{wp}(\textbf{while } r \geq y \textbf{ do begin } r := r - y; \ q := q + 1 \textbf{ end}, \ x = r + q \times y \wedge r < y \wedge r \geq 0)$$

$$\equiv (\exists j)_{j \geq 0}(A_j(R))$$

$$\equiv (\exists j)_{j \geq 0}(x = r + q \times y \wedge r < (j + 1) \times y \wedge r \geq j \times y)$$

Next, we compute

$$\text{wp}(q := 0;\ r := x, (\exists j)_{j \geq 0}(x = r + q \times y \wedge r < (j+1) \times y \wedge r \geq j \times y))$$
$$\equiv (\exists j)_{j \geq 0}(x < (j+1) \times y \wedge x \geq j \times y)$$

which is implied by the input condition $x \geq 0 \wedge y > 0$, and hence the proof that

$$(x \geq 0 \wedge y > 0)\{\text{INTDIV}\}(x = r + q \times y \wedge r < y \wedge r \geq 0)$$

Recall that $Q\{S\}R$ is a shorthand notation for the proposition "if Q is true before the execution of S then R is true after the execution, provided that S terminates." Termination of the program has to be proved separately [MANN74]. If $Q \equiv \text{wp}(S, R)$, however, termination of the program is guaranteed. In that case, we can write $Q[S]R$ instead, which is a shorthand notation for the proposition: "if Q is true before the execution of S, then R is true after the execution of S, and the execution will terminate" [BAYE75].

The Inductive Assertion Method: Top-Down Approach

In the second approach, given a program S and a predicates Q, the basic problem is to find as strong as possible a condition R such that $Q\{S\}R$. If S is an assignment statement of the form $x := E$, where x is a variable and E is an expression, we have

$$Q\{x := E\}(Q' \wedge x = E')_{x' \to E^{-1}}$$

where Q' and E' are obtained from Q and E, respectively, by replacing every occurrence of x with x', and then replacing every occurrence of x' with E^{-1} such that $x = E' \equiv x' = E^{-1}$.

In practice, the predicate $(Q' \wedge x = E')_{x' \to E^{-1}}$ is constructed as follows. Given Q and $x := E$:

1. Write $Q \wedge x = E$.
2. Replace every occurrence of x in Q and E with x' to yield $Q' \wedge x = E'$.
3. If x' occurs in E' construct $x' = E^{-1}$ from $x = E'$ such that $x = E' \equiv x' = E^{-1}$; else E^{-1} does not exist.
4. If E^{-1} exists, replace every occurrence of x' in $Q' \wedge x = E'$ with E^{-1}. Otherwise, replace every atomic predicate in $Q' \wedge x = E'$ having at least one occurrence of x' with T (the constant predicate TRUE).

The following examples should clarify the definition given above.

Q	$x := E$	$(Q' \wedge x = E')_{x' \to E^{-1}}$	Which can be simplified to:
$x = 0$	$x := 10$	$T \wedge x = 10$	$x = 10$
$a > 1$	$x := 1$	$a > 1 \wedge x = 1$	$a > 1 \wedge x = 1$
$x < 10$	$x := x + 1$	$x - 1 < 10$	$x < 11$
$x \neq y$	$x := x - y$	$x + y \neq y$	$x \neq 0$

In essence, $(Q' \wedge x = E')_{x' \to E^{-1}}$ denotes the strongest postcondition for the final state if an execution of $x := E$, with the initial state satisfying Q, terminates.

As explained earlier, it is convenient to use $\vdash P$ to denote the fact that P is a theorem (i.e., always true). A verification rule may be stated in the form "if $\vdash X$, then $\vdash Y$," which says that if proposition X has been proved as a theorem, Y is thereby also proved as a theorem. Note that $\vdash Q[S]R$ implies that $\vdash Q\{S\}R$, but not the other way around. The student should find an example of this fact.

We now proceed to give some useful verification rules. As given previously, for an assignment statement of the form $x := E$, we have

$$\vdash Q\{x := E\}(Q' \wedge x = E')_{x' \to E^{-1}} \qquad \text{(Rule 1)}$$

For a conditional statement of the form **if** B **then** S_1 **else** S_2, we have

If $\vdash Q \wedge B\{S_1\}R_1$ and $\vdash Q \wedge \neg B\{S_2\}R_2$ then $\vdash Q\{\textbf{if } B \textbf{ then } S_1 \textbf{ else } S_2\}(R_1 \vee R_2)$
$$\text{(Rule 2)}$$

For a loop construct of the form **while** B **do** S, we have

If $\vdash Q \supset R$ and $\vdash (R \wedge B)\{S\}R$ then $\vdash Q\{\textbf{while } B \textbf{ do } S\}(\neg B \wedge R)$ $\qquad$ (Rule 3)

The relation above is commonly known as the invariant-relation theorem, and any predicate R satisfying the premise is called a *loop invariant* of the loop construct **while** B **do** S. Thus, the partial correctness of program S with respect to input condition I and output condition $\emptyset$ can be proved by showing that $I\{S\}Q$ and $Q \supset \emptyset$. The proof can be constructed in smaller steps if S is a long sequence of statements. Specifically, if S is $S_1; S_2; \ldots; S_n$, then $I\{S_1; S_2; \ldots; S_n\}\emptyset$ can be proved by showing that $I\{S_1\}P_1$, $P_1\{S_2\}P_2$, …, and $P_{n-1}\{S_n\}\emptyset$ for some predicates $P_1, P_2, \ldots$, and P_{n-1}. P_i's are called *inductive assertions*, and this method of proving program correctness is called the *inductive assertion method*.

Required inductive assertions for constructing a proof often have to be found by guesswork, based on one's understanding of the program in question, especially if a loop construct is involved. No algorithm for this purpose exists, although some heuristics have been developed to aid the search.

To illustrate, consider again the problem of proving the partial correctness of

INTDIV: **begin**
        $q := 0; r:=x;$
        while $r \geq y$ **do begin** $r := r - y; q := q + 1$ **end**
    end.

with respect to the input condition $I \equiv x \geq 0 \wedge y > 0$ and output condition $\emptyset \equiv x = r + q \times y \wedge r < y \wedge r \geq 0$. By Rule 1 we have

$$(x \geq 0 \wedge y > 0)\{q := 0\}(x \geq 0 \wedge y > 0 \wedge q = 0)$$

and

$$(x \geq 0 \wedge y > 0 \wedge q = 0)\{r := x\}(x \geq 0 \wedge y > 0 \wedge q = 0 \wedge r = x)$$

From the output condition $\emptyset$ we can guess that $x = r + q \times y \wedge r \geq 0$ is a loop invariant. This can be verified by the fact that

$$(x \geq 0 \wedge y > 0 \wedge q = 0 \wedge r = x) \supset (x = r + q \times y \wedge r \geq 0)$$

and

$$(r \geq y \wedge x = r + q \times y \wedge r \geq 0)\{r := r - y; q := q + 1\}(x = r + q \times y \wedge r \geq 0)$$

Hence, by Rule 3, we have

$$(r \geq y \wedge x = r + q \times y \wedge r \geq 0)\{\textbf{while } r \geq y \ \textbf{ do begin } r := r - y; q := q + 1 \textbf{ end}\}$$
$$(r < y \wedge x = r + q \times y \wedge r \geq 0)$$

Thus, we have shown, by transitivity of implication, that

$$(x \geq 0 \wedge y > 0)\{\text{INTDIV}\}(x = r + q \times y \wedge r < y \wedge r \geq 0)$$

There are many variations of the inductive-assertion method. The version above is designed, as an integral part of this section, to show that a correctness proof can be constructed in a top-down manner. As such, we assume that a program is composed of a concatenation of statements and an inductive assertion is to be inserted between such statements only. The problem is that most programs contain nested loops and compound statements, which may render applications of Rules 2 and 3 hopelessly complicated. This difficulty can be alleviated by using a variant of the inductive-assertion method described below.

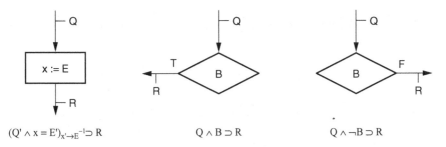

Figure 6.5 Elements of a path in a flowchart.

The complication induced by nested loops and compound statements can be eliminated by representing the program as a flowchart. Appropriate assertions are then placed on various points in the control flow. These assertions "cut" the flowchart into a set of paths. The *path* between assertions Q and R is formed by a single sequence of statements that will be executed if the control flow traverses from Q to R in an execution, and contains no other assertions. It is possible that Q and R are the same.

Since programs are assumed to be written in a Pascal-like language as stated before, each node in the flowchart of a program is either a branch predicate or an assignment statement. It follows that the flowchart of any program is formed by three types of simple path depicted in Figure 6.5. The intended function of each basic path is described by the associated lemma that in effect states that if the starting assertion is true, the ending assertion will also become true when the control reaches the end of the path. In this method we let the input predicate be the starting assertion at the program entry, and let the output predicate be the ending assertion at the program exit. To prove the correctness of the program is to show that every lemma associated with a basic path is a theorem (i.e., always true). If we succeeded in doing that then due to transitivity of the implication relation, it implies that if the input predicate is true at the program entry, the output predicate will be true also if and when the control reaches the exit (i.e., if the execution terminates). Therefore, it constitutes a proof of the partial correctness of the program.

In practice, we work with composite paths instead of simple paths to reduce the number of lemmas need that to be proved. A *composite path* is a path formed by a concatenation of more than one simple path. The lemma associated with a composite path can be constructed by observing that the effect produced by a composite path is the conjunction of that produced by its constituent simple paths. At least one assertion should be inserted into each loop so that any path is of finite length.

There are other details that can best be explained by using an example. Let us consider program INTDIV used in the previous discussion. The flowchart of that program is shown in Figure 6.6. Three assertions are used for this example: A is the input predicate, C is the output predicate, and B is the assertion used to cut the loop. Note that assertion B cannot be simply $q = 0$ and $r = x$ because B is not merely the ending point of path AB—it is also the beginning and ending points of path BB. Therefore, we have to guess the assertion at that point that will lead us to a successful

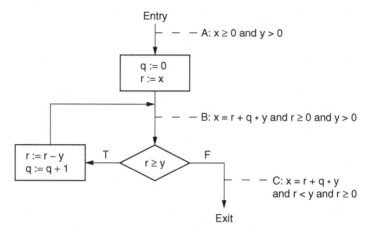

Figure 6.6   Flowchart of program INTDIV.

proof. In this case it is not difficult to guess because the output predicate provides a strong hint as to what we need at that point.

There are three paths between assertions in this flowchart: paths AB, BB, and BC. These paths lead us to the following lemmas that must be proved.

- *Path AB:* $x \geq 0 \wedge y > 0 \wedge q = 0 \wedge r = x \supset x = r + q * y \wedge r \geq 0 \wedge y > 0$.
- *Path BB:* $x = r + q * y \wedge r \geq 0 \wedge y > 0 \wedge r' = r - y \wedge q' = q + 1 \supset x = r' + q' * y \wedge r' \geq 0 \wedge y > 0$. (Here q' and r' denote the new values of q and r after the loop body is executed.)
- *Path BC:* $x = r + q * y \wedge r \geq 0 \wedge y > 0 \wedge \neg(r \geq y) \supset x = r + q * y \wedge r < y \wedge r \geq 0$.

These three lemmas can be readily proved as follows.

- *Lemma for path AB.* Substitute 0 for q and r for x in the consequence.
- *Lemma for path BB.* Substitute q with $q' - 1$ and r with $r' + y$ for every occurrence of q and r and simplify.
- *Lemma for path BC.* Use the fact that $\neg(r \geq y)$ is $r < y$, and simplify.

A common error made in constructing a correctness proof is that the assertion that we guess is either stronger or weaker than the correct one. Let P be the correct inductive assertion to use in proving $I\{S_1; S_2\}\emptyset$; that is, $I\{S_1\}P$ and $P\{S_2\}\emptyset$ are both theorems. If the assertion that we guess is too weak, say, $P \vee \Delta$, where Δ is some extraneous predicate, $I\{S_1\}(P \vee \Delta)$ is still a theorem but $(P \vee \Delta)\{S_2\}\emptyset$ may not be. On the other hand, if the assertion that we guess is too strong, say, $P \wedge \Delta$, $(P \wedge \Delta)\{S_2\}\emptyset$ is still a theorem but $I\{S_1\}(P \wedge \Delta)$ may not be. Consequently, if one failed to construct a proof by using the inductive-assertion method, it does not necessarily mean that the program is incorrect. Failure of a proof could result either from an incorrect program or an incorrect choice of inductive assertions. In comparison, the bottom-up (predicate transformation) method does not have this disadvantage.

EXERCISES

6.1 Find two examples (other than those given in the text) of programming constructs in C++ that are syntactically correct but semantically faulty.

6.2 Consider the following C++ program.

```
1   #define YES 1
2   #define NO 0
3   main()
4   {
5        int c, nl, nw, nc, inword;
6        inword = NO;
7        nl = 0;
8        nw = 0;
9        nc = 0;
10       cin >> c;
11       while (c != EOF) {
12            nc = nc + 1;
13            if (c == '\n')
14                 nl = nl + 1;
15            if (c == ' ' || c == '\n' || c == '\t')
16                 inword = NO;
17            else if (inword == NO) {
18                 inword = YES;
19                 nw = nw + 1;
20            }
21            cin >> c;
22       }
23       cout << nl << endl;
24       cout << nw << endl;
25       cout << nc << endl;
26   }
```

Construct the minimum slice with the slicing criterion C = (26, c).

6.3 In addition to technical competency, what personal traits will make a software engineer (or a programmer) a more effective moderator in software inspection?

6.4   Are there any additional materials that may be distributed to the participants of code inspection to make them more effective?

6.5   What are the main technical bottlenecks that prevent the methods of proving program correctness from becoming practical?

6.6   If you are assigned to meet a sales representative who claims that his or her company has succeeded in developing a software tool that makes it practical to prove program correctness, what questions would you ask to ascertain that the claim is valid? The claim is likely to remain invalid for some time to come, and you do not want to waste a lot of time with this sales representative. On the other hand, you may want to keep your door open in the unlikely event that there is a major technical breakthrough.

6.7   Which concepts and techniques developed in proving program correctness are also used in program testing?

7 Program Instrumentation

Normally, a computer program is designed to produce outputs that are useful only to its users. If test execution of the program produces an incorrect result, it is very significant to the tester in that it attests directly to the presence of faults in the program, and possibly includes some clues about the nature and whereabouts of the faults. On the other hand, if it produces a correct result, its significance to the tester is rather limited. The only conclusion the tester can draw from a successful test execution is that the program works correctly for that particular input. It would be beneficial to the tester if we could make a program to produce additional information useful for fault-detection and process-management purposes.

In this chapter we explore the idea of inserting additional statements (commonly known as *software instruments*) into a program for information-gathering purposes. By test-executing the instrumented program for a properly chosen set of test cases, the program will automatically produce information useful to the tester.

Possible applications of program instrumentation include:

- *Test-coverage measurement.* In performing code-based testing it is important to know, and is often necessary to provide, verifiable evidence to the contracting agency as to what extent the test requirements have been satisfied. Such information can be obtained readily by instrumenting the program with counters.

- *Test-case effectiveness assessment.* A number of methods require that a test case be selected arbitrarily from a subdomain. Unfortunately, as explained later, not all elements in a subdomain are equally apt in revealing a fault. The ineffectiveness of a test case may be measured in terms of the number of times the test case was "blindsided" during test execution, and can be measured automatically through instrumentation.

- *Assertion checking.* In using the inductive-assertion method to construct a correctness proof of a program (see Section 6.5), we insert appropriate assertions at strategic points in the program and show that those assertions are tautological (i.e., always true). If any one of the assertions was violated during an execution, it implies that there is a fault in the program. Violation of assertions during a test execution can be detected through program instrumentation.

- *Data-flow-anomaly detection.* Data-flow anomalies, which we discussed in Section 6.1, can be detected through static analysis or program instrumentation. In

Software Error Detection through Testing and Analysis, By J. C. Huang
Copyright © 2009 John Wiley & Sons, Inc.

this chapter we describe how to instrument a program for that purpose and discuss the advantages and the disadvantages of data-flow-anomaly detection through instrumentation.

- *Symbolic-trace generation.* In earlier chapters we demonstrated the usefulness of a symbolic trace in program analysis and testing. It turns out that the symbolic trace of an execution path can be generated automatically through instrumentation, as described later in the chapter.

7.1   TEST-COVERAGE MEASUREMENT

Two test-case selection criteria are in common use in the software industry. They are known as:

- *C1* (or *statement test*). Each statement in the program is exercised at least once during the test.
- *C2* (or *branch test*). Each branch in its control-flow graph is traversed at least once during the test.

Given a program P and a test set T, how can we utilize the technique of program instrumentation to determine the extent to which the test coverage is achieved by test-executing P with T? Follow the steps given below.

1. Identify a set of points in the control flow of the program such that if we know the number of times each point is crossed during execution, we will be able to determine the number of times that each statement is executed (or each branch is traversed).
2. Instrument the program with appropriate software counters at these points.
3. Test-execute the instrumented program with the test set.
4. Examine the counter values to determine the extent of coverage achieved.

How can a software counter be built? It can be implemented by using a function (method) named, for example, *count(j)*, which makes use of an integer array *counter[1..n]*. Every element of this array is associated with a certain point in the control flow of the program and is set to zero initially. At each such point in the control flow, say point j, the program is instrumented with a call to function *count[j]*. When that point is crossed during execution, *count(j)* is invoked and the value of *counter[j]* is incremented by 1. After the test we will be able to determine how many times each point was crossed during execution by examining the values of elements in *counter*.

The question now is: Where should we place the counters? A possible answer is to place a counter on each branch in the control-flow diagram that emanates from an entry node or from any node with two or more branches emanating from it. Such a branch is at the head of a path in the control flow diagram called a *decision-to-decision path* [MILL74]. When that branch is traversed, every branch on that decision-to-decision path is traversed once and only once. This method is easy to apply, but the number of counters required is not necessarily minimal.

After a test execution of the program, the values of the counters can be dumped to determine the extent of coverage achieved. If all the counters have a nonzero count, it signifies that C2 has been achieved (i.e., every branch in the control flow has been traversed at least once during the test). If any counter has a zero count, choose an additional test case to exercise it. It is also possible that despite all efforts to change a zero count, it persisted. In that event, effort should be redirected to proving that the counter is unreachable.

Incidentally, the counter values also point out which portions of the program are executed many more times than others and thus have a greater optimization payoff. Because of this feature, many seasoned programmers have an automatic software tool for counter instrumentation in their tool box. They may never have to monitor the test coverage, but as a programmer they all have to optimize their programs at times.

Observe that the number of counters needed to determine satisfaction of C1 and C2 can be fewer than the number of decision-to-decision paths in the program. An interesting question in this regard is: Given a program, what is the minimum number of counters required to determine satisfaction of C1 (or C2)? This question, which represents a nontrivial abstract graph-theoretical problem, is mostly of theoretical interest only because in practice the cost of determining the required number of counters and the locations at which these counters have to be placed often outweighs the cost of using extra counters in the decision-to-decision-path method.

7.2   TEST-CASE EFFECTIVENESS ASSESSMENT

By the *effectiveness* of a test case here we mean its capability to reveal faults in the program. A test case is ineffective if it causes the program to produce fortuitously correct results for certain elements in the input domain, even though the program is faulty.

One reason a program may produce a fortuitously correct result is that it contains expressions of the form *exp1 op exp2*, and the test case used causes *exp1* to assume a special value such that *exp1 op exp2 = exp1* regardless of the value of *exp2*. In that event, if there is an error in *exp2*, it will never be reflected in the test result. Here are some examples of such expressions and test cases:

$(a + b) * (c - d)$ if the test case used is such that $a + b = 0$
$P(x)$ and $Q(y, z)$ if the test case used is such that predicate $P(x)$ becomes false
$P(x, y)$ or $Q(z)$ if the test case used is such that predicate $P(x, y)$ becomes true

We say that such expressions are *multifaceted* and such test cases *singularly focused* because test-executing a program with a test case is in many ways like inspecting an object in the dark with a flashlight. If the light were singularly focused on only one facet of a multifaceted object, the inspector would not be able to see a flaw on the other facets.

The *singularity index* of a test case with respect to a program is defined as the number of times that a test case is singularly focused on the multifaceted expressions encountered during a particular test run. To compute the singularity index of a test case automatically, a thorough inspection and analysis of every expression contained in the program is required. If we limit ourselves to multifaceted expressions of the form *exp1 op exp2*, the instrumentation tool can be designed to instrument every facet in a multifaceted expression to count the number of times that a test case is focused singularly on a facet.

For example, suppose that a statement in the program contains the following expression:

```
a * (c + (d / e))
```

Since there are three facets in this expression, a, (c + (d / e)), and d, a tool can be designed to instrument this expression:

```
if (a == 0) si++;
if ((c + (d / e)) == 0) si++;
if (d == 0) si++;

a * (c + (d / e));
```

Here si is a variable used to store the singularity index of the test case. The greater the value of the singularity index, the higher the probability that the test case is unable to reveal an error and hence that the test case is less effective.

A measure of the singularity index can be used to determine the relative effectiveness of a test case. Suppose that a program has been tested using two different test sets. If one of the two sets revealed more faults, the relative effectiveness of these two sets is obvious. Nevertheless, if both test sets revealed the same number of faults, the relative effectiveness of the two sets becomes open to question. A way to settle the question is to measure their singularity indices: The one with a higher singularity index is likely to be less effective, for the reason given above.

7.3 INSTRUMENTING PROGRAMS FOR ASSERTION CHECKING

Often, the intended function of a program can be expressed in terms of assertions that must be satisfied, or values that must be assumed by some variables, at certain strategic points in the program. Software instruments can be used to monitor the values of variables or to detect violations of assertions. The instruments can be constructed using the host language. Use of a special language will, however, facilitate construction of the instruments and make the process less error-prone.

For example, a special high-level language was first used in the program evaluator and tester (PET) developed by Stucki and Foshee [STFO75]. This language allows the user to describe the desired instrumentation precisely and concisely. A PET preprocessor translates all instruments into statements in the host language before compilation.

An interesting feature of PET is that all instruments are inserted into the program as comments in the host language. After the program is tested and debugged thoroughly, all instruments can be removed simply by recompiling the program without using the preprocessor. In general, the instruments make the source code of a program more readable. There is no reason to remove them physically after the program is completely tested and debugged.

In the following we use examples adapted from Stucki and Foshee [STFO75] to illustrate the syntax of this special instrumentation language and its applications. (*Note:* Expressions enclosed in brackets are optional. The vertical bar delimits alternatives.)

Local Assertions

ASSERT (*extended logical expression*) [HALT on *n*[VIOLATIONS]]

Here by *local assertion* we mean that the assertion needs to be satisfied only at the point in control flow at which the instrument is located. By *extended logical expression* we mean a logical expression expressed in the instrumentation language, which is not necessarily a grammatically correct logical expression in the host language.

ASSERT ORDER (*array cross section*)
[ASCENDING |DESCENDING] [HALT ON *n* VIOLATIONS]]

Examples:

ASSERT(MOVE.LT. 9) HALT ON 10

Remark: The report produced by PET includes the total amount of time this instrument was executed, the number of times the assertion was violated, and values of MOVE that violated the assertion.

ASSERT ORDER($A(*, 3)$) ASCENDING

Remark: If there were a violation of this assertion, PET would produce a report indicating the array elements and their values that caused the violation.

TRACE[FIRST |LAST |OFF] *n* [VIOLATIONS]

This construct allows the user to control the number of execution snapshots reported for local assertion violations.

Global Assertions

Global assertions can be used to replace the use of several similar assertions within a particular program region. Such assertions appear in the declaration section of the program module and allow us to extend our capacity to inspect certain behavioral patterns for entire program modules. Possible assertions of this type include:

> ASSERT RANGE (*list of variables*) (*min, max*)
> ASSERT VALUES (*list of variables*) (*list of legal values*)
> ASSERT VALUES (*list of variables*) NOT (*list of illegal values*)
> ASSERT SUBSCRIPT RANGE (*list of array specifications*)
> ASSERT NO SIDE EFFECTS (*parameter list*)
> HALT ON *n* [VIOLATIONS]

The last assertion is designed to stop program execution after *n* global assertion violations are detected. It is useful in preventing the tool from producing a prohibitively voluminous violation report when there is an assertion violation in a loop and that loop is iterated a great number of times during program execution.

Monitors

> MONITOR[NUMERIC |CHARACTER] [RANGE]
>   FIRST[*n* VALUES] LAST [*n* VALUES] [ALL |(*list of variables*)]
> MONITOR SUBSCRIPT RANGE [ALL |(*list of array names*)]

Examples:

> MONITOR RANGE FIRST LAST ALL
> MONITOR CHARACTER RANGE (*X*VAR, *Y*VAR)
> MONITOR RANGE (*A*(∗, 3))
> MONITOR SUBSCRIPT RANGE (*A*, *B*, *C*)

Assertion checking is potentially an effective means to detect programming errors. When a fault is detected through this mechanism, it not only shows the user how that fault manifests itself in the program execution but also indicates the vicinity, if not the exact location, of that fault. This valuable information is generally not available from an incorrect program output resulting from an ordinary test execution. A programmer may, however, find it difficult to use this technique in practice. To be effective, the programmer has to place the right assertions at the right places in the program, which is not easy to do. The problem of finding the right assertions in this application is the same as that in proving program correctness. There is no effective procedure for this purpose. Thus, when a violation is detected, the user has to find out if it is caused by a programming error or an inappropriate assertion. This difficulty often is the source of frustration in applying the technique of assertion checking, and deters the technique from being commonly used in practice.

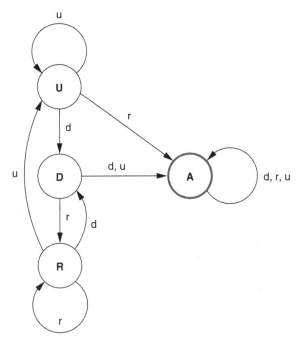

Figure 7.1   State-transition graph of the states assumable by variables in a program.

7.4   INSTRUMENTING PROGRAMS FOR DATA-FLOW-ANOMALY DETECTION[1]

The concept of a data-flow anomaly as a potential symptom of possible programming fault has discussed in Section 6.1. In the following we present a unique method for detecting data-flow anomalies by means of program instrumentation.[1] For this purpose it is useful to regard a variable as being in one of four possible states during program execution: state U: undefined; state D: defined but not referenced; state R: defined and referenced; and state A: abnormal state. For error-detection purposes it is proper to assume that a variable is in the state of being undefined when it is declared implicitly or explicitly. Now if the action taken on this variable is *define*, it will enter the state of being defined but not referenced. Then, depending on the next action taken on this variable, it will assume a different state, as shown in Figure 7.1. Note that each edge in this state diagram is associated with d, r, or u, which stand for *define*, *reference*, and *undefine*, respectively. The three types of data-flow anomalies mentioned previously can thus be denoted by ur, du, and dd in this shorthand notation. It is easy to verify that if a sequence of actions taken on the

[1]Portions of this section were adapted, with permission, from "Detection of Data Flow Anomaly Detection through Program Instrumentation," *IEEE Transactions on Software Engineering*, vol. 5, no. 3, May 1979, pp. 226–236. © 1979, IEEE.

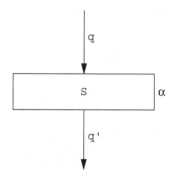

Figure 7.2 Computation of the next state $q' = f(q, \alpha)$.

variable contains either ur, du, or dd as a subsequence, the variable will enter state A, which indicates the presence of a data-flow anomaly in the execution path. We let the variable remain in state A once that state is entered. Its implications and possible alternatives will be discussed later.

It is obvious from the discussion above that there is no need to compute the sequence of actions taken on a variable along the entire execution path. Instead, we need only to know if the sequence will contain ur, du, or dd as a subsequence. Since such a subsequence will invariably cause the variable to enter state A, all we need to do is to monitor the states assumed by the variable during execution. This can be accomplished readily by means of program instrumentation.

To see how this can be done, let us consider a fragment of a flowchart shown in Figure 7.2. Suppose that we wish to detect data-flow anomalies with respect to a variable, say x. If x is in state q before statement S is executed, and if α is the sequence of actions that will be taken on x by S, an execution of S will cause x to enter state q' as depicted in Figure 7.2. Given q and α, q' can be determined based on the state diagram in Figure 7.1. However, for the discussion that follows, it is convenient to write

$$q' = f(q, \alpha)$$

where f is called the *state transition function* and is defined completely by the state diagram shown in Figure 7.1. Thus, for example, $f(U, d) = D$ and $f(D, u) = A$. For cases where α is a sequence of more than one action, the definition of f can be given as follows. Let $\alpha = a\beta$, where a is either d, r, or u, and β is a sequence of d's, r's, and u's. Then

$$f(q, a\beta) = f(f(q, a), \beta)$$

for any q in $\{A, D, R, U\}$. Thus, $f(U, dur) = f(f(U, d), ur) = f(D, ur) = f(f(D, u), r) = f(A, r) = A$.

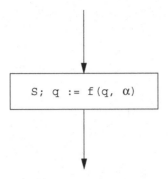

Figure 7.3   Program instrumented with $q := f(q, \alpha)$.

Next, we observe that the computation specified by the expression $q' = f(q, \alpha)$ can be carried out by using a program statement of the form

$$q := f(q, \alpha).$$

Now if we insert the statement above next to statement S in Figure 7.2, as shown in Figure 7.3, the new state assumed by variable x will be computed automatically upon execution. The augmented program depicted in Figure 7.3 is said to have been *instrumented* with the statement $q := f(q, \alpha)$. This statement should be constructed such that there will be no interference between the statement inserted and the original program. A simple way to accomplish this is to use variables other than those that appeared in the program to construct the statement inserted.

To illustrate the idea presented above, let us consider the execution path shown in Figure 7.4. Suppose that we wish to detect possible data-flow anomalies with respect to variable x along this path. According to the method described above, we need to instrument the program with statbv ements of the form $x$state $:= f(x$state, $\alpha)$, as shown in Figure 7.5. The variable "$x$state" contains the state assumed by x. At the entry, the variable x is assumed to be undefined, and therefore the variable $x$state is initialized to U. By an execution along the path, $x$state will be set to different values, as indicated on the right-hand side of Figure 7.5. Note that there is no need to place an instrument following a statement unless that statement will act on variable x. To see if there is a data-flow anomaly with respect to x on the path, all we need to do is to print out the value of $x$state by instrumenting the program with an appropriate output statement at the exit. In this example, the data flow with respect to x is anomalous in that x is defined and defined again, and the value of $x$state will be set to A to reflect this fact.

In practice, it is more appropriate to instrument programs with procedure calls instead of assignment statements. The use of a procedure allows us to save the identification of an instrument, the state assumed by the variable, and the type of data-flow anomaly detected. This information will significantly facilitate anomaly analysis.

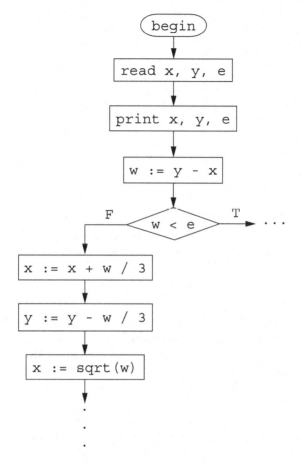

Figure 7.4   Execution path.

Data Flow of Array Elements

To instrument a program for detection of data-flow anomalies as described above, we must be able to identify the actions taken by each statement in the program as well as the objects of actions taken. This requires additional considerations if array elements are involved. The sequence of actions taken by a statement on a subscripted variable can be determined as usual. Identification of the object, however, may become a problem if the subscript is a variable or an arithmetic expression. First, without looking elsewhere we do not know which element of the array that variable is meant to be. Second, the object of action taken may be different every time that statement is executed.

   This problem becomes very difficult when data-flow anomalies are to be detected by means of static analysis. In the method described by Fosdick and Osterweil [FOOS76], this problem is circumvented entirely by ignoring subscripts and treating all elements of an array as if they were a single variable. It is interesting to see what is entailed when this approach is taken. For this purpose, let us consider the familiar

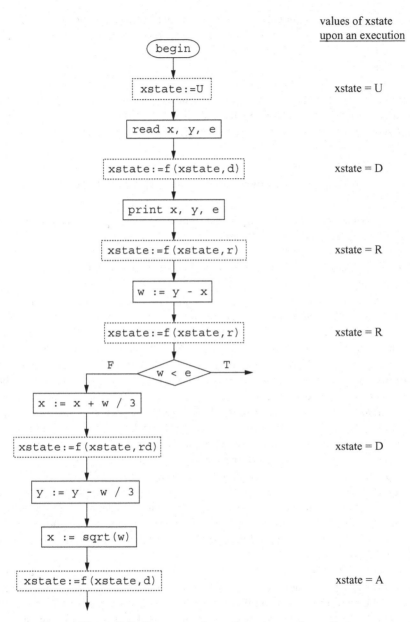

Figure 7.5 Instruments inserted on an execution path.

sequence of three statements given below, which exchanges the values of $a[j]$ and $a[k]$:

$$temp := a[j];$$
$$a[j] := a[k];$$
$$a[k] := temp;$$

It is obvious that the data flow for every variable involved is not anomalous, provided that $j \neq k$. However, if $a[j]$ and $a[k]$ are treated as the same variable, the data flow becomes anomalous because it is defined and defined again by the last two statements. This example shows that a false alarm may be produced if we treat all elements of an array as if they were a single variable. False alarms are a nuisance, and most important, a waste of programmer time and effort. In some cases, a data-flow anomaly will not be detected if we treat all elements of an array as if they were a single variable. For example, let us consider the following program:

$$i := 1;$$
$$\textbf{while } i <= 10 \textbf{ do begin } a[i] := a[i + 1]; \ i := i + 1 \textbf{ end};$$

If $a[i]$ is written mistakenly as $a[1]$, the data flow for $a[1]$ becomes anomalous because it is defined repeatedly, 10 times. This is not so if all elements of the array are treated as a single variable.

These examples clearly demonstrate that if we treat all elements of an array as the same variable, as is done in the static analysis method, it is inevitable that false alarms will be produced in some cases and that anomalies will be overlooked in others. Obviously, separate handling of array elements is highly desirable. The problem posed by array elements can be solved easily if the present method of program instrumentation is used. In this method data-flow anomalies are to be detected by software instruments placed among program statements. When it comes to executing a software instrument involving a subscripted variable, the value of its subscript has already been computed (if the subscript is a single variable) or can be computed readily (if it is an arithmetic expression). Therefore, in the process of instrumenting a program for checking the data flow of a subscripted variable, there is no need to know which element of the array that variable is meant to be. The true object of actions taken on this variable can be determined dynamically at execution time.

To implement the idea outlined above on a computer, we need (1) to allocate a separate memory location to every element in the array for the purpose of storing the state presently assumed by that element, and (2) to instrument the program with statements that will change the state of the right array element at the right place. The complexity of statements required depends on the data structure used in storing the states of the array elements.

One simple structure that can be used is to store the states of elements of an array in the corresponding elements of another array of the same dimension. Statements of the form shown in Figure 7.5 can then be used to monitor the states assumed by the array elements. For example, suppose that a program makes use of a two-dimensional array $a[1:10, 1:20]$. To instrument the program to monitor the data flow of elements in this array, we can declare another integer array of the same size, say, $sta[1:10, 1:20]$, for the purpose of storing the states of elements in array a. Specifically, the state of $a[i, j]$ will be stored in $sta[i, j]$. If the program contains the statement

$$a[i, \ j] := a[i, \ k] * a[k, \ j]$$

the instruments required for this statement will be

$$sta[i, \ k] := f(sta[i, \ k], \ r);$$
$$sta[k, \ j] := f(sta[k, \ j], \ r);$$
$$sta[i, \ j] := f(sta[i, \ j], \ d)$$

Here f is the state-transition function defined by the state diagram shown in Figure 7.1.

Selection of Input Data

After having a program instrumented as described above, possible data-flow anomalies can be detected by executing the program for a properly chosen set of input data. The input data used determine the execution paths and therefore affect the number of anomalies that can be detected in the process. The question now is: How do we select input data so that all data-flow anomalies can be detected? It turns out that there is a relatively simple answer to this question. Roughly speaking, we need to select a set of input data that will cause the program to be executed along all possible execution paths that iterate a loop zero or two times. For example, if the program has the path structure depicted in Figure 7.6, we need to choose a set of input data that will cause the program to be executed along paths *ae*, *abd*, and *abccd*. In the remainder of this section we show how this selection criterion is derived and discuss how a set of input data satisfying this criterion can be found.

It is intuitively clear that all data-flow anomalies will be detected if the instrumented program is executed along all possible execution paths. However, it is

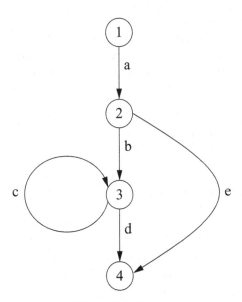

Figure 7.6 Graph.

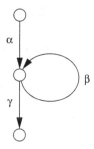

Figure 7.7   Path with a loop construct.

impractical, if not impossible, to do so because in general the number of possible execution paths is very large, especially if the program contains a loop and the number of times the loop will be iterated is input dependent. The crucial problem then is to determine the minimum number of times that a loop must be iterated to ensure detection of all data-flow anomalies.

To facilitate discussion of the problem stated above, we adopt the following notational convention. We use the special symbols α, β, and γ to denote strings of d's, r's, and u's. If α is a string and n is a nonnegative integer, α^n denotes a string formed by concatenating n α's. For any string α, α^0 is defined to be an empty string; that is, $\alpha^0 = \lambda$, where $\lambda x = x\lambda = x$ for any x.

Now let us consider the data flow with respect to a variable, say x, on an execution path. Let β represent the sequence of actions taken on x by the constituent statements of a loop on this path, as depicted in Figure 7.7. If the loop is iterated n times in an execution, the sequence of actions taken by this loop structure can be represented by β^n. Thus, if the program is executed along this path, the string representing the sequence of actions taken on x will be of the form $\alpha\beta^n\gamma$. Recall that to determine if there is a data-flow anomaly with respect to x is to determine if dd, du, or ur is a substring of $\alpha\beta^n\gamma$. Therefore, the present problem is to find the least integer k such that if $\alpha\beta^n\gamma$ (for some $n > k$) contains either dd, du, or ur as a substring, so does $\alpha\beta^k\gamma$.

For convenience, we use *.substr.* to denote the binary relation "is a substring of": thus, r.*substr.* rrdru and ur.*substr.* ddrurd.

Theorem 7.1   Let α, β, and γ be any nonempty strings, and let τ be any string of two symbols. Then, for any integer $n > 0$,

$$\tau.substr.\ \alpha\beta^n\gamma \text{ implies } \tau.substr.\ \alpha\beta^2\gamma$$

Proof: For $n > 0$, τ can be a substring of $\alpha\beta^n\gamma$ only if τ is a substring of α, β, γ, $\alpha\beta$, $\beta\beta$, or $\beta\gamma$. However, all of these are a substring of $\alpha\beta^2\gamma$. Thus, the proof follows immediately from the transitivity of the binary relation.*substr.*.

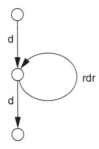

Figure 7.8   Example execution path in which the data flow becomes anomalous only if the loop is not executed.

Note that dd, du, and ur are strings of two symbols, representing the sequences of actions that cause data-flow anomalies. Theorem 7.1 says that if there exists a data-flow anomaly on an execution path that traverses a loop at least once, the anomaly can be detected by iterating the loop twice during execution. Such a data-flow anomaly may not be detected by iterating the loop only once because dd, du, and ur may be a substring of $\beta\beta$, and $\beta\beta$ is not necessarily a substring of $\alpha\beta\gamma$.

Observe that Theorem 7.1 does not hold for the case $n = 0$. This is so because τ.*substr.* $\alpha\gamma$ implies that τ is a substring of α, γ, or $\alpha\gamma$, and $\alpha\gamma$ is not necessarily a substring of $\alpha\beta^n\gamma$ for any $n > 0$. The significance of this fact is that a certain type of data-flow anomaly may not be detected if a loop is traversed during execution. Figure 7.8 exemplifies this type of data-flow anomaly. In general, if the data-flow anomaly is caused by exclusion of a loop from the execution path, it may not be detected if the loop is traversed during execution.

Based on Theorem 7.1 and the discussion above, we can conclude that *to ensure detection of all data-flow anomalies, each loop in a program has to be iterated zero and two times in execution.* Unfortunately, it is not clear how this result can be applied to the cases where a loop consists of more than one path. For example, if we have the path structure shown in Figure 7.9, we are certain that paths *abbd*, *accd*, and *ad* have to be covered in input data selection. However, it is not clear whether paths such as *abbccd*, *abcbcd*, or *abcd* have to be covered.

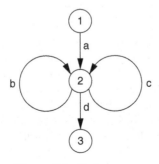

Figure 7.9   Path structure.

According to the result presented above, we need only to iterate the loop zero and two times to ensure detection of all data-flow anomalies. Thus, if a path description contains p^* as a subexpression (see Section 1.4), we can replace it with $(\lambda + p^2)$ to yield the description of the paths that have to be traversed in execution.

Does the same method apply if p is a description of a set of two or more paths? In that case, an execution of statements on p will result in having two or more sequences of actions taken on the variable. Therefore, the answer hinges on whether or not we can extend Theorem 7.1 to cases where β is a set of strings. It turns out that the answer is affirmative. To see why this is so, we first restate Theorem 7.1 for cases where α, β, and γ are sets of strings. Note that the concatenation of two sets is defined as usual. That is, if α and β are sets of strings, $\alpha\beta = \{ab \mid a \text{ in } \alpha \text{ and } b \text{ in } \beta\}$ is again a set of strings.

Theorem 7.2 Let α, β, and γ be any nonempty sets of nonempty strings, τ be any string of two symbols, and n be an integer greater than zero. If τ is a substring of an element in $\alpha\beta^n\gamma$, then τ is a substring of an element in $\alpha\beta^2\gamma$.

Theorem 7.2 is essentially the same as Theorem 7.1 except that the binary relation of "is a substring of" is changed to that of "is a substring of an element in." As such, it can be proved in the same manner. The proof of Theorem 7.1 *mutatis mutandis* can be used as the proof of Theorem 7.2.

For convenience, we now introduce the notion of a zero–two (ZT) subset. Given an expression E that describes a set of paths, we can construct another expression E_{02} from E by substituting $(\lambda + p^2)$ for every subexpression of the form p^* in E. For example, if E is a^*bc^*d, then E_{02} is $(\lambda + a^2)b(\lambda + c^2)d$. The set of paths described by E_{02} is called a *ZT subset* of that described by E.

The development presented above shows that to ensure detection of all data-flow anomalies, it suffices to execute the instrumented program along the paths in a ZT subset of the set of all possible execution paths. The question now is: How do we select input data to accomplish this? Described in the following are the steps that may be taken to find the required set of input data for a given program.

1. Find all paths from the entry to the exit in the flowchart of the program. A flowchart is essentially a directed graph, and several methods are available for finding all paths between two nodes in a directed graph (see, e.g., [LUNT65, SLOA72]).

2. Find a ZT subset of the set of paths found in step 1. Note that the regular-expression representation of a set of paths is not unique in general. For example, the set of paths between nodes 1 and 3 in Figure 7.8 can be described by $a(b + c)^*d$ or, equivalently, by $a(b^*c^*)^*d$. Since a ZT subset is defined based on the set description, a set may have more than one ZT subset. In this example, there are two. One is described by $a(\lambda + (b + c)^2)d$ and the other by $a(\lambda + ((\lambda + b^2)(\lambda + c^2))^2)d$. However, this is of no consequence because in the light of Theorem 7.2 the use of either one is sufficient to ensure detection of all data-flow anomalies.

3. For each path in the set obtained in step 2, find input data that will cause the program to be executed along that path. This may prove to be a rather difficult task in practice. Methods available are described at length in the literature (e.g., [HOWD75, HUAN75, CLAR76]). Note that the set obtained in step 2 may contain paths that cannot be executed at all. If a path is not executable because there is a loop on the path that has to be iterated a fixed number of times other than that specified, disregard the number of times the loop will be iterated in execution. Just select input data that will cause the path (and the loop) to be executed. If a path is found to be infeasible because a loop can only be traversed a number of times other than that specified, replace it with an executable path that traverses the loop two or more times. If a path is found to be infeasible because it is so intrinsically, it can be excluded from the set. The result is a set of input data that will ensure detection of all data-flow anomalies.

Concluding Remarks

The state diagram shown in Figure 7.1 is such that once a variable enters state A, it will remain in that state all the way to the end of the execution path. This implies that once the data flow with respect to a variable is found to be anomalous at a certain point, the error condition will be indicated continuously throughout that particular execution. No attempt will be made to reset the state of the variable and continue to analyze the rest of the execution path. This appears to be a plausible thing to do because in general it takes a close examination of the program by the programmer to determine the nature of the error committed at that point. Without knowing the exact cause of the anomalous condition, it is impossible to reset the state of that variable correctly.

A possible alternative would be to abort the program execution once a data-flow anomaly is detected. This can be accomplished by instrumenting programs with procedure calls that invoke a procedure with this provision. By halting program execution upon discovery of a data-flow anomaly, we may save some computer time, especially if the program is large.

As explained by Fosdick and Osterweil [FOOS76], the presence of a data-flow anomaly does not imply that execution of the program will definitely produce incorrect results. It implies only that execution may produce incorrect results. Thus, we may wish to register the existence of a data-flow anomaly when it is detected and then continue to analyze the rest of the execution path. In that case we can design the software instrument in such a way that once a variable enters state A, it will properly register the detection of a data-flow anomaly and then reset the state of the variable to state R. The reason for resetting it to state R is obvious in the light of our earlier discussion. Another alternative is to use the state diagram shown in Figure 7.10 instead of the one shown in Figure 7.1. The data flow with respect to a variable is anomalous if the variable enters either the state define–define (DD), the state define–undefine (DU), or the state undefine–reference (UR). The use of this state diagram has the additional advantage of being able to identify the type of data-flow anomaly detected.

To simplify the discussion, we have limited ourselves to analysis of data flow with respect to a single variable. However, the method presented can extended be readily

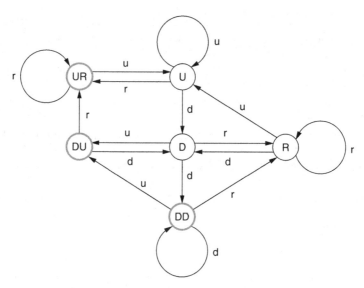

Figure 7.10   Alternative to the state diagram shown in Figure 7.1.

to analyze more than one variable at the same time. All we need to do is modify the method of handling vectors of variables, states, and sequences of actions instead of single actions.

The utility of data-flow analysis in error detection is obvious and has been confirmed for FORTRAN programs by practical experience [OSFO76]. Fosdick and Osterweil have developed a static analysis method to obtain the desired information [FOOS76]. In this book we present another method to achieve the same goal by instrumenting a program properly and then executing it for a set of input data. By comparison, the present method has the following advantages:

1. The present method is conceptually much simpler than that described by Fosdick and Osterweil [FOOS76] and therefore is much easier to implement.
2. From the nature of computation involved, it is obvious that the present method requires a much smaller program to implement on a computer.
3. From a user's point of view, the present method is easier and more efficient because it produces information about the locations and types of data-flow anomalies in a single process. In the method developed by Fosdick and Osterweil, additional effort is required to locate the anomaly once it is detected.
4. As indicated previously, the present method can readily be applied to monitor the data flow of elements of an array, which cannot be handled adequately when using the static method. Thus, the present method has a greater error-detection capability and will produce fewer false warnings.
5. In the present method, there is no need to determine the order in which the functions are invoked, and thus the presence of a recursive subprogram will not be a problem.

The method presented in this chapter is particularly advantageous if it is used in conjunction with a conventional program test to enhance the error-detection capability. In a conventional test, a program has to be exercised as thoroughly as possible (see, e.g., [HUAN76]), and therefore the task of finding a suitable set of input data to carry out the data-flow analysis will not be an extra burden on the programmer.

It is difficult to compare the cost. Very roughly speaking, the cost of applying the method described by Fosdick and Osterweil [FOOS76] is linearly proportional to the number of statements in the program, whereas that of applying the present method is linearly proportional to the execution time. Therefore, it may be more economical to use Fosdick and Osterweil method if the program is of the type that consists of a relatively small number of statements, but it takes a long time to execute (e.g., a program that iterates a loop a great number of times is of this type).

7.5 INSTRUMENTING PROGRAMS FOR TRACE-SUBPROGRAM GENERATION

The symbolic traces or trace subprograms of a program can be generated automatically through static analysis or program instrumentation. To generate symbolic traces through static analysis, we determine the syntax of the program first, construct its program graph as defined in Chapter 1, find all paths of interest, and then represent the paths as a regular expression over the edge symbols. For any path described by a regular expression, its symbolic trace can be obtained simply by replacing all edge symbols with the corresponding program components.

For example, consider the following C++ program.

```
int main()
{
    int x, y, z;

    cin >> x >> y;
    z = 1;
    while (y != 0) {
        if (y % 2 == 1)
            z = z * x;
        y = y / 2;
        x = x * x;
    }
    cout << z << endl;
}
```

Figure 7.11 shows the program graph of this program. The set of all paths from the entry to the exit can be denoted by a regular expression such as $\alpha(\beta(\gamma + \delta)\varepsilon)^*\eta$. (*Note:* It can be represented equivalently by many other regular expressions.) Now

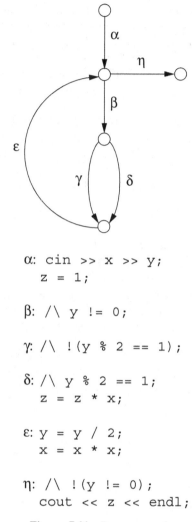

```
α: cin >> x >> y;
   z = 1;

β: /\ y != 0;

γ: /\ !(y % 2 == 1);

δ: /\ y % 2 == 1;
   z = z * x;

ε: y = y / 2;
   x = x * x;

η: /\ !(y != 0);
   cout << z << endl;
```

Figure 7.11   Program graph.

suppose that for some reason we are interested in the set of two paths {αβδεη, αβγεη}. The symbolic traces of these two paths can be obtained by replacing the edge symbols with the corresponding program components shown below.

```
αβδεη:  cin >> x >> y;
        z = 1;
        /\ y != 0;
        /\ y % 2 == 1;
        z = z * x;
```

```
y = y / 2;
x = x * x;
/\ !(y != 0);
cout << z << endl;
```

αβγεη:
```
cin >> x >> y;
z = 1;
/\ y != 0;
/\ !(y % 2 == 1);
y = y / 2;
x = x * x;
/\ !(y != 0);
cout << z << endl;
```

It should be relatively straightforward to build a software tool to automate this process. The problem with this method is that it will generate symbolic traces representing feasible as well as infeasible execution paths. Since all programs have many infeasible paths that are of interest to no one, and since it requires a considerable amount of effort to identify such paths, this method of symbolic-trace generation is not suitable for applications where efficiency matters.

This problem can be overcome by using the technique of program instrumentation. The idea is to insert additional statements into the program to print out the statement that has just been executed in an appropriate format. The symbolic trace will then be produced automatically by executing that instrumented program along the path. The syntax of the host programming language and the format of statements in trace subprograms dictate the way instrumentation is to be done. The format of statements should be chosen to facilitate analysis. For example, a trace subprogram can be expressed as a constrained subprogram, as defined in earlier chapters.

For programs in C++ language, a trace subprogram may be generated as follows. First, we need to define the format in which each statement or predicate is to appear in the trace subprogram. For this purpose we use "TRACE(S) = t" as the shorthand notation for "statement S is to appear as t in the trace subprogram." The software instrumentation tool will instrument a program for symbolic trace generation as follows. For every statement S in the source code to be instrumented, the tool will find TRACE(S), assign a trace number TN(S) to S, store TN(S) as well as TRACE(S) in a file, and then replace S with INST(S), which consists of S as well as the instruments (additional statements designed to generate the trace).

Listed below are the definitions of TRACE(S) and INST(S) for a variety of statements in C++. The intention of this list is not to provide a complete blueprint for building the required software tool but rather to show how TRACE(S) and INST(S) can be defined for types of statements commonly found in a modern programming language such as C++. Therefore, no attempt has been made to list all types of statements.

1. *Expression statement*

> TRACE(E;) = E;   if *E* is an expression statement.

Examples: The trace subprogram of assignment statement x = 1 is simply x = 1 itself and that of cin >> first >> character is cin >> first >> character itself.

The syntax of C++ allows the use of certain shorthand notations in writing an expression statement. To facilitate symbolic analysis, such notations should be rewritten in full in a trace subprogram as exemplified below.

Statement	Trace Subprogram
++n;	n = n + 1
--n;	n = n - 1
x = ++n;	n = n + 1
	x = n
x = n++;	x = n
	n = n + 1
i += 2;	i = i + 2
x *= y + 1;	x = x * (y + 1)

2. *Conditional statement*

(a) TRACE(if (P) S) = /\ P;
                              TRACE(S);   if *P* is true,
     TRACE(if (P) S) = /\ !(P);   otherwise.

P is enclosed in parentheses because it may contain an operator with a priority lower that that of the unary operator "!." Incorrect interpretation of *P* may result if the parentheses are omitted.

Example: The trace subprogram of the statement

if (c == '\n') ++n;

is dependent on the value of *c* just before this statement is executed. If it is '\n' (new line), the trace subprogram is

/\ c == '\n'
++n;

Otherwise, it is

/\ !(c == '\n');

(b) ```TRACE(if (P) S₁ else S₂) = /\ P```
                                    ```TRACE(S₁)```   if P is true,

    ```TRACE(if (P) S₁ else S₂) = /\ !(P)```
                                    ```TRACE(S₂)```   otherwise.

(c) ```TRACE(if (P₁) S₁;```
      ```else if (P₂) S₂;```
      ```else if (P₃) S₃;```

         .

         .

         .

      ```else if (Pₙ) Sₙ;```
      ```else Sₙ₊₁)```

=   ```/\ !(P₁);```
    ```/\ !(P₂);```

     .

     .

     .

   ```/\ Pᵢ;```
   ```TRACE(Sᵢ);```   if P_i is true for some $1 \leq i \leq n$,

=   ```/\ !(P₁);```
    ```/\ !(P₂);```

     .

     .

     .

  ```/\ !(Pₙ);```
  ```TRACE(Sₙ₊₁);```   otherwise.

3. *WHILE statement*

```
TRACE(while (B) S)  =   /\ B;
                        TRACE(S);
                        /\ B
                        TRACE(S);
                          .

                          .

                          .
                        /\ B
                        TRACE(S);
                        /\ !(B);
```
```

Example: For the following statements

```
i = 1;
while (i <= 3)
    i = i + 1;
```

the trace subprogram is defined to be

```
i = 1;
/\ i <= 3;
i = i + 1;
/\ i <= 3;
i = i + 1;
/\ i <= 3;
i = i + 1;
/\ !(i <= 3);
```

4. *DO statement*

```
TRACE(do S while (B)) =  TRACE(S);
                         /\ B;
                         TRACE(S);
                         /\ B;

                             .

                             .

                             .

                         TRACE(S);
                         /\ !(B);
```

5. *FOR statement*

```
TRACE(for (E₁, E₂, E₃) S) =  E₁;
                             /\ E₂;
                             TRACE(S);
                             E₃;
                             /\ E₂;
                             TRACE(S);
                             E₃;

                                 .

                                 .

                                 .

                             /\ !(E₂);
```

Example: The trace subprogram of the statement

```
for( x = 1; x <= 3; x = x + 1 )
      sum = sum + x;
```

is defined to be

```
x = 1;
/\ x <= 3;
sum = sum + x;
x = x + 1;
/\ x <= 3;
sum = sum + x;
x = x + 1;
/\ x <= 3;
sum = sum + x;
x = x + 1;
/\ !(x <= 3);
```

6. *SWITCH statement*

```
TRACE(switch (C) {
        case C₁: S₁;
        case C₂: S₂;

            .

            .

            .

        case Cₙ: Sₙ;
        default: Sₙ₊₁;});
```

$$=\quad \text{/\ C == C_i;}$$
$$\text{TRACE(S_i);}$$

if $C = C_i$ for some $1 \leq i \leq n$, assuming that S_i ends with a "break" statement,

$$=\quad \text{/\ C != (C_1);}$$
$$\text{/\ C != (C_2);}$$

.

.

.

$$\text{/\ C != (C_n);}$$
$$\text{TRACE(S_{n+1});}$$

otherwise.

Note: Parentheses are needed around C_i's because C_i's may contain operators such as "&," "$*\wedge*$," and "|," which have a precedence lower than that of "==" and "!=."

7. *BREAK statement*

```
TRACE(break;)  =  empty string (i.e., need not generate a trace
                  subprogram for such a statement)
```

8. *CONTINUE statement*

```
TRACE(continue;)  =  empty string
```

9. *RETURN statement*

   (a)   `TRACE(return;) = return`
   (b)   `TRACE(return E;) = return E`

10. *EXIT statement*

   (a)   `TRACE(exit;) = exit;`
   (b)   `TRACE(exit E;) = exit E;`

11. *GOTO statement*

```
TRACE(goto LABEL;)  =  empty string
```

12. *Labeled statement*

```
TRACE(LABEL: S;)  =  TRACE(S);
```

13. *Null statement*

```
TRACE( ;) = empty string
```

14. *Compound statement*

```
TRACE({declaration-list, statement-list}) =
      TRACE(statement-list)
TRACE(S₁; S₂;) =   TRACE(S₁)
                   TRACE(S₂)
```

The instrumentation tool examines each statement in the program, constructs its trace as defined above, assigns an identification number called TN (trace number) to the trace, and stores the trace with its TN in a file. The tool then constructs INST(S), which stands for "the instrumented version of statement S," and writes it into a file created for storing the instrumented version of the program. Production of the trace is done by the program execution monitor pem(·). A function call pem(TN(S)) causes the trace of S numbered TN(S) to be fetched from the file and appended to the trace being constructed. The definition of INST(S) is given below.

1. *Expression statement.* If E is an expression, then

$$\text{INST}(E;) = \text{pem (TN}(E));$$
$$E;$$

For example, if 35 is the trace number associated with the statement

$$\text{cout} << \text{"This is a test"} << \text{endl};$$

then

$$\text{INST(cout} << \text{"This is a test"} << \text{endl};) = \text{pem (35)};$$
$$\text{cout} << \text{"This is a test"} << \text{endl};$$

2. *Condition statement*

$$\text{INST(if } (P)S) = \text{if } (P) \{$$
$$\quad \text{pem (TN}(P));$$
$$\quad \text{INST}(S)$$
$$\}$$
$$\text{else}$$
$$\quad \text{pem (TN}(!(P)));$$

$$\text{INST(if } (P) \; S_1 \text{ else } S_2) = \text{if } (P) \{$$
$$\quad \text{pem(TN}(P));$$
$$\quad \text{INST}(S_1)$$
$$\}$$
$$\text{else } \{$$
$$\quad \text{pem (TN}(!(P)));$$
$$\quad \text{INST}(S_2)$$
$$\}$$

Note that an "if" statement may be nested; that is, S_1 or S_2 above may be another "if" statement. With the instrumentation method described recursively as shown above, we do not need a special rule to deal with nested "if" statements, or to instrument "if" statements of the form (c) given previously.

3. *WHILE statement*

$$INST(\text{while } (P)\ S) = \text{while } (P)\{$$
$$\text{pem } (TN(P));$$
$$INST(S)$$
$$\}$$
$$\text{pem } (TN(!(P)));$$

4. *DO statement*

$$INST(\text{do } S \text{ while } (P);) = \_do\_?:$$
$$INST(S)$$
$$\text{if } (P)\ \{$$
$$\text{pem } (TN(P));$$
$$\text{goto\_do\_?};$$
$$\}$$
$$\text{else}$$
$$\text{pem } (TN(!(P)));$$

The question mark here will be replaced by an integer assigned by the analyzer–instrumentor. Note that it is incorrect to instrument the DO statement as shown below:

```
do {
      INST(S)
      if (P) pem (TN(P));
}
while (P);
pem (TN(!(P)));
```

The reason is that predicate P will be evaluated twice here. If P contains a shorthand or assignment operator, the instrumented program will no longer be computationally equivalent to the original program.

5. *FOR statement*

$$INST(\text{for } (E_1;\ E_2;\ E_3)\ S) = \text{pem } (TN(E_1));$$
$$\text{for } (E_1;\ E_2;\ E_3)\ \{$$
$$\text{pem } (TN(E_2));$$
$$INST(S)$$
$$\text{pem } (TN(E_3));$$
$$\}$$
$$\text{pem } (TN(!(E_2)));$$

6. *SWITCH statement*

INST(switch (C) {
        case C_1 : S_1
        case C_2 : S_2

        .

        .

        case C_n : S_n
        default : S_{n+1}})
= { int $\_i\_$;
    $\_i\_ = 0$;
    switch (C) {
        case C_1 :   if $(\_i\_ + + == 0)$ pem (TN($C == (C_1)$));
                    INST(S_1)
        case C_2 :   if $(\_i\_ + + == 0)$ pem (TN($C == (C_2)$));
                    INST(S_2)

        .

        .

        .

        case C_n :   if $(\_i\_ + + == 0)$ pem (TN($C == (C_n)$));
                    INST(S_n)
        default :   if $(\_i\_ + + == 0)$ {
        pem (TN($C \; ! = (C_1)$));
        pem (TN($C \; ! = (C_2)$));

        .

        .

        .

        pem (TN($C \; ! = (C_n)$));
        }
        INST(S_{n+1})
    }
}

The reason we use $\_i\_$ here is that cases serve just as labels. After the code
for one case has been completed, execution falls through to the next unless
one takes explicit action to escape. The flag $\_i\_$ is used to ensure that only the
condition that is true is included in the trace subprogram.

7. *RETURN statement*

INST(return;) = pem (TN(return));
        return;

INST(return E;) = pem (TN(return E));
        return E;

8. *EXIT statement*

$$\text{INST(exit;) = pem (TN(exit));}$$
$$\text{exit;}$$

$$\text{INST(exit } E;) = \text{pem (TN(exit } E));$$
$$\text{exit } E;$$

9. *Labeled statement*

$$\text{INST(LABEL : } S) = \text{LABEL : INST}(S)$$

10. *Compound statement*

$$\text{INST({declaration-list statement-list}) = \{}$$
$$\text{declaration-list}$$
$$\text{INST(statement-list)}$$
$$\}$$

$$\text{INST}(S_1; \ S_2) = \text{INST}(S_1)$$
$$\text{INST}(S_2)$$

11. *Other statements*

$$\text{INST(break;) = break;}$$

$$\text{INST(continue;) = continue;}$$

$$\text{INST(goto LABEL;) = goto LABEL;}$$

$$\text{INST(;) =;}$$

EXERCISES

Because Exercises 7.3 and 7.4 may each take one person-semester or more to complete, they should be assigned as software development projects rather than classroom exercises.

7.1 Design and implement a software tool that will automatically instrument a program with software counters such that a nonzero count of every counter implies traversal of all branches during test execution.

7.2 Discuss the mechanisms that may be used to detect the global violation of an assertion.

7.3   Design and implement a software tool that will instrument a program automatically for test-case effectiveness measurement.

7.4   Design and implement a software tool that will instrument a program automatically for data-flow-anomaly detection.

7.5   Certain modern compilers are capable of detecting some types of data-flow anomalies. Investigate the capabilities of the compiler you use most often in this respect, and test it to see if it is capable of detecting all types of data-flow anomaly all the time.

7.6   The static method for data-flow-anomaly detection may produce false alarms: that is, may indicate that there is a data-flow anomaly, whereas in fact there is none. Find an example significantly different from the ones given in the text that will trigger a false alarm if the static method is used but will not if the dynamic (instrumentation) method is used.

7.7   Define the TRACE($\cdot$) and INST($\cdot$) functions in Section 7.5 for a programming language of your choice.

7.8   Enumerate the situations under which use of the instrumentation method may become technically undesirable or unacceptable.

APPENDIX A
Logico-Mathematical Background

To determine if a given program will do what it is intended to do through analysis or testing, we often need to:

- Interpret the program specification correctly
- Determine if any part of the program specification is violated (i.e., is not satisfied)
- Prove that a certain assertion is a theorem (i.e., is always true)
- Argue for (or against) the correctness of a given program

These tasks can be facilitated by using the concepts, notations, and formalisms discussed in this appendix.

A.1 THE PROPOSITIONAL CALCULUS

A *proposition* is a declarative sentence that is either true or false. For example:

- Disney World is located in Florida.
- $x + y = y + x$.
- Eleven is divisible by 3.
- The number 4 is a prime number.

are propositions. The first two sentences are true, whereas the last two false.

Given propositions, we can form new propositions by combining them with connectives such as "not," "and," "or." The propositional calculus is a method for computing the truth values of propositions that involves connectives. The connectives of the propositional calculus include:

- Negation: ¬, not
- Conjunction: ∧, and
- Disjunction: ∨, or

Software Error Detection through Testing and Analysis, By J. C. Huang
Copyright © 2009 John Wiley & Sons, Inc.

- Implication: $\supset$, implies, if ... then ...
- Equivalence: $\equiv$, ... if and only if ...

The definitions of these connectives are:

p	q	$\neg p$	$p \wedge q$	$p \vee q$	$p \supset q$	$p \equiv q$
F	F	T	F	F	T	T
F	T	T	F	T	T	F
T	F	F	F	T	F	F
T	T	F	T	T	T	T

Formally, the *propositional calculus* is a mathematical system in which $\{T, F\}$ is the underlying set and the connectives are the operations defined on this set. A *propositional variable* is a variable that may assume a value of T or F. It denotes a proposition.

A *well-formed formula* (wff) in the language of the propositional calculus is a syntactically correct expression. It is composed of connectives, propositional variables (such as $p, q, r, s, \ldots$), constants (T and F), and parentheses.

The syntax of a wff can be defined recursively as follows:

1. A propositional variable standing alone is a wff.
2. If α is a wff, then $\neg(\alpha)$ is a wff.
3. If α and β are wffs, then $(\alpha) \wedge (\beta)$, $(\alpha) \vee (\beta)$, $(\alpha) \supset (\beta)$, and $(\alpha) \equiv (\beta)$ are wffs.
4. Those expressions and only those expressions obtained by rules 1, 2, and 3 are wffs.

A wff obtained by the definition above may contain many parentheses and thus not be suitable for human consumption. The use of parentheses can be reduced by using the following precedence (listed in descending order):

$$\neg, \wedge, \vee, \supset, \equiv$$

The *truth table* of a wff lists the truth values of the formula for all possible combinations of assignments to the values of variables involved.

In practice, analysis of a statement can often be facilitated by translating it into a well-formed formula first.

Example A.1   Suppose that policy of a pharmaceutical company includes the following statement:

Proposition Alpha: If a drug passes both an animal test and a clinical test, the company will market it if and only if it can be produced and sold profitably and the government does not intervene.

Now let us further suppose that the company is developing a new drug with an enormous market potential, and an ambitious manager has just decided to put the drug on the market immediately despite the fact that the drug has failed the clinical test. Does this decision to market the drug violate the policy stated as Proposition Alpha?

The policy is not violated if it is not made false. To facilitate determination of its truth value, we shall translate it into a well-formed formula:

$$A_1 : a \wedge c \supset (m \equiv p \wedge \neg g)$$

where a: the drug passes an animal test
    c: the drug passes a clinical test
    m: the company will market the drug
    p: the drug can be produced and sold profitably
    g: the government intervenes

It is obvious that if the drug failed the clinical test (i.e., if c is false), formula A_1 is true regardless of the assignment of values made to other variables. That is, even though the drug failed to pass the clinical test, the decision to market the drug does not violate the policy represented by A_1.

Note, however, that the formula A_1 represents only one possible translation of Proposition Alpha. The same statement can also be taken in such a way that it is translated into the following formula:

$$A_2: \quad a \wedge c \supset m \equiv p \wedge \neg g$$

In this case, "$\equiv$" is the main connective (i.e., the one to be evaluated last, in accordance with the precedence relation defined previously). If c is false, the left-hand side of the "$\equiv$" connective is always true, and the formula becomes false only when the right-hand side of the connective becomes false. Since the truth values of p and g are not given for the question in hand, there are insufficient information to determine the truth value of the formula, and thus the tool should indicates that there is insufficient data to evaluate that proposal to market the drug.

The second translation (A_2) appears to be more plausible. It is difficult to imagine that a company would adopt a policy allowing marketing of a drug that did not pass the clinical test.

Definition A.2   If for every assignment of values to its variables a wff has the value T, the wff is said to be *valid*, or the wff is said to be a *tautology*; if it always has the value F, it is said to be *contradictory* (or, a *contradiction*). A wff is said to be *satisfiable* if and only if it is not contradictory. A wff is said to be *contingent* if and only if it is neither valid nor contradictory.

Notation A.3   If A is a tautology, we write $\vdash A$, where "$\vdash$" is "T" written sideways.

Note that A is a tautology if and only if $\neg A$ is a contradiction.

It is useful to define certain relationships among propositions so that if we know the truth value of a proposition, we may be able to say something about the truth values of its relatives. The first relation, a strong one, is logical equivalence.

Definition A.4   Two wffs A and B are said to be *logically equivalent* if and only if they have the same truth table.

Theorem A.5 A and B are logically equivalent if and only if $\vdash A \equiv B$.

A weaker relation, more frequently encountered in practical applications, is logical consequence.

Definition A.6 B is a *logical consequence* of A (denoted by $A \vdash B$) if for each assignment of truth value to the variables of A and B such that A has the value T, then B also has the value T.

A is called the *antecedent* and B the *consequence* if $A \vdash B$.

Theorem A.7 $A \vdash B$ if and only if $\vdash A \supset B$.

One possible application of the theorems above is to establish a rule of inference known as *modus ponens*. This rule says that if we can show that A and $A \supset B$ are both true, we can immediately assert that B is also true. The validity of this rule can be established by showing that $\vdash (A \wedge (A \supset B)) \supset B$.

Alternatively, the inference rule can be stated as:

$$\text{if } A \text{ and } A \supset B \text{ then } B.$$

Here A corresponds to the premise, $A \supset B$ to the argument, and B to the conclusion.

To show that an argument is valid is to show that whenever the premise is true, the conclusion is also true. In symbolic form, it is to show that $\vdash A \supset B$. If the argument is valid, the truthfulness of the conclusion can be established simply by showing that the premise is true. Note that if the premise is a contradiction, there is no way to establish the truthfulness of the conclusion through the use of the argument $A \supset B$. Thus, in practical applications, we should check the consistency of the argument. An argument is said to be *consistent* if its premise is satisfiable.

By definition of the implication ($\supset$) connective, $A \supset B$ can be false only if A is true and B is false. Hence, a common technique for showing $\vdash A \supset B$ is to show that if B is false, it is not possible to (find an assignment of truth values to all prepositional variables involved that will) make A true.

We write $A_1, A_2, \ldots, A_n \vdash B$ if the antecedent consists of n propositions such that B is true whenever every component in the antecedent is true.

Theorem A.8 $A_1, A_2, \ldots, A_n \vdash B$ if and only if $\vdash A_1 \wedge A_2 \wedge \cdots \wedge A_n \supset B$.

The relationship $A_1, A_2, \ldots, A_n \vdash B$ is useful in that it has the following two properties:

1. When every A_i is true, B is also true.
2. B is false only if some A_i is false.

This relationship can be used to analyze the validity of a decision. A decision is said to be *valid* if it does not violate any constraints imposed or contradicts any known facts. Constraints may be company policies, government regulations, software requirements, rules of physics, and the like. Let $A_1, A_2, \ldots, A_n$ be the constraints and B be the decision. Then to show that the decision is valid is to show that B is the consequence of $A_1, A_2, \ldots, A_n$: that is, $\vdash A_1 \wedge A_2 \wedge \cdots \wedge A_n \supset B$. A common way to construct the proof of $\vdash A_1 \wedge A_2 \wedge \cdots \wedge A_n \supset B$ is to show that if we let B be false, it would be impossible to make all A_i's true at the same time.

It is interesting to see what will happen if additional constraints are imposed on the decision-making process. Let us suppose that in addition to the policy expressed as Proposition Alpha, which is repeated below for convenience.

A_1 or A_2:   If the drug passes both an animal test and a clinical test, the company will market it if and only if it can be produced and sold profitably and the government does not intervene.

the company further stipulates that:

A_3:   If the drug cannot be produced and sold profitably, it should not be marketed.

and requires its decision makers to keep in mind that:

A_4:   If the drug failed the animal test or the clinical test and the drug is marketed, the government will definitely intervene.

Also remember that the drug failed the clinical test. This fact is to be denoted A_5. Let us see if the following is a tautology:

$$\vdash A_2 \wedge A_3 \wedge A_4 \wedge A_5 \supset B$$

where A_2: $a \wedge c \supset m \equiv p \wedge \neg g$
      A_3: $\neg p \supset \neg m$
      A_4: $(\neg a \vee \neg c) \wedge m \supset g$
      A_5: $\neg c$
      B: $\neg m$

The proof can be constructed as follows.

1. Assume that B is false by assigning F to m (i.e., $m \leftarrow T$).
2. To make A_5 true, $c \leftarrow F$.
3. To make A_3 true, $p \leftarrow T$.
4. To make A_4 true, $g \leftarrow T$.
5. To make A_2 true, we need to do $g \leftarrow F$. This contradicts what we have done in step 4.

This shows that it is impossible to make B false and all antecedents (i.e., A_2, A_3, A_4, and A_5) true at the same time, and thus $A_2 \wedge A_3 \wedge A_4 \wedge A_5 \supset B$ is a tautology. That is, the policies represented by A_2, A_3, and A_4, and the fact represented by A_5 dictate that the drug should not be marketed. It is impossible to market the drug without contradicting A_5 or violating at least one of the policies represented by A_2, A_3, and A_4. Note that the constraints A_2 through A_5 are consistent in that it is possible to find an assignment to all propositional variables involved so that all the constraints are true at the same time. See rows 2 and 18 of Table A.1 .

It is interesting to observe that $A_1 \wedge A_3 \wedge A_4 \wedge A_5 \supset B$ is not a tautology. The disproof can be constructed in exactly the same way as demonstrated above except that in step 5, we will have to find an assignment to make $A_1 : a \wedge c \supset (m \equiv p \wedge \neg g)$ true. We will have no problem doing that because A_1 is already made true in step 2, when we set c to F.

Table A.1 may be helpful in clarifying the preceding discussions. Rows corresponding to interesting cases are highlighted. In particular, rows 7 and 23 correspond to the case where a negative decision can be made without violating any constraints if Proposition Alpha is translated into A_1 instead of A_2. Table A.1 is the truth table for the following formulas:

$$
\begin{array}{ll}
A_1 : & a \wedge c \supset (m \equiv p \wedge \neg g) \\
A_2 : & a \wedge c \supset m \equiv p \wedge \neg g \\
A_3 : & \neg p \supset \neg m \\
A_4 : & (\neg a \vee \neg c) \wedge m \supset g \\
A_5 : & \neg c \\
B : & \neg m
\end{array}
$$

A.2   THE FIRST-ORDER PREDICATE CALCULUS

The power of the propositional calculus is quite limited in that it can only deal with propositions (i.e., sentences that are either true or false). In many applications we have to deal with sentences such as:

- She is a graduate student.
- $x > 0$.

TABLE A.1   Truth Table of the Well-Formed Formulas Involved

	a	c	m	p	g	A_1	A_2	A_3	A_4	A_5	B
0	F	F	F	F	F	T	F	T	T	T	T
1	F	F	F	F	T	T	F	T	T	T	T
2	F	F	F	T	F	T	T	T	T	T	T
3	F	F	F	T	T	T	F	T	T	T	T
4	F	F	T	F	F	T	F	F	F	T	F
5	F	F	T	F	T	T	F	F	T	T	F
6	F	F	T	T	F	T	T	T	F	T	F
7	F	F	T	T	T	T	F	T	T	T	F
8	F	T	F	F	F	T	F	T	T	F	T
9	F	T	F	F	T	T	F	T	T	F	T
10	F	T	F	T	F	T	T	T	T	F	T
11	F	T	F	T	T	T	F	T	T	F	T
12	F	T	T	F	F	T	F	F	F	F	F
13	F	T	T	F	T	T	F	F	T	F	F
14	F	T	T	T	F	T	T	T	F	F	F
15	F	T	T	T	T	T	F	T	T	F	F
16	T	F	F	F	F	T	F	T	T	T	T
17	T	F	F	F	T	T	F	T	T	T	T
18	T	F	F	T	F	T	T	T	T	T	T
19	T	F	F	T	T	T	F	T	T	T	T
20	T	F	T	F	F	T	F	F	F	T	F
21	T	F	T	F	T	T	F	F	T	T	F
22	T	F	T	T	F	T	T	T	F	T	F
23	T	F	T	T	T	T	F	T	T	T	F
24	T	T	F	F	F	T	T	T	T	F	T
25	T	T	F	F	T	T	T	T	T	F	T
26	T	T	F	T	F	F	F	T	T	F	T
27	T	T	F	T	T	T	T	T	T	F	T
28	T	T	T	F	F	F	F	F	T	F	F
29	T	T	T	F	T	F	F	F	T	F	F
30	T	T	T	T	F	T	T	T	T	F	F
31	T	T	T	T	T	F	F	T	T	F	F

Without knowing who she is, or what the value of x is, we will not be able to tell if these sentences are true or false. However, once a particular person is assigned to the pronoun *she*, or a number is assigned to x, these sentences will become either true or false. These are called *sentential forms*. They cannot be treated in the propositional calculus.

The *first-order predicate calculus* can be viewed as an extension of the propositional calculus that includes facilities for handling sentential forms as well as propositions. The language of the first-order predicate calculus includes all symbols for the logical operations and for propositions. In addition, it makes use of the following symbols:

- *For individual constants* (names of individuals): $a, b, c, \ldots$
- *For individual variables* (pronouns): $x, y, z, \ldots$
- *For function letters* (to denote functions): $f, g, h, \ldots$
- *For predicate letters* (to denote predicates): $F, G, H, \ldots$
- *For quantifiers*: universal quantifier $(\forall x)$, existential quantifier $(\exists x)$.

The syntax of the language can be defined recursively as follows:

Definition A.9   A *term* is defined as follows:

1. Individual constants and individual variables are terms.
2. If f is an *n*ary functional letter and $t_1, t_2, \ldots, t_n$ are terms, then $f(t_1, t_2, \ldots, t_n)$ is a term.
3. Those expressions and only those expressions obtained by 1 and 2 are terms.

Definition A.10   A string is an *atomic formula* if it is either:

1. A propositional variable standing alone, or
2. A string of the form $F(t_1, t_2, \ldots, t_n)$, where F is an *n*ary predicate letter and $t_1, t_2, \ldots, t_n$ are terms.

Definition A.11   A *well-formed formula (wff)* in the language of the first-order predicate calculus is defined as follows:

1. An atomic formula is a wff.
2. If A is a wff and x is an individual variable, then $(\forall x)A$ and $(\exists x)A$ are wffs.
3. If A and B are wffs, then $\neg A, (A) \wedge (B), (A) \vee (B), (A) \supset (B)$, and $(A) \equiv (B)$ are wffs.
4. Those expressions and only those expressions obtained by 1, 2, and 3 are wffs.

The notation $(\forall x)P$ is to be read as "for all x (in the domain) ..." and $(\exists x)P$ is to be read as "there exists an x (in the domain) such that. ..."

The *scope* of a quantifier is the subexpression to which the quantifier is applied. The occurrence of an individual variable, say x, is said to be *bound* if it is either an occurrence $(\forall x)$, $(\exists x)$, or within the scope of a quantifier $(\forall x)$ or $(\exists x)$. Any other occurrence of a variable is a *free* occurrence. For example, in the wff

$$P(x) \wedge (\exists x)(Q(x) \equiv (\forall y)R(y))$$

the first occurrence of x is free because it is not within the scope of any quantifier, while the second and third occurrences of x and the occurrences of y are all bound. Thus, a variable may have both free and bound occurrences within a wff.

A variable may be within the scope of more than one quantifier. In that case, an occurrence of a variable is bound by the innermost quantifier of that variable within whose scope that particular occurrence lies.

Definition A.12   An *interpretation* of a wff consists of a nonempty domain D and an assignment to each $n$ary predicate letter of an $n$ary predicate on D, to each $n$ary function letter of an $n$ary function on D, and to each individual constant of a fixed element of D.

Definition A.13   A wff is *satisfiable* in a domain D if there exists an interpretation with domain D and assignments of elements of D to the free occurrences of individual variables in the formula such that the resulting proposition is true.

Definition A.14   A wff is *valid* in a domain D if for every interpretation with domain D and assignment of elements of D to free occurrences of individual variables in the formula, the resulting proposition is true.

A wff is satisfiable if it is satisfiable in some domain. A wff is valid if it is valid in all domains.

Example A.15   Consider the wff $(\forall x)P(f(x, a), b)$. A possible interpretation of this wff would be

$$D : \text{the set of all integers}$$
$$P(u, v) : u > v$$
$$f(y, z) : y + z$$
$$a : 1$$
$$b : 0$$

This interpretation of the wff yields the following statement:

$$\text{For every integer } x, x + 1 > 0.$$

which is obviously false.

Example A.16   Consider the wff $(\forall x)(\exists y)P(f(x, y), a)$. A possible interpretation of this wff would be:

$$D : \text{the set of all integers}$$
$$P(u, v) : u \text{ is equal to } v$$
$$f(x, y) : x + y$$
$$a : 0$$

The formula interpreted can be restated as $(\forall x)(\exists y)(x + y = 0)$ and is a true statement. Observe that the order in which the quantifiers are given is important and cannot be changed arbitrarily. For example, if we interchange the quantifiers of the wff above, the interpreted statement will change from

For every integer x, there exists another integer y such that $x + y = 0$.

which is true, to an entirely different statement:

There exists an integer y such that for every integer x, $x + y = 0$.

which is obviously false.

Listed below are some theorems in the first-order predicate calculus that can be used to govern the movement of quantifier in a wff.

Theorems A.17

(1) $(\exists x)(\exists y)A \equiv (\exists y)(\exists x)A$.

(2) $(\forall x)(\forall y)A \equiv (\forall y)(\forall x)A$.

(3) $(\forall x)(A \supset B) \equiv ((\exists x)A \supset B)$, where x does not occur free in B.

(4) $(\exists x)(A \supset B) \equiv ((\forall x)A \supset B)$, where x does not occur free in B.

(5) $(\forall x)(A \supset B) \equiv (A \supset (\forall x)B)$, where x does not occur free in A.

(6) $(\exists x)(A \supset B) \equiv (A \supset (\exists x)B)$, where x does not occur free in A.

The correctness of these theorems can readily be verified informally by considering cases in which the domain is a finite set, say $D = \{x_1, x_2, \ldots, x_n\}$. Theorem (3), for example, can then be rewritten as

$$(A(x_1) \supset B) \wedge (A(x_2) \supset B) \wedge \cdots \wedge (A(x_n) \supset B)$$
$$\equiv (A(x_1) \vee A(x_2) \vee \cdots \vee A(x_n)) \supset B$$

and theorem (4) as

$$(A(x_1) \supset B) \vee (A(x_2) \supset B) \vee \cdots \vee (A(x_n) \supset B)$$
$$\equiv (A(x_1) \wedge A(x_2) \wedge \cdots \wedge A(x_n)) \supset B$$

Since these can be treated as formulas in the propositional calculus, the equivalence relations can be verified readily using a truth table.

To illustrate the necessity of the qualifier "where x does not occur free in B" for (3), let us consider the following interpretation, where x occurs free in $B(x, y)$:

D: the set of all positive integers
$A(x, y)$: x divides y
$B(x, y)$: $x \leq y$

With this interpretation (3) reads $(\forall x)(\text{"}x \text{ divides } y\text{"} \supset x \leq y) \equiv (\exists x)(x \text{ divides } y) \supset x \leq y$. Although the left-hand side of the "$\equiv$" is true, the truth value of the right-hand side depends on the assignment made to the free variable x, and thus the equivalence relation does not hold.

Now if we interpret $B(x, y)$ to be $(\exists x)((y \div x)x = y)$, (3) reads $(\forall x)(\text{"}x \text{ divides } y\text{"} \supset (\exists x)((y \div x)x = y)) \equiv (\exists x)(x \text{ divides } y) \supset (\exists x)((y \div x)x = y)$. The equivalence relation holds because x does not occur free in B. Note that the equivalence relation also holds if x does not occur in B at all. For example, if we interpret $B(x, y)$ to be "y is not prime," then (3) reads $(\forall x)(\text{"}x \text{ divides } y\text{"} \supset \text{"}y \text{ is not prime"}) \equiv (\exists x)(x \text{ divides } y) \supset \text{"}y \text{ is not prime."}$

In many cases, the truth value of a wff can be evaluated more readily if we transform the wff into the canonical form described below.

Definition A.18 A wff is said to be in the *prenex normal form* if it is of the form

$$(Q_1 x_1)(Q_2 x_2) \cdots (Q_n x_n)M$$

where each $(Q_i x_i)$ is either $(\forall x_i)$ or $(\exists x_i)$, and M is a formula containing no quantifiers. $(Q_1 x_1)(Q_2 x_2) \cdots (Q_n x_n)$ is called the *prefix* and M the *matrix* of the formula.

The following rules (logically equivalent relations) can be utilized to transform a given wff into its prenex normal form:

(1a) $\neg((\exists x)A(x)) \equiv (\forall x)(\neg A(x))$.
(1b) $\neg((\forall x)A(x)) \equiv (\exists x)(A(x))$.
(2a) $(Qx)A(x) \vee B \equiv (Qx)(A(x) \vee B)$, where x does not occur free in B.
(2b) $(Qx)A(x) \wedge B \equiv (Qx)(A(x) \wedge B)$, where x does not occur free in B.
(3a) $(\exists x)A(x) \vee (\exists x)C(x) \equiv (\exists x)(A(x) \vee C(x))$.
(3b) $(\forall x)A(x) \wedge (\forall x)C(x) \equiv (\forall x)(A(x) \wedge C(x))$.
(4a) $(Q_1 x)A(x) \vee (Q_2 x)C(x) \equiv (Q_1 x)(Q_2 y)(A(x) \vee C(y))$.
(4b) $(Q_3 x)A(x) \wedge (Q_4 x)C(x) \equiv (Q_3 x)(Q_4 y)(A(x) \wedge C(y))$.

In (4a) and (4b), y is a variable that does not occur in $A(x)$. Q, Q_1, Q_2, Q_3, and Q_4 are either $\exists$ or $\forall$. In order to make the rules above applicable, it may be necessary to rename variables and rewrite the formula into an equivalent one using the $\neg$, $\wedge$, and $\vee$ connectives only.

Example A.19   Consider the wff $(\forall x)P(x) \wedge (\exists x)Q(x) \vee \neg(\exists x)R(x)$, which can be rewritten into the prenex normal form as follows.

$$(\forall x)P(x) \wedge (\exists x)Q(x) \vee \neg(\exists x)R(x)$$
$$(\forall x)P(x) \wedge (\exists x)Q(x) \vee (\forall x)(\neg R(x)) \qquad \text{by (1a)}$$
$$(\forall x)(\exists y)(P(x) \wedge Q(y)) \vee (\forall x)(\neg R(x)) \qquad \text{by (4b)}$$
$$(\forall x)(\exists y)(\forall z)(P(x) \wedge Q(y) \vee \neg R(z)) \qquad \text{by (4a)}$$

This sequence of transformation is valid provided that x does not occur free in Q and R, y does not occur free in P and R, and z does not occur free in P and Q. In applying the transformation rules, always select a new variable name such that no free variable becomes bound in the process.

To illustrate, let us consider the following logical expression:

$$b - a > e \wedge b + 2a \geq 6 \wedge 2(b - a)/3 \leq e \qquad \text{(A)}$$

In program testing, expression (A) may represent the condition under which a specific program path will be traversed, and the problem is to find an assignment of values to the input variables a, b, and e such that the condition is satisfied.

An inequality solver can be used to find possible solutions to (A). Alternatively, if we find it easier to work with equalities, we can restate formula (A) in terms of equality by observing that

$$a > b \equiv (\exists d)_{d>0}(a = b + d)$$
$$a \geq b \equiv (\exists d)_{d\geq0}(a = b + d)$$
$$a < b \equiv (\exists d)_{d>0}(a = b - d)$$
$$a \leq b \equiv (\exists d)_{d\geq0}(a = b - d)$$

Formula (A) thus becomes

$$(\exists x)_{D_1}(x = b - a - e) \wedge (\exists x)_{D_2}(x = b + 2a - 6) \wedge (\exists x)_{D_2}(x = e - 2(b - a)/3)$$

where D_1 is the set of all real numbers greater than zero, and D_2 is the set of all real numbers greater than or equal to zero.

The task can be made more manageable by rewriting it into its prenex normal form:

$$(\exists x)_{D_1}(\exists y)_{D_2}(\exists z)_{D_2}(x = b - a - e \wedge y = b + 2a - 6 \wedge z = e - 2(b - a)/3)$$
$$\text{(B)}$$

The three equations above are indeterminate because there are more than three variables involved. Therefore, we cannot obtain the desired assignment directly by solving the equations. However, we can combine these three equations to form a new equation in such a way that the number of variables involved in the new equation will be minimal. This can be accomplished using the same techniques that we use in solving simultaneous equations. In the present example, we can combine the three equations to yield

$$(\exists x)_{D_1}(\exists y)_{D_2}(\exists z)_{D_2}(3x - y + 3z = 6 - 3a) \tag{C}$$

As indicated in expression (C), the requirements on the assignments to x, y, and z are that $x > 0$, $y \geq 0$, and $z \geq 0$. So let us begin by making the following assignments:

$$x \leftarrow 0.1 \qquad y \leftarrow 0 \qquad z \leftarrow 0$$

Then (C) can be satisfied by letting

$$a \leftarrow 1.9$$

To satisfy the second component in (B) we must have $0 = b + 2 \times 1.9 - 6 = b - 2.2$; that is, we have to make the assignment

$$b \leftarrow 2.2$$

Finally, the first and the third components of (B) can be satisfied by letting

$$e \leftarrow 0.2$$

In summary, logical expression (A) can be satisfied by the following assignment:

$$a \leftarrow 1.9 \qquad b \leftarrow 2.2 \qquad e \leftarrow 0.2$$

A.3 PRINCIPLE OF MATHEMATICAL INDUCTION

The set of (nonnegative) integers have many interesting properties, chief among them being that (1) the numbers can be constructed (or generated) from zero uniquely, and (2) if a property that holds for one number also holds for the next number in the generation, that property holds for all integers. The second property noted is the gist of the principle of mathematical induction, which has so many applications in computer programming that it requires some discussion.

Definition A.20 *Principle of mathematical induction.* If zero has a property P, and if any integer n is P, then $n + 1$ is also P, so every integer is P. The principle is used in proving statements about integers or, derivatively, in proving statements about sets of objects of any kind that can be correlated with integers.

The procedure is to prove that

(a) 0 is P (induction basis)

to assume that

(b) n is P (induction hypothesis)

to prove that

(c) $n + 1$ is P (induction step)

using (a) and (b); and then to conclude that

(d) n is P for all n.

For example, suppose we wish to prove that

$$\sum_{i=0}^{n} i = \frac{n(n+1)}{2}$$

To begin, we must state the property that we want to prove. This statement is called the *induction proposition*. In this case P is given directly by

$$n \text{ is } P \Leftrightarrow \sum_{i=0}^{n} i = \frac{n(n+1)}{2}$$

(a) For the basis of the induction we have for $n = 0$, $0 = 0(0+1)/2$, which is true.

(b) The induction hypothesis is that k is P for some arbitrary choice of k:

$$\sum_{i=0}^{k} i = 0 + 1 + 2 + \cdots + k = \frac{k(k+1)}{2}$$

(c) For the induction step, proving that $k + 1$ is P, we have

$$\sum_{i=0}^{k+1} i = \sum_{i=0}^{k} i + (k+1)$$
$$= \frac{k(k+1)}{2} + (k+1) \quad \text{(using the induction hypothesis)}$$
$$= \frac{kk + k + 2k + 2}{2}$$
$$= \frac{(k+1)[(k+1)+1]}{2}$$

(d) Hence $k + 1$ has the property P.

The principle of induction is also valid if at step (b), the induction hypothesis, we assume that every $k \leq n$ is P. Moreover, one may choose any integer as a basis and then prove that some property of interest holds for the set of integers greater than or equal to the basis.

A closely related concept, which is commonly used in computer programming, is the inductive definition of a set or property having the following standard form:

Definition A.21 *Inductive definition of a set or property* P. Given a finite set A:

(a) The elements of A are P (basis clause).
(b) The elements of B, all of which are constructed from A, are P (inductive clause).
(c) The elements constructed as in (a) and (b) are the only elements of P (extremal clause).

We have already seen many examples of inductive definitions in the preceding section, where all well-formed formulas are defined inductively.

A.4 DIRECTED GRAPHS AND PATH DESCRIPTIONS

As explained in Chapter 5, the path structures in a directed graph can conveniently be described using regular expressions. For example, the set of paths between nodes 1 and 4 in Figure A.1 can be described by using a regular expression, such as

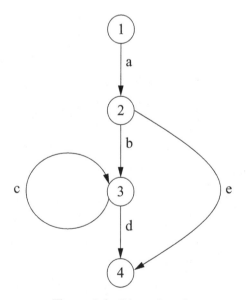

Figure A.1 Directed graph.

a(e+bc*d) or ae+abd+abc*d. The question now is: Given a directed graph, how do we go about finding a regular expression that describes the path structure between a pair of nodes in the graph? Presented below is a method that can be used to answer this question systematically [LUNT65]. It is easy to understand, and it is relatively easy to implement on a computer.

Let G be a directed graph in which each edge is labeled by an element of set E of symbols. If there are n nodes in G, then G can be represented by an $n \times n$ matrix as follows. First, the nodes in G are to be ordered in some way. Then we form an $n \times n$ matrix $[G] = [g_{ij}]$, where g_{ij} (the element on the ith row and jth column) is a regular expression denoting the set of all paths of length 1 (i.e., the paths formed by a single edge) leading from the ith node to the jth node. For example, the graph given above can be represented by the following matrix:

$$
\begin{bmatrix}
\varnothing & a & \varnothing & \varnothing \\
\varnothing & \varnothing & b & e \\
\varnothing & \varnothing & c & d \\
\varnothing & \varnothing & \varnothing & \varnothing
\end{bmatrix}
$$

where $\varnothing$ is a special symbol representing the empty set.

The operations of concatenation, disjunction (+), and the star operation (*) are now to be extended over the matrices with regular expressions as elements. Let $[X]$, $[Y]$, $[Z]$, and $[W]$ be $n \times n$ matrices. We define

$$[X] + [Y] = [Z] = [z_{ij}]$$

where $z_{ij} = x_{ij} + y_{ij}$,

$$[X][Y] = [W] = [w_{ij}]$$

where $w_{ij} = \overset{n}{\underset{k=1}{+}} x_{ik} y_{kj}$, and

$$[X]^* = [X]^0 + [X]^1 + [X]^2 + [X]^3 + \cdots,$$

where $[X]^0$ is defined to be an $n \times n$ matrix in which every element on the main diagonal is λ and all other elements are identically $\varnothing$. If we consider concatenation as multiplication and disjunction as addition, the first two matrix operations defined above are similar to matrix addition and matrix multiplication, respectively, defined in the theory of matrices.

Now given $[G] = [g_{ij}]$, the matrix representation of a graph G having n nodes, we may construct a $(n-1) \times (n-1)$ matrix B by simultaneously eliminating the

kth row and the kth column of $[G]$ (for some $1 \leq k \leq n$) as follows:

$$[G] = \begin{bmatrix} g_{11} & \cdots & g_{1k} & \cdots & g_{1n} \\ \cdots & & & & \cdots \\ g_{k1} & \cdots & g_{kk} & \cdots & g_{kn} \\ \cdots & & & & \cdots \\ g_{n1} & \cdots & g_{nk} & \cdots & g_{nn} \end{bmatrix}$$

$$[B] = \begin{bmatrix} g_{11} & \cdots & g_{1(k-1)} & g_{1(k+1)} & \cdots & g_{1n} \\ \cdots & & & & & \cdots \\ g_{(k-1)1} & \cdots & g_{(k-1)(k-1)} & g_{(k-1)(k+1)} & \cdots & g_{(k-1)n} \\ g_{(k+1)1} & \cdots & g_{(k+1)(k-1)} & g_{(k+1)(k+1)} & \cdots & g_{(k+1)n} \\ \cdots & & & & & \cdots \\ g_{n1} & \cdots & g_{n(k-)1} & g_{n(k+1)} & & g_{nn} \end{bmatrix}$$

$$+ \begin{bmatrix} g_{1k} \\ \cdots \\ g_{(k-1)k} \\ g_{(k+1)k} \\ \cdots \\ g_{nk} \end{bmatrix} [g_{kk}]^* \begin{bmatrix} g_{k1} & \cdots & g_{k(k-1)} & g_{k(k+1)} & \cdots & g_{kn} \end{bmatrix}$$

It should be easy to see that eliminating a row and the corresponding column in $[G]$ in this way does not alter the path information between any pair of the remaining nodes. On the right-hand side of the equation above, the first term represents all the paths that do not go through the node to be eliminated, and the second term represents all the paths that do. In other words, matrix $[B]$ represents the graph obtained by eliminating the kth node in the original graph without removing the associated edges.

Thus, to find the paths leading from the ith node to the jth node in G, we simply use the method described above to eliminate successively (in any order) all nodes other than the ith and jth nodes. We will then be left with a 2×2 matrix (assuming that $i < j$):

$$[B'] = \begin{bmatrix} b_{ii} & b_{ij} \\ b_{ji} & b_{jj} \end{bmatrix}$$

Then p_{ij}, the regular expression denoting the paths leading from the ith node to the jth node, can be constructed from the elements in $[B']$ as follows:

$$p_{ij} = (b_{ii} + b_{ij}\, b_{jj}^* b_{ji})^* b_{ij} (b_{jj} + b_{ji}\, b_{ii}^* b_{ij})^*$$

If $b_{ii} = b_{ji} = b_{jj} = \emptyset$, which is almost always the case in many applications, we have

$$p_{ij} = b_{ij}$$

because $\emptyset* = \lambda$ and $\lambda a = a\lambda = a$ for any regular expression a.

To illustrate, let us suppose that we wish to find the set of all paths leading from node 1 to node 4 in Figure A.1 . The matrix representation of the graph is repeated below for convenience.

$$\begin{bmatrix} \emptyset & a & \emptyset & \emptyset \\ \emptyset & \emptyset & b & e \\ \emptyset & \emptyset & c & d \\ \emptyset & \emptyset & \emptyset & \emptyset \end{bmatrix}$$

According to the method described above, we can eliminate, for example, column 2 and row 2 (i.e., node 2) first to yield the following 3×3 matrix:

$$\begin{bmatrix} \emptyset & \emptyset & \emptyset \\ \emptyset & c & d \\ \emptyset & \emptyset & \emptyset \end{bmatrix} + \begin{bmatrix} a \\ \emptyset \\ \emptyset \end{bmatrix} [\emptyset]^* [\emptyset \quad b \quad e]$$

$$= \begin{bmatrix} \emptyset & \emptyset & \emptyset \\ \emptyset & c & d \\ \emptyset & \emptyset & \emptyset \end{bmatrix} + \begin{bmatrix} \emptyset & ab & ae \\ \emptyset & \emptyset & \emptyset \\ \emptyset & \emptyset & \emptyset \end{bmatrix}$$

$$= \begin{bmatrix} \emptyset & ab & ae \\ \emptyset & c & d \\ \emptyset & \emptyset & \emptyset \end{bmatrix}$$

Now column 2, row 2 corresponds to the node labeled by integer 3. It can be similarly eliminated to yield the following 2×2 matrix.

$$\begin{bmatrix} \emptyset & ae \\ \emptyset & \emptyset \end{bmatrix} + \begin{bmatrix} ab \\ \emptyset \end{bmatrix} [c]^* [\emptyset \quad d]$$

$$= \begin{bmatrix} \emptyset & ae \\ \emptyset & \emptyset \end{bmatrix} + \begin{bmatrix} \emptyset & abc^*d \\ \emptyset & \emptyset \end{bmatrix}$$

$$= \begin{bmatrix} \emptyset & ae + abc*d \\ \emptyset & \emptyset \end{bmatrix}$$

Hence, the set of paths leading from node 1 to node 4 is described by ae+abc*d.

The reader may wonder what will happen if we eliminate the nodes in a different order. In general, different regular expressions may result if the nodes are eliminated in different orders, but the resulting regular expressions will be equivalent in the sense that they all denote the same set. Therefore, we may say that the order in which the nodes are eliminated is immaterial insofar as the membership of the path set is concerned. But in some applications the resulting regular expression represents a program composed of a set of path subprograms. The complexity of the regular expression reflects the complexity of the program. In such applications, therefore, it may be desirable to eliminate the nodes in the order that will yield a regular expression of the least (syntactic) complexity. An algorithm for determining such an order, however, remains unknown.

APPENDIX B
Glossary

Assertion checking   When a program is being executed, its variables should assume values in a certain range, or satisfy a certain assertion, at various points in its control flow. Any violation constitutes a symptom of programming error. Such violations can be detected by inserting appropriate instruments (additional statements) into the program and then executing the instrumented program with an appropriate set of inputs. This dynamic technique for software fault detection is called assertion checking (Section 7.3).

Backward substitution   The process of computing the weakest precondition of an assignment statement: The result is to be obtained by substituting the right-hand side of the assignment statement for every occurrence of the left-hand-side variable in the postcondition (Section 5.1).

Boundary–interior testing   An abbreviated version of path testing. Path testing is impractical because any program with loop constructs has a prohibitively large number of execution paths. One way to make it practical is to allow the tester to sample the execution paths to be traversed. This is one such method (Section 2.4).

Boundary-value analysis   A specification-based test-case selection method: For each input and output variable defined in the range between the lower bound LB and the upper bound UB, choose LB, UB, LB $- \delta$, and UP $+ \delta$ as the test cases, where δ is the smallest value assumable by the variables (Section 3.3).

Branch testing   A test-case selection criterion: requires the use of a set of test cases that causes every branch in the control-flow diagram to be traversed at least once during the test (Section 2.3).

Code inspection   Also known as *walkthrough*; refers to a process in which a program is scrutinized systematically by the peers of its creator in a meeting for the purpose of fault discovery (Section 6.4).

Component (to be tested)   When a program is executed, not every component is involved. If a program component is not involved in a test execution and if the component is faulty, the fault will not be revealed by the test. That is why it is essential that all components be exercised at least once during a test. Different choices of component lead to the development of different test-case selection methods, such as statement and branch tests (Section 1.2).

Software Error Detection through Testing and Analysis, By J. C. Huang
Copyright © 2009 John Wiley & Sons, Inc.

Computation fault   A type of programming fault induced by a failure to provide a correct sequence of steps to compute the value for a specific input even though the input is in the subdomain prescribed by the specification (Section 1.3).

Computationally coupled inputs   Two inputs to a program are said to be (tightly) coupled computationally if the fact that the program executes correctly with one input will make it more likely that the program will execute correctly with the other input as well (Section 1.1).

Conditional probability   Let A and B be two events. The probability that event A will occur given that event B has actually occurred is called the conditional probability of A given B and is denoted $P(A|B)$. Event A is said to be independent of event B if $P(A|B) = P(A)$.

Cost-effectiveness   The cost-effectiveness of a test set is Defined to be the probability of revealing a fault during the test, divided by the number of elements in the test set.

Coupling coefficient   The coupling coefficient between two test cases t_1 and t_2 is defined to be the conditional probability that the program will execute correctly with t_2 given that the program executed correctly with t_1, minus the probability that the program will execute correctly with t_2 (Section 1.2). Its values lie between zero and 1. It can be argued that the smaller this coefficient, the greater the probability that the test set consisting of these two test cases would reveal a fault in the test using this test set.

c-use   A term used in data-flow testing. A variable is said to have a c-use if it is used (referenced) in an assignment statement or other type of computational statement (Section 2.5).

Cyclomatic number   A graph-theoretical measure of the complexity of a graph: It is relevant to McCabe's test method because it is the maximum cardinality of a set of linearly independent paths that can be constructed from a graph: in other words, the number of test cases one needs to choose in McCabe's method (Section 2.4).

Data flow   When a program component such as a statement is being executed, it will take a sequence of actions on the data structure, such as a variable. The possible actions are *define* (assign a value to the variable), *reference* (make use of the value of the variable), and *undefine* (cause the value of the variable to become undefined). *Data flow* refers to sequences of such actions that take place during program execution (Section 2.5).

Data-flow anomaly   When a program is being executed, its components will act on the data in three ways: define, reference, or undefine. When a datum is created by the program, it is undefined. The program has to define it first and then make use of it by referencing it. If for some reason the program makes use of a datum without defining it first, defines a datum and defines it again without using it, or defines a datum and undefines it without using the definition first, we say that there is a data-flow anomaly. A data-flow anomaly is a symptom of possible fault in the program (Sections 6.1 and 7.4).

Data-flow testing A family of test-case selection methods that require various types of segments of execution paths to be traversed during the test. Each data-flow testing method is a variation of the path testing method abbreviated in different ways and to a different degree (Section 2.5).

Debug (vs. operational) testing A testing process aimed at detecting (and subsequently removing) faults in a program to improve its reliability. It uses a test set that is believed to have a high probability of revealing at least one fault during the test.

Decision table A tabular description of the computation embodied by a program or prescribed by a program specification. Based on the decision table, one can select test cases to perform subfunction test (Section 3.4).

Domain fault A type of programming fault that is induced by a failure to create a subdomain in the program that is contained completely in a subdomain prescribed by the specification (Section 1.3)

Domain-strategy testing A code-based test-case selection method: for every straight line used to define a subdomain, three test cases need to be selected to check the correct positioning of that line. A test set selected by using this criterion will be particularly effective in revealing domain errors (Section 2.6).

Equivalence partitioning A method designed to select test cases from the program specification. For each predicate found in a program specification, this method adds to the test set being constructed one test case that satisfies the predicate and another that does not. It is called predicate testing in this book (Section 3.2).

Equivalent mutant A mutant that is logically equivalent to the original program. It presents a problem in doing a program mutation test because no test case can cause an equivalent mutant to produce a test result different from that of the original program (Section 2.7).

Error guessing A test-case selection method: using the tester knowledge about the program and its authors to select test cases that are most likely to reveal latent faults (Section 3.1).

Error seeding A process for assessing the fault-detection capability of a test method: Faults (errors) are introduced into a program deliberately to see how many of the artificially inserted faults can be revealed by the test method used (Section 2.7).

Fault-discovery capability The fault-discovery capability of a test set is defined to be the probability that at least one fault will be revealed by test-executing the program with that set.

Ideal test set A set of test cases selected using a selection criterion that is both reliable and valid. It has the property that if its use leads to a successful test, it constitutes a direct proof of correctness. In other words, if a program works correctly with every element of an ideal test set, that program will work correctly with every element in the input domain (Section 4.1).

Input (output) domain The set of all possible inputs (outputs) to a program, including valid and invalid ones as well.

Linearly independent paths A path (in a graph) is said to be a linear combination of others if its vector representation is equal to that formed by a linear combination of their vector representations. A set of paths is said to be linearly independent if no path in the set is a linear combination of any other paths in the set (Section 2.4).

Loop invariant The loop invariant of a loop construct is a condition that is true before the loop is entered, and true after each iteration of the loop body (Section 6.5). It is an abstract entity useful in communicating precisely and concisely the working of a loop construct.

McCabe's test method As mentioned elsewhere, path testing is impractical because most programs have a prohibitively large number of execution paths. It can be made practical by allowing the tester to sample the paths to be traversed. This is one such method. It requires that a maximal set of linearly independent paths in the program be traversed during the test (Section 2.4).

Memoryless program A type of computer programs that always produces the same output when executed with the same input. Its behavior is similar to that of a combinational circuit in digital hardware.

Mutant A program that has been altered by using a set of mutation rules: It is created to mimic the working of a faulty program statement (Section 2.7).

Operational profile Distribution of the probability that elements of the input domain will be used in production runs (Section 4.2).

Operational testing A method of program testing using a set of test cases selected based on the operational profile of the program (Section 4.2). The test cases used are those that have the highest probabilities of being used in production runs. Therefore, it can be used to assess the reliability of the program as well.

Optimum test set A test set is said to be *optimal* if it is constructed in such a way that it satisfies both the first and second principles of test-case selection, and its cardinality is minimal.

Oracle Any person or thing that is capable of responding unequivocally to an inquiry about the correctness of a particular test execution.

Output domain The set of all possible outputs of a program.

Path testing The test-case selection criterion that requires all feasible execution paths in the program to be traversed at least once during the test.

Postcondition A condition that is to be satisfied by the output upon termination of the program execution.

Precondition A condition that is to be satisfied by the input just before the program is executed.

Predicate Logically speaking, a predicate is a sentence that has the form of a statement or proposition, but the truth value of which cannot be determined because it contains pronouns, variables, or quantifiers. An interpretation has to be made before its truth value can be evaluated.

Predicate testing A specification-based test-case selection method: Simply put, an application of the method entails finding predicates in the program specification, and for each found, selecting a test case that satisfies the predicate and selecting another that does not (Section 3.2). It is also known as the *method of equivalence partitioning*.

Principle of test-case selection (first)   In choosing a new element for a test set being constructed, preference should be given to those candidates that are computationally as loosely coupled as possible to all the existing elements in the set.

Principle of test-case selection (second)   In constructing a test set, include in it as many test cases as needed to cause every component to be exercised at least once during the test.

Program analysis   The process of examining the text of a computer program for the purpose of extracting a certain attribute of the program.

Program correctness   A program is said to be correct (with respect to its specification) if every one of its input/output pairs satisfies the specification.

Program graph   A directed-graph representation of a program in which every edge is associated with a pair of the form $< /\backslash C, S >$, where C is the condition under which that edge will be traversed in execution and S a program component to be executed in the process (Chapter 2).

Program instrumentation   The process of inserting additional statements (instruments) into the source code for the purpose of extracting certain information about the program (Chapter 7).

Program mutation   The process in which program mutants are created by using a set of rules to alter statements in the program (Section 2.7). It can be viewed as a way to seed a program with predefined types of faults.

Program mutation test   A test-case selection criterion that requires building of a test set that distinguishes the program from all of its mutants: that causes every mutant to produce at least one test result different from that of the original program (Section 2.7).

Program slicing   A method for creating a subprogram from a given program. The subprogram is produced by removing some or all of statements that would not contribute to the program behavior specified. The program behavior is specified in terms of the values assumed by certain variables at a specific point in the control flow (Section 6.3).

Program testing   A process in which the program is executed for the purpose of determining if it has a certain property, such as correctness, termination, or speed.

Program with memory   A program that is capable of assuming different initial states. Therefore, execution of the program with the same input does not entail production of the same output. The program output will be determined not only by the present input but by previous ones as well. The behavior of such a program is similar to that of a sequential circuit in digital hardware.

p-use   A term in data-flow testing. A variable is said to have a p-use if it is referenced in a branch predicate (Section 2.5).

Regression test In a regression test, the program is tested with all the test cases used previously. It is performed after the program has been modified (debugged) to ensure that no new faults have been introduced into the program (Section 4.5).

Reliability of a test-case selection criterion A test-case selection criterion is said to be reliable if the program will test successfully (or unsuccessfully) with any test set selected by using that criterion (Section 4.1).

Singularity index The number of times a test case was blindsided by program statements during test execution, a possible measure for ineffectiveness of a test case (Section 7.2).

Software counter A type of software instrument inserted into the program source code for the purpose of counting the number of times the control crossed that point in control flow (Section 7.1).

Statement testing A test-case selection criterion that requires every statement in the program to be exercised at least once during the test (Section 2.2).

Static analysis A process in which the source code of the program in question is examined systematically for the purpose of extracting certain attributes. No execution of the program is involved in the process (Chapter 6).

Successful test A program test is said to be successful if each and every input/output pair produced in the test satisfies the program specification (Section 4.1).

Subfunction testing A testing process in which the test cases are selected based on the program specification to exercise each and every subfunction to be implemented in the program (Section 3.1).

Symbolic execution A process in which a program is executed with symbolic inputs (versus real inputs) to produce symbolic outputs (Section 6.2). If the program is executed with a real input, and if it produced a correct output, all we can conclude from that fact is that the program works correctly for that particular input. If the program executed correctly with a symbolic input, we should be able to draw a wider conclusion from that. That is the rationale behind the development of this technique.

Symbolic trace The symbolic trace of an execution path in a program is a linear list of path predicates (evaluated to be true) and program statements encountered on the path (Chapter 5 and Section 7.5). It is a textual representation of an execution path in a program.

Test Short for *test execution*, it refers to an instance of executing a program with one or more test cases for determining certain properties of the program.

Test case An input of a program that is chosen specifically to test-execute the program.

Test-case selection criterion A condition (or property) used to prescribe the formation of a test set. Any subset of the input domain that satisfies the condition (or has the prescribed property) is a test set prescribed by the criterion. *Example:* a set of inputs that causes every statement in the program to be exercised at least once during the test.

Test coverage   The extent to which the source code of a program is involved in a test, measured in terms of the percentage of components chosen to be exercised during the test.

Test set   A set of test cases (inputs) that is specifically chosen for the purpose of test-executing a program.

Tester   A person who is technically responsible for the testing process. The most important technical decision that must be made before the inception of a testing process is the choice of test-case selection criterion to be used. This decision is customarily made by the originating organization of the software project, and stipulated explicitly in the contract. Otherwise, it is the responsibility of the tester to make the choice. In any case, it is the ultimate responsibility of the tester to ensure, and to verify it to the stakeholders, that the test-case selection criterion is used correctly and faithfully in the testing process.

Theorem   A statement or proposition that is always true.

Validity of a test-case selection criterion   A test-case selection criterion is said to be valid (Section 4.1) if at least one of the test sets selected by using that criterion is capable of revealing the fault (if any) in the program.

Walkthrough   A process also known as *code inspection* (Section 6.4) in which a program is scrutinized systematically by the peers of its creator in a meeting for the purpose of fault discovery.

Weakest precondition   It is useful to use a condition to characterize certain inputs of program S having the property that if we use any of them to execute S, the execution will terminate and S will produce an output that satisfies postcondition R. The weakest of such conditions (i.e., the one that defines the largest subset of the input domain) is called the weakest precondition (Section 5.1).

APPENDIX C
Questions for Self-Assessment

Circle only one answer for each of the questions posed below. If you find any question that appears to have more than one correct answer, choose the one that is most specific or appropriate. (The answers are given at the end of this appendix.)

1. There are many reasons why it is impractical to do exhaustive testing (i.e., to test a program for all possible input cases) for a real-world program, some of which are listed below. Of course, not every one of these is valid for all programs. Among these reasons, however, there is one that is valid for almost all nontrivial programs and thus can be used to assert categorically that it is impractical to do exhaustive testing for a nontrivial program. Which one is it?

   (a) Most programs do not terminate for every possible input.

   (b) Expected output for some input may be difficult to determine.

   (c) There is no effective procedure for generating all possible inputs.

   (d) The membership of all possible inputs is mostly unknown.

   (e) The number of all possible inputs, although finite, is prohibitively large.

2. The concept of computational coupling between two test cases is central to the establishment of the first principle of test-case selection. Let $p(OK(t_2)|OK(t_1))$ denote the probability that a program will execute correctly with test case t_2, given the fact that the program executes correctly with test case t_1. By definition,

   i. $1 \geq p(OK(t_2)|OK(t_1)) \geq 0$.

   ii. The value of $p(OK(t_2)|OK(t_1))$ approaches that of $p(OK(t_2))$ if t_1 and t_2 are strongly coupled.

   iii. The value of $p(OK(t_2)|OK(t_1))$ approaches 1 if t_1 and t_2 are very weakly coupled.

   Which of the foregoing statements is true?

   (a) All

   (b) (i) only.

   (c) (ii) only.

Software Error Detection through Testing and Analysis, By J. C. Huang
Copyright © 2009 John Wiley & Sons, Inc.

(d) (iii) only.

(e) None of (a) through (d) is a correct answer.

3. The first principle of test-case selection says that in choosing a new element for a test set being constructed, preference should be given to those candidates that are computationally coupled as loosely as possible to all existing elements in the set. Which of the following statements about this principle are true?

   i. It tells us how to avoid selection of a new element that is redundant in the sense that its inclusion in the test set would not increase its fault-detection capability significantly.

   ii. It helps us to find the test case that has the highest probability of error detection.

   iii. It tells us how to construct a test set that is effective in the sense that it can achieve a high probability of fault detection with few test cases.

   (a) All.

   (b) All but (i).

   (c) All but (ii).

   (d) All but (iii).

   (e) None of (a) through (d) is a correct answer.

4. The second principle of test-case selection says that we should include as many elements in the test set as possible so that every (predetermined type of programming) construct in the program will be exercised at least once during the test execution. This is based on:

   (a) the fact that correctness of a program is implied by the correctness of its parts.

   (b) the observation that it is the only practical way to reduce to a manageably small number the test cases required.

   (c) a theoretical work showing that it will afford the highest probability of error detection.

   (d) the fact that the presence of an error will not be reflected in the test results unless the faulty construct is involved in the test execution.

   (e) the lessons learned from hardware testing.

5. There are two commonly used test-case selection criteria in the defense industry known as C1 and C2. C1 requires the test set to "exercise the program to the extent that each statement in the program is executed at least once, whereas C2 requires that each branch in its control flow be traversed at least once. C2 is more thorough (i.e., tends to reveal more latent faults) than C1 because:

   (a) the use of C2 entails that all conditional statements in the program will be exercised during the test.

   (b) satisfaction of C1 implies satisfaction of C2.

   (c) satisfaction of C2 entails that all errors undetectable by the use of C1 will be detected.

(d) the use of C2 entails that more statements will be executed more than once during the test.

(e) C2 covers C1, and certain programming errors may be detected when using C2 but not when using C1.

6. Consider the following C++ program, whose graph is shown in Figure C.1.

```
main()
{
    int x, y, z;

    cin >> x >> y;
    z = 1;
    while (y != 0) {
        if (y % 2 == 1)
            z = z * x;
        y = y / 2;
        x = x * x;
    }
    cout << z << endl;
}
```

There is a potential execution path denoted by αβδεη. Which of the following is its path predicate?

(a) y != 0 && y % 2 != 1 && y == 0

(b) y != 0 || y % 2 != 1 || y == 0

(c) y / 2 == 0

(d) y != 0 && y % 2 != 1 && y / 2 == 0

(e) None of (a) through (d) is a correct answer.

7. To find a set of test cases satisfying C2 (branch testing) is to find a set of inputs that causes each element in a certain set of paths (from the entry to the exit) to be traversed at least once during the test. Assuming that this set of paths is described by a regular expression, which of the following are the necessary conditions that must be satisfied by that set of paths?

    i. The program graph is constructed such that none of the edge symbols is associated with a conditional (branch) statement or a loop construct.

    ii. Every edge symbol occurs at least once in the regular expression.

    iii. It does not contain a star operation, (i.e., a subexpression of the form a^*).

    iv. Each path described by this regular expression is a feasible execution path.

(a) All.

(b) All but (i).

(c) All but (ii).

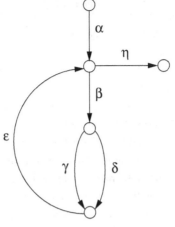

where α: cin >> x >> y;
          z = 1;

β: /\ y != 0;

γ: /\ !(y % 2 == 1);

δ: /\ y % 2 == 1;
    z = z * x;

ε: y = y / 2;
    x = x * x;

η: /\ !(y != 0);
    cout << z << endl;

Figure C.1   Program graph.

(d) All but (iii).
(e) All but (iv).

8. Which of the following is a well-known maxim regarding program testing?
   (a) Program testing is not necessary if the clean-room approach to software development is practiced.
   (b) Only incompetent programmers need to do testing.
   (c) An exhaustive test is the only practical way of constructing a correctness proof.
   (d) Program testing can be used to discover the presence of errors but not their absence.
   (e) None of (a) through (d) is a correct answer.

9. Suppose that a C++ programmer mistakenly writes

```
if (B)        instead of      if (B) {
    S1;                           S1;
    S2;                           S2;
                              }
```

Which of the following statements are true?

    i. It needs only one test case to do a statement test for both programs.

    ii. It requires at least two test cases to do a branch test for both programs.

    iii. This error will never be reflected in the test result if only one test case is used to do the statement test.

(a) All.

(b) (i) and (ii) only.

(c) (i) and (iii) only.

(d) (ii) and (iii) only.

(e) None of (a) through (d) is a correct answer.

10. It is the loop constructs that make the number of possible execution paths in a program prohibitively large. Which of the following test methods can be viewed as a variation of all-path testing, requiring only a much smaller subset of execution paths to be traversed during the test?

    i. The branch test.

    ii. The statement test.

    iii. The method for test-case selection proposed by McCabe (using a maximal set of linearly independent paths).

Which of the above are correct?

(a) All.

(b) All but (i).

(c) All but (ii).

(d) All but (iii).

(e) None of (a) through (d) is a correct answer.

11. In graph theory, a strongly connected graph $G = <E, N>$ can have as many as $v(G) = |E| - |N| + 1$ linearly independent paths. McCabe's complexity measure, the cyclomatic number, is purported to measure the same attribute of a control-flow graph with $|E|$ edges and $|N|$ nodes, but is given as $v(G) = |E| - |N| + 2$ instead. Why?

(a) One is added to increase the test coverage.

(b) One edge from the exit to the entry has to be added to make a control-flow diagram strongly connected.

(c) The number of edges is counted in a different way.

(d) The number of nodes is counted in a different way.

(e) None of (a) through (d) is a correct answer.

12. The essence of program testing is to choose certain components of the program to be exercised during the test. In data-flow testing, the components to be exercised are:

(a) Data structures in the program.

(b) Paths in the data-flow diagram.

(c) Segments of an execution path that starts with a definition of some datum and ends with the use of that definition.

(d) Segments of an execution path that starts with a definition of some datum and ends with the next definition of that datum.

(e) None of (a) through (d) is a correct answer.

13. Figure C.2 depicts the coverage relation among the test-case selection methods.

    i. Method *A* covers method *B* if node *B* is a descendant of node *A* in the graph.

    ii. According to this graph, the all-c/some-p method covers the all-def method.

    iii. According to this graph, the all-c/some-p method also covers the statement method.

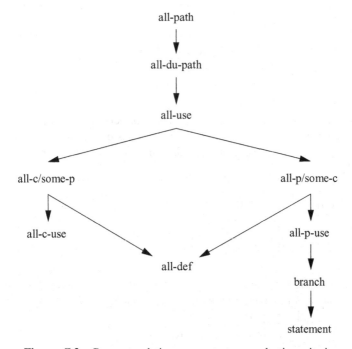

Figure C.2 Coverage relation among test-case selection criteria.

Which of the statements above are true?

(a) All.

(b) All but (i).

(c) All but (ii).

(d) All but (iii).

(e) None of (a) through (d) is a correct answer.

14. Which of the following are assumptions made in developing domain-strategy testing?

    i. Coincidental (fortuitous) correctness of the program may not occur for any "off" point.

    ii. The path corresponding to each adjacent domain computes a different subfunction.

    iii. Functions defined in two adjacent subdomains yield the same value for the same test point near the border.

(a) All.

(b) All but (i).

(c) All but (ii).

(d) All but (iii).

(e) None of (a) through (d) is a correct answer.

15. Consider a program with the path domains D_i in a two-dimensional space defined by the following predicates:

$$x - 2 <= 0$$
$$x + y > 0$$
$$2x - y >= 0$$

Which of the following sets of x–y pairs is a correct choice of the three test cases (on–off–on points) needed to test the correctness of a boundary defined by the predicate $x - 2 >= 0$, assuming that the smallest real number on the machine is 0.001?

(a) $\{(2, 3), (1.9, 1), (2, -1)\}$.

(b) $\{(2.001, 3), (2, 1), (2.001, -1)\}$.

(c) $\{(2.001, 3), (2, 1), (1.999, -1)\}$.

(d) $\{(1.999, 3), (2, 1), (1.999, -1)\}$.

(e) None of the above.

16. It can be argued that any set of test cases used in a mutation test must cause every statement in the program to be executed at least once during the test. This argument is valid only if:

(a) all mutants generated are nonequivalent.

(b) no more than one mutation rule is applied to generate a mutant.

(c) there is at least one mutation rule applicable to every executable statement in the program.

(d) no two mutation rules will produce an identical mutant.

(e) no two mutation rules will produce logically equivalent mutants.

17. Program mutation is in essence a systematic method for seeding the type of error that a programmer is likely to commit. Thus, it can be theorized that a set of test cases D_t adequately tests a program P:

(a) if all nonequivalent mutants of P are differentiated from P.

(b) if all mutants of P execute incorrectly for at least one element of D_t.

(c) if every mutant did not terminate for at least one element of D_t.

(d) if any mutant of P produced an incorrect result.

(e) if the result produced by every mutant is very close to that produced by P.

18. Major problems involved in applying the technique of program mutation include:

    i. requiring deep understanding of the program in question and all of its mutants.

    ii. difficulty in detecting the equivalence between the program and its mutants.

    iii. the large number of mutants most programs yield.

(a) All.

(b) All but (i).

(c) All but (ii).

(d) All but (iii).

(e) None of (a) through (d) is a correct answer.

19. What is the competent programmer's assumption made in connection with program mutation?

(a) A competent programmer does not misread program specifications.

(b) A competent programmer can commit only typographical errors.

(c) A competent programmer will never introduce new errors into a program when correcting an error.

(d) Errors that can be generated by using mutation rules are the only type of programming error a competent programmer might commit.

(e) None of (a) through (d) is a correct answer.

20. In the method of predicate testing (also known as equivalence partitioning) we find relevant predicates by identifying:

(a) parts of a program specification that are logically equivalent.

(b) the equivalence relations (in mathematical sense) defined in the program specification.

(c) different combinations of conditions for which the same computation is to be applied.

   (d) the conditions stated in the specification that require the inputs to be treated differently in the program.

   (e) items other than those mentioned above.

21. Specification-versus code-based test-case selection methods: In view of the component chosen to be exercised during the test, the method of predicate testing can be regarded as the counterpart of that of:

    (a) domain-strategy testing.

    (b) path testing.

    (c) data-flow testing.

    (d) branch testing.

    (e) program mutation.

22. Although there are similarities, the method of boundary-value analysis is most distinctly different from the method of predicate testing in that:

    (a) identification of input variables is not required in its application.

    (b) deep understanding of the program specification is not required.

    (c) instead of selecting test cases based on the input conditions alone, it also requires derivation of test cases based on output conditions.

    (d) it can only be applied to numerical programs.

    (e) it can only be applied to programs with linear branch predicates.

23. Which test-case selection method makes explicit assumption that the program to be tested does not differ from the correct program in a major way?

    (a) Branch testing.

    (b) Domain-strategy testing.

    (c) Error guessing.

    (d) Subfunction testing.

    (e) None of (a) through (d) is a correct answer.

24. Shown in Figure C.3 is a set of curves showing the relationship among risk reduction, total cost of testing, and net benefit of testing plotted using the theoretical model discussed in Chapter 4. Refer to these curves in answering this and the following questions. What quantity is represented by t_γ in the graph?

    (a) Real time.

    (b) Test time measured in computer time.

    (c) The time it takes to repair the faults detected through testing.

    (d) Test execution time plus the time required to fix the program.

    (e) None of (a) through (d) is a correct answer.

25. What are represented by the three curves in Figure C.3?

    (a) 1: total cost of testing; 2: risk reduction; 3: net benefit.

    (b) 1: risk reduction; 2: net benefit of testing; 3: total cost of testing.

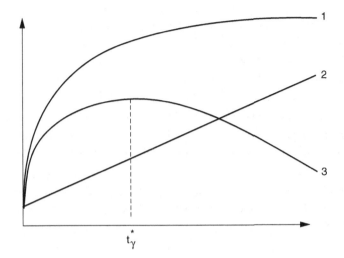

Figure C.3   Cost, risk reduction, and net benefit of testing.

(c) 1: risk reduction; 2: total cost of testing; 3: net benefit of testing.

(d) 1: net benefit of testing; 2: risk reduction; 3: total cost of testing.

(e) None of (a) through (d) is a correct answer.

26. In reference to the notation of Goodenough and Gerhart [GOGE77], let $F(d) = d$ mod 3 for all $d \in D$, where D is the set of all nonnegative integers. Furthermore, let $OK(d) = (d \bmod 5 = F(d))$. That is, program F is supposed to compute the remainder of $d \div 5$, but instead, computes that of $d \div 3$, where $\div$ denotes the operation of integer division. Which of the test-case selection criteria listed below is reliable?

(a) $C(T) \equiv (T = \{t\} \text{ and } t \in D)$

(b) $C(T) \equiv (T = \{1\} \text{ or } T = \{4\})$

(c) $C(T) \equiv (T = \{t\} \text{ and } t \in \{0, 1, 2, 3, 4\})$

(d) $C(T) \equiv (T = \{t, t + 1, t + 2\} \text{ and } t \in D)$

(e) None of (a) through (d) is a correct answer.

27. As a continuation of question 26, which of the following test-data selection criteria is valid?

  i. $C(T) \equiv (T = \{1, 10, 100, 1000, 10000\})$

  ii. $C(T) \equiv (T = \{1, 15, 31, 47\})$

  iii. $C(T) \equiv (T = \{t_1, t_2, t_3, t_4, t_5\} \text{ and } T \text{ is a subset of } D)$

  iv. $C(T) \equiv (T = \{t\} \text{ and } (t = 0 \text{ or } t = 1 \text{ or } t = 2 \text{ or } t = 3))$

(a) All.

(b) All but (i).

(c) All but (ii).

(d) All but (iii).

(e) None of (a) through (d) is a correct answer.

28. By definition, if a program is known to be correct, then for that program:

    (a) the empty set is the only set of test cases that can be both reliable and valid.

    (b) any selection criterion C is reliable but not valid.

    (c) any selection criterion C is valid but not reliable.

    (d) any selection criterion C is both reliable and valid.

    (e) the set of all possible inputs is the only set of test cases that can be both reliable and valid.

29. Let P be a program and C be a test-case selection criterion. If C is such that it does not exclude any input from being selected as a test case, we can immediately conclude that:

    (a) C is reliable.

    (b) C is valid.

    (c) C is neither reliable nor valid.

    (d) C is reliable but not valid.

    (e) C is valid but not reliable.

30. Let P be a program and C a test-case selection criterion. Suppose that we use C to select two different nonempty sets of test cases T_1 and T_2 and find that $\neg$SUCCESSFUL(T_1) and $\neg$SUCCESSFUL(T_2). This implies that:

    (a) C is neither reliable nor valid.

    (b) C is reliable.

    (c) C is reliable and valid.

    (d) C is valid.

    (e) none of the above.

31. Static analysis is a practical method for:

    (a) determining the thoroughness of a test.

    (b) detecting data-flow anomaly involving an array element.

    (c) determining the effectiveness of a test case.

    (d) detecting assertion violation in a program.

    (e) none of the above.

32. No automatic symbolic execution system has been built to run in a batch mode because:

    (a) the truth value of a branch predicate cannot be determined.

    (b) the assignment of symbolic values cannot be done in batch mode.

    (c) the computation of symbolic values can only be done interactively.

    (d) the identification of input variables cannot be automated.

    (e) of technical difficulties other than those mentioned in (a) through (d).

33. The symbolic execution tree of a program becomes infinite when:
    (a) and only when there is an infinite loop in the program.
    (b) the value of an output variable becomes infinite.
    (c) there is a loop construct or a recursive procedure call in the program.
    (d) and only when loop constructs are improperly nested.
    (e) and only when assignment of truth value to a branch predicate is done improperly.

34. If along the path we symbolically execute the C++ program

```
cin >> x >> y;
z = 1;
/\ y != 0;
/\ y % 2 == 1;
z = z * x;
y = y / 2;
x = x * x;
/\ !(y != 0);
cout << z << endl;
```

by assigning the symbolic values A to x and B to y at the input, it will yield:
    i. $x = A * A$
    ii. $y = B/2$
    iii. $z = A$

Which of the expressions above are true?
    (a) All.
    (b) All but (i).
    (c) All but (ii).
    (d) All but (iii).
    (e) None of (a) through (d) is a correct answer.

35. The technique of program instrumentation can be utilized to prove:
    (a) the reliability of a test criterion.
    (b) that an execution of a given program always terminates.
    (c) that a branch test has been achieved.
    (d) the validity of a test-case selection criterion.
    (e) none of (a) through (d) is a correct answer.

36. In instrumenting programs for assertion checking, the instruments may be implemented as comments in the host language. The purpose there is to:
    (a) reduce execution overhead while performing assertion checking.
    (b) facilitate their construction.

(c) facilitate their removal.

(d) increase their error-detection capability.

(e) prevent interference with the computation performed by the program.

37. The presence of a data-flow anomaly indicates that

     i. the program is definitely in error.

     ii. the program is possibly in error.

     iii. a datum is defined and then used repeatedly without being redefined.

Which of the foregoing statements are true?

(a) All.

(b) All but (i).

(c) All but (ii).

(d) All but (iii).

(e) None of (a) through (d) is a correct answer.

38. In practice, existing program testing methods are such that:

(a) their capabilities complement one another.

(b) some have error-detection capabilities identical to others.

(c) some can be used to obtain a direct proof of program correctness.

(d) they are easy to implement and economical to use.

(e) none of (a) through (d) is true.

39. Which of the following statements regarding regression testing are true?

     i. It is designed to verify that a particular modification of the program is done successfully.

     ii. It is designed to verify that no new errors have been introduced in the debugging process.

     iii. Its test cases include all of those used in previous tests.

(a) All.

(b) All but (i).

(c) All but (ii).

(d) All but (iii).

(e) None of (a) through (d) is a correct answer.

40. An oracle (in software testing) is:

(a) the generic name of any automatic software testing tool.

(b) any program designed to automate the test process.

(c) any means by which the correctness of a test result is determined.

(d) an utterance given by a tester in response to an inquiry about a test result.

(e) a database management system specifically designed for management of software testing process.

41. *Integration testing*: Instead of using the "big-bang" approach, in which all components are integrated into a system for testing at the same time, it is better to use a top-down, bottom-up, or sandwich testing strategy to do it incrementally because:

(a) it is easier to determine what the correct test result should be.

(b) it requires less time to complete each test execution.

(c) it is easier to find appropriate test cases that way.

(d) unit testing of the added program unit can be done simultaneously.

(e) errors can be isolated and located more readily.

42. A stub used in integration testing is:

(a) a driver used in a unit test.

(b) a subprogram designed to generate and feed the test cases.

(c) a simulator of a called program (dummy program unit) used in a top-down integration test.

(d) a program segment designed to prevent a "runaway" program from damaging other programs during a test.

(e) a simulator of a calling program (dummy program unit) used in a bottom-up integration test.

43. A test driver in integration testing is:

(a) a simulator of a calling program (dummy program unit) used in a bottom-up integration test.

(b) a program unit designed to feed the test cases automatically.

(c) a special input/output routine used to control the input device.

(d) a simulator of a calling program (dummy program unit) used in a top-down integration test.

(e) a program designed to generate test data automatically.

44. The disadvantages of top-down integration testing include:

    i. It may sometimes be difficult to find top-level input data that will exercise a lower-level module in a particular manner desired.

    ii. The evolving system may be very expensive to run as a test harness for new routines.

    iii. It may be costly to relink and reexecute a system each time a new routine is added.

(a) All.

(b) All but (i).

(c) All but (ii).

(d) All but (iii).

(e) None of (a) through (d) is a correct answer.

45. In what way does encapsulation in object-oriented programs affect software testing?

    i. The basic testable unit will no longer be a subprogram.

    ii. Traditional strategies for integration testing are no longer applicable.

    iii. The test results are no longer repeatable.

(a) All.

(b) All but (i).

(c) All but (ii).

(d) All but (iii).

(e) None of (a) through (d) is a correct answer.

46. Which of the following is among the reasons that the traditional top-down integration testing strategy cannot be applied directly to an object-oriented program?

(a) There is no invocation relationship among classes.

(b) The invocation order may not be repeatable in an object-oriented program.

(c) There is no clear top or bottom in an invocation relationship among classes.

(d) Certain test results may not be visible.

(e) None of (a) through (d) is a correct answer.

47. Many flow-graph-based test-case selection methods can be applied to object-oriented programs if we change the definition of a flow graph. For example, the changes could include:

    i. Each node is associated with a message.

    ii. Each edge is associated with the order in which the messages can be issued.

    iii. There will be no edge connecting node A to node B if an issuance of message A cannot be followed by an issuance of message B.

Which of these changes were included in the message graph described in Section 4.4?

(a) All.

(b) All but (i).

(c) All but (ii).

(d) All but (iii).

(e) None of (a) through (d) is a correct answer.

48. Consider the following statements about program slicing.

    i. A slice of a program is an executable subprogram of the original.

    ii. No loop construct can be included in a slice.

    iii. Data-flow analysis is performed to determine if a particular program statement can be excluded from the slice being constructed.

Which of these statements are true?

(a) All.

(b) All but (i).

(c) All but (ii).

(d) All but (iii).

(e) None of (a) through (d) is a correct answer.

49. Consider the following symbolic trace:

```
i = 0;
/\ !(isspace(s[i]));
/\ !(s[i] == '-');
sign = 1;
/\ !(s[i] == '+' || s[i] == '-');
n = 0;
/\ (isdigit(s[i]));
n = 10 * n + (s[i] - '0');
i = i + 1;
/\ !(isdigit(s[i]));
return sign * n;
```

It shows that this execution path was traversed because:

    i. the first input character, $s[0]$, was not a space.

    ii. the second input character, $s[1]$, was a digit.

    iii. the third input character, $s[2]$, was not a digit.

Which of these statements is (are) true?

(a) All.

(b) (i) Only.

(c) (ii) Only.

(d) (iii) Only.

(e) None of (a) through (d) is a correct answer.

50. The rules developed in Chapter 5 can be used to simplify the symbolic trace given in question 49. For example, we can do the following.

    i. We can move a constraint upstream over an assignment statement by performing backward substitution on the constraint. In particular, if we have $S; /\backslash C$, we can replace it with $/\backslash wp(S, C); S$, where S is a statement, C is some condition, and wp stands for "weakest precondition".

    ii. We can move a constraint upstream over an assignment statement without changing anything provided that no new value is assigned by the assignment statement to any variable that occurs in the constraint.

    iii. The symbolic trace given in question 49 can thus be equivalently transformed into the following trace.

```
i = 0;
/\ !(isspace(s[i]));
/\ !(s[i] == '-');
/\ !(s[i] == '+' || s[i] == '-');
/\ (isdigit(s[i]));
/\ !(isdigit(s[i+1]));
sign = 1;
n = 0;
n = 10 * n + (s[i] - '0');
i = i + 1;
return sign * n;
```

Which of these statements are true?

(a) All.

(b) All but (i).

(c) All but (ii).

(d) All but (iii).

(e) None of (a) through (d) is a correct answer.

KEY

1.	e	2.	b	3.	c	4.	d
5.	e	6.	e	7.	a	8.	d
9.	a	10.	a	11.	b	12.	c
13.	d	14.	d	15.	e	16.	c
17.	a	18.	b	19.	d	20.	d
21.	d	22.	c	23.	e	24.	b
25.	c	26.	e	27.	c	28.	d
29.	b	30.	d	31.	e	32.	a
33.	c	34.	a	35.	c	35.	c
37.	e	38.	a	39.	a	40.	c
41.	e	42.	c	43.	a	44.	a
45.	d	46.	c	47.	a	48.	c
49.	b	50.	a				

Bibliography

ABBO84 C. Abbott, Intervention Schedules for Real-Time Programming, *IEEE Trans. Software Engineering*, vol. 10, no. 3, May 1984, pp. 268–274.

ACM82 ACM, Special Issues on Rapid Prototyping: Working Papers from the ACM SIGSOFT Rapid Prototyping Workshop, *ACM Software Engineering Notes*, vol. 7, no. 5, Dec. 1982.

ADBC82 W. R. Adrion, M. A. Branstad, and J. C. Cherniavsky, Validation, Verification, and Testing of Computer Software, *ACM Computing Surveys*, vol. 14, no. 2, June 1982, pp. 159–192.

AHSU86 A. V. Aho, R. Sethi, and J. D. Ullman, *Compilers: Principles, Techniques, and Tools*, Addison-Wesley, Reading, MA, 1986.

ALAV84 M. Alavi, An Assessment of the Prototyping Approach to Information Systems Development, *Commun. ACM*, vol. 27, no. 6, June 1984, pp. 556–563.

ALCO76 F. E. Allen and J. Cocke, A Program Data Flow Analysis Procedure, *Commun. ACM*, vol. 19, no. 3, Mar. 1976, pp. 137–147.

ANDE79 R. B. Anderson, *Proving Programs Correct*, Wiley, New York, 1979.

ASMA70 E. Ashcroft and Z. Manna, *The Translation of GOTO Programs to WHILE Programs*, Tech. Rep. CS-188, Computer Science, Department, Stanford University, 1970.

BAGO99 I. Bashir and A. L. Goel, *Testing Object-Oriented Software: Life Cycle Solutions*, Springer-Verlag, New York, 1999.

BALA00 T. Ball and J. R. Larus, Using Paths to Measure, Explain, and Enhance Program Behavior, *IEEE Computer*, July 2000, pp. 57–65.

BAMI75 S. K. Basu and J. Misra, Proving Loop Programs, *IEEE Trans. Software Engineering*, vol. 1, no. 1, Mar. 1975, pp. 76–86.

BASE87 V. R. Basili and R. W. Selby, Comparing the Effectiveness of Software Testing Strategies, *IEEE Trans. Software Engineering*, vol. 13, no. 12, Dec. 1987, pp. 1278–1296.

BAYE75 S. K. Basu and R. T. Yeh, Strong Verification of Programs, *IEEE Trans. Software Engineering*, vol. 1, no. 3, Sept. 1975, pp. 339–345.

Software Error Detection through Testing and Analysis, By J. C. Huang

BDER79   G. Bristow, C. Drey, B. Edwards, and W. Riddle, *Anomaly Detection in Concurrent Programs*, Tech. Rep. CU-CS-147-79, Computer Science Deptarment, University of Colorado at Boulder, 1979.

BDHP73   J. R. Brown, A. J. DeSalvio, D. E. Heine, and J. G. Purdy, Automatic Software Quality Assurance, in *Program Test Methods*, W. C. Hetzel (Ed.), Prentice-Hall, Englewood Cliffs, NJ, 1973, pp. 181–203.

BDLS78   T. Budd, R. A. DeMillo, R. A. Lipton, and F. G. Sayward, The Design of a Prototype Mutation System for Program Testing, *Proc. AFIPS National Computer Conference*, vol. 47, 1978, pp. 623–627.

BDLS80   T. Budd, R. A. DeMillo, R. A. Lipton, and F. G. Sayward, Theoretical and Empirical Studies on Using Program Mutation to Test the Functional Correctness of Programs, *Proc. 7th ACM Symposium on Principles of Programming Languages*, Jan. 1980, pp. 220–233.

BEIZ84   B. Beizer, *Software System Testing and Quality Assurance*, Van Nostrand Reinhold, New York, 1984, p. 300.

BEIZ90   B. Beizer, *Software Testing Techniques*, 2nd ed., International Thomson Computer Press, London, 1990.

BEMA94   A. Bertolino and M. Marre, Automatic Generation of Path Covers Based on the Control Flow Analysis of Computer Programs, *IEEE Trans. Software Engineering*, vol. 20, no. 12, Dec. 1994, pp. 885–899.

BERA94   E. V. Berard, Issues in Testing OO Software, *IEE Electro/49 International*, IEE, London, 1994.

BERG62   C. Berge, *Theory of Graphs and Its Applications*, Wiley, New York, 1962.

BINK97   D. Binkley, Semantics Guided Regression Test Cost Reduction, *IEEE Trans. Software Engineering*, vol. 23, no. 8, Aug. 1997, pp. 498–516.

BLAC07   R. Black, *Pragmatic Software Testing*, Wiley, Hoboken, NJ, 2007.

BOKM02   C. Boyapati, S. Khurshid, and D. Marinov, Korat: Automated Testing Based on Java Predicates, *Proc. ACM International Symposium on Software Testing and Analysis*, July 2002.

BOSC03   P. J. Boland, H. Singh, and B. Cukic, Comparing Partition and Random Testing via Majorization and Schur Functions, *IEEE Trans. Software Engineering*, vol. 29, no. 1, Jan. 2003, pp. 88–94.

BROW88   M. H. Brown, *Algorithm Animation*, MIT Press, Cambridge, MA, 1988.

BRPL04   L. C. Briand, M. Di Penta, and Y. Labiche, Assessing and Improving State-Based Class Testing: A Series of Experiments, *IEEE Trans. Software Engineering*, vol. 30, no. 11, Nov. 2004, pp. 770–793.

BSRR02   M. Burnett, A. Sheretov, B. Ren, and G. Rothermel, Testing Homogeneous Spreadsheet Grids with the "What You See Is What You Test" Methodology, *IEEE Trans. Software Engineering*, vol. 28, no. 6, Aug. 2002, pp. 576–594.

BUKO70   B. Bussell and R. A. Koster, Instrumenting Computer Systems and Their Programs, *AFIPS Conferene Proc.*, vol. 37, 1970, pp. 525–534.

CADM02   J. W. Cangussu, R. A. DeCarlo, and A. P. Mathur, A Formal Model of the Software Test Process, *IEEE Trans. Software Engineering*, vol. 28, no. 8, Aug. 2002, pp. 782–796.

CATA91   R. Carver and K. C. Tai, Replay and Testing for Concurrent Programs, *IEEE Software*, vol. 8, no. 2, Mar. 1991, pp. 66–74.

CDFP97   D. M. Cohen, S. R. Dalal, M. L. Fredman, and G. C. Patton, The AETG System: An Approach to Testing Based on Combinatorial Design, *IEEE Trans. Software Engineering*, vol. 23, no. 7, July 1997, pp. 437–444.

CHBC93   J. K. Chaar, M. J. Halliday, I. S. Bhandari, and R. Chillarege, In-Process Evaluation for Software Inspection and Test, *IEEE Trans. Software Engineering*, vol. 19, no. 11, Nov. 1993, pp. 1055–1070.

CHHT79   T. E. Cheatham, Jr., G. H. Holloway, and J. A. Townley, Symbolic Evaluation and the Analysis of Programs, *IEEE Trans. Software Engineering*, vol. 5, no. 4, July 1979, pp. 402–417.

CHLE73   C. L. Chang and R. C. T. Lee, *Symbolic Logic and Mechanical Theorem Proving*, Academic Press, New York, 1973.

CHMC85   E. Charniak and D. McDermott, *Introduction to Artificial Intelligence*, Addison-Wesley, Reading, MA, 1985, p. 147.

CHUS87   T. Chusho, Test Data Selection and Quality Estimation Based on the Concept of Essential Branches for Path Testing, *IEEE Trans. Software Engineering*, vol. 13, no. 5, May 1987, pp. 509–517.

CHYU94   T. Y. Chen and Y. T. Yu, On the Relationship Between Partition and Random Testing, *IEEE Trans. Software Engineering*, vol. 20, no. 12, Dec. 1994, pp. 977–979.

CHYU96   T. Y. Chen and Y. T. Yu, On the Expected Number of Failures Detected by Subdomain Testing and Random Testing, *IEEE Trans. Software Engineering*, vol. 22, no. 2, Feb. 1996, pp. 109–119.

CLAR76   L. Clarke, A System to Generate Test Data and Symbolically Execute Programs, *IEEE Trans. Software Engineering*, vol. 2, no. 3, Sept. 1976, pp. 215–222.

COBL83   G. Collins and G. Blay, *Structured Systems Development Techniques: Strategic Planning to System Testing*, John Wiley, 1983.

COPI65   I. M. Copi, *Symbolic Logic*, Macmillan, New York, 1965.

CRIS84   F. Cristian, Correct and Robust Programs, *IEEE Trans. Software Engineering*, vol. 10, Mar. 1984, pp. 163–174.

CRJA02   R. D. Craig and S. P. Jaskiel, *Systematic Software Testing*, Artech House, Norwood, MA, 2002.

CUBC02   R. Culbertson, C. Brown, and G. Cobb, *Rapid Testing*, Prentice Hall, Upper Saddle River, NJ, 2002.

CYKL05   D. Coppit, J. Yang, S. Khurshid, W. Le, and K Sullivan, Software Assurance by Bounded Exhaustive Testing, *IEEE Trans. Software Engineering* vol. 31, no. 4, Apr. 2005, pp. 328–339.

DADH72   O. J. Dahl, E. W. Dijkstra, and C. A. R. Hoare, *Structured Programming*, Academic Press, New York, 1972.

DAVI78   C. G. Davis, The Testing of Large, Real Time Software Systems, *Proc. 7th Texas Conference on Computing Systems*, 1978.

DELS78   R. A. DeMillo, R. J. Lipton, and F. G. Sayward, Hints on Test Data Selection: Help for the Practicing Programmer, *Computer*, vol. 11, no. 4, Apr. 1978, pp. 34–41.

DENN91   R. Denney, Test-Case Generation from Prolog-Based Specifications, *IEEE Software*, vol. 8, no. 2, Mar. 1991, pp. 49–57.

DEOF91   R. A. DeMillo and A. J. Offutt, Constraint-Based Automatic Test Data Generation, *IEEE Trans. Software Engineering*, vol. 17, no. 9, Sept. 1991, pp. 900–911.

DIJK75   E. W. Dijkstra, Guarded Commands, Nondeterminancy and Formal Derivation of Programs, *Commun. ACM*, vol. 18, no. 8, Aug. 1975, pp. 453–457.

DIJK76   E. W. Dijkstra, *A Discipline of Programming*, Prentice-Hall, Englewood Cliffs, NJ, 1976.

DIJK90   E. W. Dijkstra, *Formal Development of Programs and Proofs*, Addison-Wesley, Reading, MA, 1990.

DKST05   D. P. Darcy, C. F. Kemerer, S. A. Slaughter, and J. E. Tomayko, The Structural Complexity of Software: An Experimental Test, *IEEE Trans. Software Engineering*, vol. 31, no. 11, Nov. 2005, pp. 982–995.

DMMP87   R. A. DeMillo, W. M. McCraken, R. J. Martin, and J. F. Passafiume, *Software Testing and Evaluation*, Benjamin/Cummings, Menlo Park, CA, 1987.

DUNT84   J. W. Duran and S. C. Ntafos, An Evaluation of Random Testing, *IEEE Trans. Software Engineering*, vol. 10, no. 4, July 1984, pp. 438–444.

DURP99   E. Dustin, J. Rashka, and J. Paul, *Automated Software Testing*, Addison-Wesley, Reading, MA, 1999.

DURW03   A. Dunsmore, M. Roper, and M. Wood, The Development and Evaluation of Three Diverse Techniques for Object-Oriented Code Inspection, *IEEE Trans. Software Engineering*, vol. 29, no. 8, Aug. 2003, pp. 677–686.

EGKM02   S. G. Eick, T. L. Graves, A. F. Karr, A. Mockus, and P. Schuster, Visualizing Software Changes, *IEEE Trans. Software Engineering*, vol. 28, no. 4, Apr. 2002, pp. 396–412.

ELDI05   S. Elbaum and M. Diep, Profiling Deployed Software: Assessing Strategies and Testing Opportunities, *IEEE Trans. Software Engineering*, vol. 31, no. 4, Apr. 2005, pp. 312–327.

ELME73   W. R. Elmendorf, *Cause-Effect Graphs in Functional Testing*, TR-00.2487, IBM System Development Division, Poughkeepsie, NY, 1973.

EVMM07   G. D. Everett, R. McLeod, Jr., and R. McLeod, *Software Testing*, Wiley, Hoboken, NJ, 2007.

FAIR75   R. E. Fairley, An Experimental Program Testing Facility, *IEEE Trans. Software Engineering*, vol. 1, no. 4, 1975, pp. 350–357.

FAIR79   R. E. Fairley, ALADDIN: Assembly Language Assertion Driven Debugging Interpreter, *IEEE Trans. Software Engineering*, vol. 5, no. 4, July 1979, pp. 426–428.

FBKA91   S. Fujiwara, G. Bochmann, F. Khendek, M. Amalou, and A. Ghedamsi, Test Selection Based on Finite State Models, *IEEE Trans. Software Engineering*, vol. 17, no. 6, June 1991, pp. 591–603.

FEGR99   M. Fewster and D. Graham, *Software Test Automation: Effective Use of Text Execution Tools*, Addison-Wesley, Reading, MA, 1999.

FENE99   N. E. Fenton and M. Neil, A Critique of Software Defect Prediction Methods, *IEEE Trans. Software Engineering*, vol. 25, no. 5, Sept. 1999, pp. 675–689.

FHLS98   P. G. Frankl, R. G. Hamlet, B. Littlewood, and L. Strigini, Evaluating Test Methods by Delivered Reliability, *IEEE Trans. Software Engineering*, vol. 24, no. 8, Aug. 1998, pp. 586–601.

FHLS99   P. G. Frankl, R. G. Hamlet, B. Littlewood, and L. Strigini, Correction to: Evaluating Test Methods by Delivered Reliability, *IEEE Trans. Software Engineering*, vol. 25, no. 2, Mar. 1999, p. 286.

FLFQ05   C. Flanagan, S. N. Freund, and S. Qadeer, Exploiting Purity for Atomicity, *IEEE Trans. Software Engineering*, vol. 31, no. 4, Apr. 2005, pp. 275–291.

FLOY67   R. W. Floyd, Assigning Meaning to Programs, *Proceedings of a Symposium in Applied Mathematics*, vol. 19, *Mathematical Aspects of Computer Science*, J. T. Schwartz (Ed.), Providence, RI, 1967, pp. 19–32.

FMRW05   C. Fu, A. Milanova, B.G. Ryder, and D. G. Wonnacott, Robustness Testing of Java Server Applications, *IEEE Trans. Software Engineering*, vol. 31, no. 4, Apr. 2005, pp. 292–311.

FOOS76   L. D. Fosdick and L. J. Osterweil, Data Flow Analysis in Software Reliability, *ACM Computing Surveys*, vol. 8, no. 3, Sept. 1976, pp. 305–330.

FREE91   R. S. Freedman, Testability of Software Components, *IEEE Trans. Software Engineering*, vol. 17, no. 6, June 1991, pp. 553–564.

FRVO95   M. Friedman and J. Voas, *Software Assessment: Reliability, Safety, and Testability*, Wiley, New York, 1995.

FRWE88   P. G. Frankl and E. J. Weyuker, An Applicable Family of Data Flow Testing Criteria, *IEEE Trans. Software Engineering*, vol. 14, no. 10, Oct. 1988, pp. 1483–1498.

FRWE93a   P. G. Frankl and E. J. Weyuker, A Formal Analysis of the Fault-Detecting Ability of Testing Methods, *IEEE Trans. Software Engineering*, vol. 19, no. 3, Mar. 1993, pp. 202–213.

FRWE93b   P. G. Frankl and S. N. Weiss, An Experimental Comparison of the Effectiveness of Branch Testing and Data Flow Testing, *IEEE Trans. Software Engineering*, vol. 19, no. 8, Aug. 1993, pp. 774–787.

FRWE93c   P. G. Frankl and E. J. Weyuker, Provable Improvements on Branch Testing, *IEEE Trans. Software Engineering*, vol. 19, no. 10, Oct. 1993, pp. 962–976.

FRWE93d   P. G. Frankl and S. N. Weiss, Correction to: An Experimental Comparison of the Effectiveness of Branch Testing and Data Flow Testing, *IEEE Trans. Software Engineering*, vol. 19, no. 12, Dec. 1993, p. 1180.

GANA97   M. J. Gallagher and V. L. Narasimhan, ADTEST: A Test Data Generation Suite for Ada Software Systems, *IEEE Trans. Software Engineering*, vol. 23, no. 8, Aug. 1997, pp. 473–485.

GELL78   M. Geller, Test Data as an Aid in Proving Program Correctness, *Commun. ACM*, vol. 21, no. 5, May 1978, pp. 368–375.

GHSC99   A. Ghosh and M. Schmid, An Approach to Testing COTS Software for Robustness to Operating System Exceptions and Errors, *Proc. 10th International Symposium on Software Reliability Engineering*, IEEE Computer Society Press, Los Alamos, CA, 1999, pp. 166–174.

GIRG93   M. R. Girgis, Corrigendum for: Constraint-Based Automatic Test Data Generation, *IEEE Trans. Software Engineering*, vol. 19, no. 6, June 1993, p. 640.

GIVO03   D. D. Givone, *Digital Principles and Design*, McGraw-Hill, New York, 2003.

GOGE77   J. B. Goodenough and S. L. Gerhart, Toward a Theory of Testing: Data Selection Criteria, in *Current Trends in Programming Methodology*, vol. II, *Program Validation*, R. T. Yeh (Ed.), Prentice-Hall, Englewood Cliffs, NJ, 1977, pp. 44–79.

GOUR83   J. Gourlay, A Mathematical Framework for the Investigation of Testing, *IEEE Trans. Software Engineering*, vol. 9, Nov. 1983, pp. 686–709.

GRAH02   D. Graham, Requirements and Testing: Seven Missing-Link Myths, *IEEE Software*, vol. 19, no. 5, Sept.–Oct. 2002, pp. 15–17.

GUGU02   N. Gupta and R. Gupta, Data Flow Testing, in *The Compiler Design Handbook: Optimization and Machine Code Generation*, CRC Press, Boca Roton, FL, 2002, pp. 247–267.

GUTJ99   W. J. Gutjahr, Partition Testing vs. Random Testing: The Influency of Uncertainty, *IEEE Trans. Software Engineering*, vol. 25, no. 5, Sept. 1999, pp. 661–674.

HAKI76   S. L. Hantler and J. C. King, An Introduction to Proving the Correctness of Programs, *ACM Computing Surveys*, vol. 8, no. 3, Sept. 1976, pp. 331–353.

HAML77   R. G. Hamlet, Testing Programs with the Aid of a Compiler, *IEEE Trans. Software Engineering*, vol. 3, no. 4, July 1977, pp. 279–289.

HAML89   R. G. Hamlet, Theoretical Comparison of Testing Methods, *Proc. 3rd Symposium on Software Testing, Analysis, and Verification*, Dec. 1989, pp. 28–37.

HARA69   F. Harary, *Graph Theory*, Addison-Wesley, Reading, MA, 1969.

HASO91   M. J. Harrold and M. L. Soffa, Selecting and Using Data for Integration Testing, *IEEE Software*, vol. 8, no. 2, Mar. 1991, pp. 58–65.

HATA90   D. Hamlet and R. Taylor, Partition Testing Does Not Inspire Confidence, *IEEE Trans. Software Engineering*, vol. 16, no. 12, Dec. 1990, pp. 1402–1411.

HATT07   L. Hatton, The Chimera of Software Quality, *IEEE Computer*, vol. 40, no. 7, 2007.

HECM02   D. Hendrix, J. H. Cross II, and S. Maghsoodloo, The Effectiveness of Control Structure Diagrams in Source Code Comprehension Activities, *IEEE Trans. Software Engineering*, vol. 28, no. 5, May 2002, pp. 463–477.

HEND77   P. Henderson, Structured Program Testing, in *Current Trends in Programming Methodology*, vol. II, *Program Validation*, R. T. Yeh (Ed.), Prentice-Hall, Englewood Cliffs, NJ, 1977, pp. 1–15.

HETZ73   W. C. Hetzel, *Program Test Methods*, Prentice-Hall, Englewood Cliffs, NJ, 1973.

HETZ88   B. Hetzel, *The Complete Guide to Software Testing*, 2nd ed. Wellesley, MA: QED Info. Sci., 1988.

HEUL75   M. S. Hecht and J. D. Ullman, A Simple Algorithm for Global Data Flow Analysis Problems, *SIAM J. Computing*, vol. 4, Dec. 1975, pp. 519–532.

HEWH02   C. A. Healy and D. B. Whalley, Automatic Detection and Exploitation of Branch Constraints for Timing Analysis, *IEEE Trans. Software Engineering*, vol. 28, no. 8, Aug. 2002, pp. 763–781.

HIBO94   T. Higashino and G. V. Bochmann, Automatic Analysis and Test Case Derivation for a Restricted Class of LOTOS Expressions with Data Parameters, *IEEE Trans. Software Engineering*, vol. 20, no. 1, Jan. 1994, pp. 29–42.

HMWZ92   J. C. Huang, J. Munoz, H. Watt, and G. Zvara, ECOS Graphs: A Dataflow Programming Language, *Proc. Symposium on Applied Computing*, Mar. 1992.

HOAR69   C. A. R. Hoare, An Axiomatic Basis for Computer Programming, *Commun. ACM*, vol. 12, no. 10, Oct. 1969, pp. 576–580.

HOEI77   W. E. Howden and P. Eichhorst, *Proving Properties of Programs from Program Traces*, CS Rep. 18, University of California at San Diego, 1977.

HORS96   C. Horstmann, *Mastering C++*, Wiley, New York, 1996.

HOSM02   G. J. Holzmann and M. H. Smith, An Automated Verification Method for Distributed Systems Software Based on Model Extraction, *IEEE Trans. Software Engineering*, vol. 28, no. 4, Apr. 2002, pp. 364–377.

HOST91   D. M. Hoffman and P. Strooper, Automated Module Testing in Prolog, *IEEE Trans. Software Engineering*, vol. 17, no. 9, Sept. 1991, pp. 934–944.

HOWD75   W. E. Howden, Methodology for Generation of Program Test Data, *IEEE Trans. Computers*, vol. 24, no. 5, May 1975, pp. 554–559.

HOWD76   W. E. Howden, Reliability of the Path Analysis Testing Strategy, *IEEE Trans. Software Engineering*, vol. 2, no. 3, Sept. 1976, pp. 208–214.

HOWD77   W. E. Howden, Symbolic Testing and the DISSECT Symbolic Evaluation System, *IEEE Trans. Software Engineering*, vol. 3, no. 4, July 1977, pp. 266–278.

HOWD78a   W. E. Howden, DISSECT: A Symbolic Evaluation and Program Testing System, *IEEE Trans. Software Engineering*, vol. 4, no. 1, Jan. 1978, pp. 70–73.

HOWD78b   W. E. Howden, A Survey of Dynamic Analysis Methods, in *Software Testing and Validation Techniques*, E. F. Miller and W. E. Howden (Eds.), IEEE Computer Society, Long Beach, CA, 1978, pp. 184–206.

HOWD78c   W. E. Howden, An Evaluation of the Effectiveness of Symbolic Testing and of Testing on Acutal Data, *Software Practice and Experience*, vol. 8, 1978, pp. 381–397.

HOWD80a   W. E. Howden, Functional Testing and Design Abstraction, *J. Systems and Software*, vol. 1, 1980, pp. 307–313.

HOWD80b   W. E. Howden, Functional Program Testing, *IEEE Trans. Software Engineering*, vol. 6, no. 2, Mar. 1980, pp. 162–169.

HOWD80c   W. E. Howden, Applicability of Software Validation Techniques to Scientific Programs, *ACM Trans. Programming Language and System*, vol. 2, no. 3, July 1980, pp. 307–320.

HOWD82   W. E. Howden, Validation of Scientific Programs, *ACM Computing Surveys*, vol. 14, no. 2, June 1982, pp. 193–227.

HOWD87   W. E. Howden, *Functional Program Testing and Analysis*, McGraw-Hill, New York, 1987.

HUAN75   J. C. Huang, An Approach to Program Testing, *ACM Computing Surveys*, vol. 7, no. 3, Sept. 1975, pp. 113–128.

HUAN76   J. C. Huang, A Method for Program Analysis and Its Applications to Program-Correctness Problems, *International J. Computer Mathematics*, vol. 5, no. 4, 1976, pp. 203–227.

HUAN77a   J. C. Huang, Principles of Software Validation, *Proc. 1977 Summer Computer Simulation Conference*, Chicago, 1977, pp. 705–708.

HUAN77b   J. C. Huang, Error Detection Through Program Testing, in *Current Trends in Programming Methodology*, vol. II, *Program Validation*, R. T. Yeh (Ed.), Prentice-Hall, Englewood Cliffs, NJ, 1977, pp. 16–43.

HUAN78a   J. C. Huang, Program Instrumentation and Software Testing, *Computer*, vol. 11, no. 4, Apri. 1978, pp. 25–32.

HUAN78b   J. C. Huang, Program Instrumentation: A Tool for Software Testing, *Proc. Infotech State of the Art Conference on Software Testing*, London, 1978. Also in

Infotech State of the Art Report: Software Testing, vol. 2, *Invited Papers*, Infotech International, London, 1979, pp. 147–159.

HUAN79   J. C. Huang, Detection of Data Flow Anomaly Through Program Instrumentation, *IEEE Trans. Software Engineering*, vol. 5, no. 3, May 1979, pp. 226–236.

HUAN80a   J. C. Huang, A New Verification Rule and Its Applications, *IEEE Trans. Software Engineering*, vol. 6, no. 5, Sept. 1980, pp. 480–484.

HUAN80b   J. C. Huang, Instrumenting Programs for Symbolic-Trace Generation, *IEEE Computer*, vol. 13, no. 12, Dec. 1980, pp. 17–23.

HUAN82   J. C. Huang, Experience with Use of Program Instrumentation in Software Testing, *Proc. National Security Industrial Association National Conference on Software Technology and Management*, Alexandria, VA, Oct. 1981.

HUAN87   J. C. Huang, A Depth-First and Tool-Supportable Programming Strategy, *Software: Practice and Experience*, vol. 17, no. 2, Feb. 1987, pp. 159–163.

HUAN90   J. C. Huang, State Constraints and Pathwise Decomposition of Programs, *IEEE Trans. Software Engineering*, vol. 16, no. 8, Aug. 1990, pp. 880–896.

HUAN98   J. C. Huang, Measuring the Effectiveness of a Test Case, *Proc. 1998 IEEE Workshop on Application Specific Software Engineering and Technology*, Mar. 1998, pp. 157–159.

HUAN08   J. C. Huang, *Path-Oriented Program Analysis*, Cambridge University Press, New York, 2008.

HUHL84   J. C. Huang, M. Ho, and T. Law, A Simulator for Real-Time Software Debugging and Testing, *Software Practice and Experience*, vol. 14, no. 9, Sept. 1984, pp. 845–855.

HULE99   J. C. Huang and T. Leng, Generalized Loop-Unrolling: A Method for Program Speedup, *Proc. 1999 IEEE Workshop on Application-Specific Software Engineering and Technology*, Mar. 1999, pp. 244–248.

HURL83   R. B. Hurley, *Decision Tables in Software Engineering*, Van Nostrand Reinhold, New York, 1983.

HUVY84   J. C. Huang, P. Valdes, and R. T. Yeh, A Tool-Based Approach to Software Validation and Testing, *Proc. National Computer Conference*, July 1984.

HUYE75   J. C. Huang and R. T. Yeh, A Method of Test-Case Generation, *Proc. 2nd US–Japan Computer Conference*, Tokyo, 1975, pp. 585–589.

JAAG84   J. Jachner and V. K. Agarwal, Data Flow Anomaly Detection, *IEEE Trans. Software Engineering*, vol. 10, no. 4, July 1984, pp. 432–437.

JARZ98   S. Jarzabek, Design of Flexible Static Program Analyzers with PQL, *IEEE Trans. Software Engineering*, vol. 24, no. 3, Mar. 1998, pp. 197–215.

JORG02   P. Jorgensen, *Software Testing: A Craftsman's Approach*, CRC Press, Boca Raton, FL, 2002.

JVCS07   J. Jacky, M. Veanes, C. Campbell, and W. Schulte, *Model-Based Software Testing and Analysis with C++*, Cambridge University Press, New York, 2007.

JVSJ06   P. Jalote, V. Vangala, T. Singh, and P. Jain, Program Partitioning: A Framework for Combining Static and Dynamic Analysis, *Proc. 2006 International Workshop on Dynamic Systems Analysis*, Shanghai, China, pp. 11–16.

KABP01   C. Kaner, J. Bach, and B. Pettichord, *Lessons Learned in Software Testing*, Wiley, New York, 2001.

KAFN99   C. Kaner, J. Falk, and H. Q. Nguyen, *Testing Computer Software*, 2nd ed., Wiley, New York, 1999.

KALA00   M. S. Kalambi, *Development of a Graphical Software Analysis Tool Using Software Engineering Concepts for Corporate-wide System Engineering*, M.S. thesis, Department of Computer Science, University of Houston, 2000.

KEPI99   B. W. Kernighan and R. Pike, *The Practice of Programming*, Addison-Wesley, Reading, MA, 1999.

KEPL74   B. W. Kernighan and P. J. Plaugher, *The Elements of Programming Style*, McGraw-Hill, New York, 1974.

KERI88   B. W. Kernighan and D. M. Ritchie, *The C Programming Language*, 2nd ed., Prentice-Hall, Englewood Cliffs, NJ, 1988.

KIFI95   E. Kit and S. Finzi, *Software Testing in the Real World: Improving the Process*, Addison-Wesley, Reading, MA, 1995.

KING75   J. C. King, A New Approach to Program Testing, *Proc. 1975 International Conference on Reliable Software*, Los Angeles, 1975.

KING76   J. C. King, Symbolic Execution and Program Testing, *Commun. ACM*, vol. 19, no. 7, July 1976, pp. 385–394.

KIOF91   K. King and A. J. Offut, A Fortran Language System for Mutation-Based Software Testing, *Software Practice and Experience*, vol. 21, no. 7, 1991, pp. 685–718.

KOCT02   P. V. Koppol, R. H. Carver, and K.-C, Tai, Incremental Integration Testing of Concurrent Programs, *IEEE Trans. Software Engineering*, vol. 28, no. 6, Aug. 2002, pp. 607–623.

KORF66   R. R. Korfhage, *Logic and Algorithms*, Wiley, New York, 1966.

KOVA88   W. Kobrosly and S. Vassiliadis, *A Survey of Software Functional Testing Techniques* IEEE, New York, 1988, pp. 127–134.

KRMR91   E. W. Krauser, A. P. Mathur, and V. J. Rego, High Performance Software Testing on SIMD Machines, *IEEE Trans. Software Engineering*, vol. 17, no. 6, May 1991, pp. 403–423.

KRSG73   K. W. Krause, R. W. Smith, and M. A. Goodwin, Optimal Software Test Planning Through Automated Network Analysis, *Proc. IEEE Symposium on Computer Software Reliability*, 1973.

KUHG98   D. C. Kung, P. Hsia, and J. Gao, *Testing Object-Oriented Software*, IEEE Computer Society, Los Alamitos, CA, 1998.

KUWG04   D. R. Kuhn, D. R. Wallace, and A. M. Gallo, Jr., Software Fault Interactions and Implications for Software Testing, *IEEE Trans. Software Engineering*, vol. 30, no. 6, June 2004, pp. 418–421.

LAKO83   J. W. Laski and B. Korel, A Data Flow Oriented Program Testing Strategy, *IEEE Trans. Software Engineering*, vol. 9, no. 3, May 1983, pp. 347–354.

LAMP79   L. Lamport, A New Approach to Proving the Correctness of Multiprocessor Programs, *TOPLAS*, vol. 1, no. 1, July 1979, pp. 84–97.

LARU93   J. R. Larus, Efficient Program Tracing, *IEEE Computer*, vol. 26, no. 5, May 1993, pp. 52–61.

LAVI97   G. Lanubile and G. Visaggio, Extracting Reusable Functions by Flow Graph–Based Program Slicing, *IEEE Trans. Software Engineering*, vol. 23, no. 4, Apr. 1997, pp. 246–259.

LEBL99   T. P. LeBlanc, Selection of Test Cases to Cost-Effectively Reduce the Risk of Failure of a Rule-Based Scheduling Engine, M.S. thesis, Department of Computer Science, University of Houston, May 1999.

LECA06   Y. Lei and R. H. Carver, Reachability Testing of Concurrent Programs, *IEEE Trans. Software Engineering*, vol. 32, no. 6, June 2006, pp. 382–404.

LELE88   W. Leler, *Constraint Programming Languages*, Addison-Wesley, Reading, MA, 1988.

LIEN83   B. P. Lientz, Issues in Software Maintenance, *ACM Computing Surveys*, vol. 15, no. 3, 1983, pp. 271–278.

LIJE88   T. E. Lindquist and J. R. Jenkins, Test-Case Generation with IOGen, *IEEE Software*, vol. 5, no. 1, Jan. 1988, pp. 72–79.

LIWR97   B. Littlewood and D. Wright, Some Conservative Stopping Rules for the Operational Testing of Safety-Critical Software, *IEEE Trans. Software Engineering*, vol. 23, no. 11, Nov. 1997, pp. 673–683.

LMPS04   S. Loveland, G. Miller, R. Prewitt, and M. Shannon, *Software Testing Techniques: Finding the Defects That Matter*, Charles River Media, Hingham, MA, 2004.

LOND77   R. L. London, Perspectives on Program Verification, in *Current Trends in Programming Methodology*, R. T. Yeh (Ed.), Prentice-Hall, Englewood Cliffs, NJ, 1977, pp. 151–172.

LUDB94   G. Luo, A. Das, and G. V. Bochmann, Software Testing Based on SDL Specifications with Save, *IEEE Trans. Software Engineering*, vol. 20, no. 1, Jan. 1994, pp. 72–87.

LUNT65   A. G. Lunts, A Method of Analysis of Finite Automata, *Soviet Physics Doklady*, vol. 10, 1965, pp. 102–103.

LUSU79   D. C. Luckham and N. Suzuki, Verification of Array, Record, and Pointer Operations in Pascal, *TOPLAS*, vol. 1, no. 2, Oct. 1979, pp. 226–244.

MACE05   M. Mock, D. C. Atkinson, C. Chambers, and S. J. Eggers, Program Slicing with Dynamic Points-to Sets, *IEEE Trans. Software Engineering*, vol. 31, no. 8, Aug. 2005, pp. 657–678.

MANN74   Z. Manna, *Mathematical Theory of Computation*, McGraw-Hill, New York, 1974.

MANN02   C. C. Mann, Why Software Is So Bad, *MIT Technology Review*, July–Aug. 2002, pp. 32–39.

MARI95   B. Marick, *The Craft of Software Testing*, Prentice Hall, Upper Saddle River, NJ, 1995.

MAWU93   Z. Manna and R. Wuldinger, *The Deductive Foundations of Computer Programming*, Addion-Wesley, Reading, MA, 1993.

MCCA76   T. J. McCabe, A Complexity Measure, *IEEE Trans. Software Engineering*, vol. 2, no. 4, Dec. 1976, pp. 308–320.

MCGA83   P. R. McMullin and J. D. Gannon, Combining Testing with Formal Specifications: A Case Study, *IEEE Trans. Software Engineering*, vol. 9, no. 3, May 1983, pp. 328–334.

MENS02   T. Mens, A State-of-the-Art Survey on Software Merging, *IEEE Trans. Software Engineering*, vol. 28, no. 5, May 2002, pp. 449–462.

MEXI05   A. M. Memon and Q. Xie, Studying the Fault-Detection Effectiveness of GUI Test Cases for Rapidly Evolving Software, *IEEE Trans. Software Engineering*, vol. 31, no. 10, Oct. 2005, pp. 884–896.

MEYE08   B. Meyer, Seven Principles of Software Testing, *IEEE Computer*, vol. 41, no. 8, 2008, pp. 99–101.

MIHO81   E. Miller and W. E. Howden, *Tutorial: Software Testing and Validation Technique*, IEEE Computer Society Press, Los Alamitos, CA, 1981.

MILL74   E. F. Miller, Structurally Based Automatic Program Testing, *Proc. EASCON-74*, Washington, DC, 1974.

MILL86   H. D. Mills, Structured Programming: Retrospect and Prospect, *IEEE Software*, vol. 3, no. 6, Nov. 1986, pp. 58–66.

MIME75   E. F. Miller and R. A. Melton, Automated Generation of Test-Case Datasets, *Proc. 1975 International Conference on Reliable Software*, Los Angeles, CA, Apr. 1975.

MIMS01   C. C. Michael, G. McGraw, and M. A. Schatz, Generating Software Test Data by Evolution, *IEEE Trans. Software Engineering*, vol. 27, no. 12, Dec. 2001, pp. 1085–1110.

MIYI04   J. Miller and Z. Yin, A Cognitive-Based Mechanism for Constructing Software Inspection Team, *IEEE Trans. Software Engineering*, vol. 30, no. 11, Nov. 2004, pp. 811–825.

MMNP92   K. W. Miller, L. J. Morell, R. E. Noonan, S. K. Park, D. M. Nicol, B. W. Murrill, and J. M. Voas, Estimating the Probability of Failure When Testing Reveals No Failures, *IEEE Trans. Software Engineering*, vol. 18, no. 1, Jan. 1992, pp. 33–43.

MOWE77   J. H. Morris, Jr. and B. Wegbreit, Program Verification by Subgoal Induction, in *Current Trends in Programming Methodology*, vol. II, *Program Validation*, R. T. Yeh (Ed.), Prentice-Hall, Englewood Cliffs, NJ, 1977, pp. 197–227.

MUIO87   J. D. Musa, A. Iannino, and K. Okumoro, *Software Reliability: Measurement, Prediction, Application*, McGraw-Hill, New York, 1987.

MUSA93   J. D. Musa, Operational Profiles in Software-Reliability Engineering, *IEEE Software*, vol. 10, no. 2, Mar./Apr. 1993, pp. 14–32.

MUSA96   J. D. Musa, Software Reliability Engineered Testing, *IEEE Computer*, vol. 29, no. 11, Nov. 1996, pp. 61–68.

MYER79   G. F. Myers, *The Art of Software Testing*, Wiley-Interscience, New York, 1979.

NAIK07   S. Naik, *Software Testing and Quality Assurance*, Wiley, Hoboken, NJ, 2007.

NTAF84   S. C. Ntafos, An Evaluation of Required Element Testing Strategies, *IEEE Trans. Software Engineering*, vol. 10, no. 6, Nov. 1984.

NTHA79   S. C. Ntafos and S. L. Hakimi, On Path Cover Problems in Digraphs and Applications to Program Testing, *IEEE Trans. Software Engineering*, vol. 5, no. 5, Sept. 1979, pp. 520–529.

OFLE94   A. J. Offutt and S. D. Lee, An Empirical Evaluation of Weak Mutation, *IEEE Trans. Software Engineering*, vol. 20, no. 5, May 1994, pp. 337–344.

OCBA88   T. J. Ostrand and M. J. Balcer, The Category-Partition Method for Specifying and Generating Functional Tests, *Commun. ACM*, vol. 31, no. 6, Jun. 1988, pp. 676–686.

OSFO76   L. J. Osterweil and L. D. Fosdick, DAVE: A Validation, Error Detection, and Documentation System for FORTRAN Programs, *Software Practice and Experience*, vol. 6, 1976, pp. 473–486.

OSWB05   T. J. Ostrand, E. J. Weyuker, and R. M. Bell, Predicting the Location and Number of Faults in Large Software Systems, *IEEE Trans. Software Engineering*, vol. 31, no. 4, Apr. 2005, pp. 340–355.

PABC93   A. S. Parrish, R. B. Borie, and D. W. Cordes, Automated Flow Graph-Based Testing of Object-Oriented Software Modules, *Journal of Systems and Software*, vol. 23, 1993, pp. 95–109.

PABE74   M. R. Paige and J. P. Benson, The Use of Software Probes in Testing FORTRAN Programs, *Computer*, vol. 7, July 1974, pp. 40–47.

PALA03   D. L. Parnas and M. Lawford, The Role of Inspection in Software Quality Assurance, *IEEE Trans. Software Engineering*, vol. 29, no. 8, Aug. 2003, pp. 674–676.

PAZW91   A. S. Parrish and S. H. Zweben, Analysis and Refinement of Software Test Data Adequacy Properties, *IEEE Trans. Software Engineering*, vol. 17, no. 6, June 1991, pp. 565–581.

PAZW93   A. S. Parrish and S. H. Zweben, Clarifying Some Fundamental Concepts in Software Testing, *IEEE Trans. Software Engineering*, vol. 19, no. 7, July 1993, pp. 687–697.

PEPA98   D. K. Peters and D. L. Parnas, Using Test Oracles Generated from Program Documentation, *IEEE Trans. Software Engineering*, vol. 24, no. 3, Mar. 1998, pp. 161–173.

POBR87   R. M. Poston and M. W. Bruen, Counting Down to Zero Software Failures, *IEEE Software*, vol. 4, no. 5, Sept. 1987, pp. 54–61.

PRAK99   S. Prakash, Design and Development of a Software Analysis Tool, Master's thesis, Department of Computer Science, University of Houston, 1999.

RAHC76   C. V. Ramamoorthy, S. F. Ho, and W. T. Chen, On the Automated Generation of Program Test Data, *IEEE Trans. Software Engineering*, vol. 2, no. 4, Dec. 1976, pp. 293–300.

RAHO77   C. V. Ramamoorthy and S. F. Ho, Testing Large Software with Automated Software Evaluation Systems, in *Current Trends in Programming Methodology*, vol. II; *Program Validation*, R. T. Yeh (Ed.), Prentice-Hall, Englewood Cliffs, NJ, 1977, pp. 112–150.

RAKC75   C. V. Ramamoorthy, K. H. Kim, and W. T. Chen, Optimal Placement of Software Monitors Aiding Systematic Testing, *IEEE Trans. Software Engineering*, vol. 1, no. 4, Dec. 1975, pp. 403–410.

RAWE85   S. Rapps and E. Weyuker, Selecting Software Test Data Using Data Flow Information, *IEEE Trans. Software Engineering*, vol. 11, no. 4, Apr. 1985, pp. 367–375.

RESN70   M. D. Resnik, *Elementary Logic*, McGraw-Hill, New York, 1970.

RITH93   D. J. Richardson and M. C. Thompson, An Analysis of Test Data Selection Criteria Using the RELAY Model of Fault Detection, *IEEE Trans. Software Engineering*, vol. 19, no. 6, June 1993, pp. 533–553.

ROHA93   G. Rothermel and M. J. Harrold, A Safe, Efficient Algorithm for Regression Test Selection, *Proc. IEEE Software Maintenance Conference*, 1993, pp. 358–367.

ROHA96   G. Rothermel and M. J. Harrold, Analyzing Regression Test Selection Techniques, *IEEE Trans. Software Engineering*, vol. 22, no. 8, Aug. 1996, pp. 529–551.

RUES69   E. C. Russell and G. Estrin, Measurement Based Automatic Analysis of Fortran Programs, *Proc. SJCC*, 1969, pp. 723–732.

SAMA93   S. Sankar and M. Mandal, Concurrent Runtime Monitoring of Formally Specified Programs, *IEEE Computer*, vol. 26, no. 3, Mar. 1993, pp. 32–43.

SEBB87   R. Selby, V. R. Basili, and T. Baker, Cleanroom Software Development: An Empirical Evaluation, *IEEE Trans. Software Engineering*, vol. 13, no. 9, Sept. 1987, pp. 1027–1037.

SCHA08   S. R. Schach, *Object-Oriented Software Engineering*, McGraw-Hill, New York, 2008, pp. 430–439.

SHAP83   E. Y. Shapiro, *Algorithmic Program Debugging*, MIT Press, Cambridge, MA, 1983.

SHER91   S. A. Sherer, A Cost-Effective Approach to Testing, *IEEE Software*, vol. 8, no. 2, Mar. 1991, pp. 34–40.

SHER92a   S. A. Sherer, *Software Failure Risk*, Plenum Press, New York, 1992.

SHER92b   M. J. Sherman, *Development of Software Tools for Program Analysis*, M.S. thesis, Department of Computer Science, University of Houston, 1992.

SLOA72   N. J. A. Sloane, On Finding the Paths Through a Network, *Bell System Technical J.*, vol. 51, no. 2, Feb. 1972, pp. 371–390.

SORO93   J. A. Solheim and J. H. Rowland, An Empirical Study of Testing and Integration Strategies Using Artificial Software Systems, *IEEE Trans. Software Engineering*, vol. 19, no. 10, Oct. 1993, pp. 941–949.

SSGP07   S. Sampath, S. Sprenkle, E. Gibson, L. Pollock, and A. S. Greenwald, Applying Concept Analysis to User-Session-Based Testing of Web Applications, *IEEE Trans. Software Engineering*, vol. 33, no. 10, Oct. 2007, pp. 643–658.

STFO75   L. G. Stucki and G. L. Foshee, New Assertion Concepts for Self-Metric Software Validation, *Proc. 1975 International Conference on Reliable Software*, 1975, pp. 59–71.

STUC73   L. G. Stucki, Automatic Generation of Self-Metric Software, *Proc. IEEE Symposium on Computer Software Reliability*, 1973, pp. 94–100.

STUC77   L. G. Stucki, New Directions in Automated Tools for Improving Software Quality, in *Current Trends in Programming Methodology*, vol. II; *Program Validation*, R. T. Yeh (Ed.), Prentice-Hall, Englewood Cliffs, NJ, 1977, pp. 80–111.

SURI91   J. Su and P. Ritter, Experience in Testing the Motif Interface, *IEEE Software*, vol. 8, no. 2, Mar. 1991, pp. 26–33.

TAIK80   K.-C. Tai, Program Testing Complexity and Test Criteria, *IEEE Trans. Software Engineering*, vol. 6, no. 6, 1980, pp. 531–538.

TAIK80   K.-C. Tai, Theory of Fault-Based Predicate Testing for Computer Programs, *IEEE Trans. Software Engineering*, vol. 22, no. 8, Aug. 1996, pp. 552–562.

TALK92   R. N. Taylor, D. L. Levine, and C. D. Kelly, Structural Testing of Concurrent Programs, *IEEE Trans. Software Engineering*, vol. 18, no. 3, Mar. 1992, pp. 206–215.

TAOS78   R. N. Taylor and L. J. Osterweil, A Facility for Verification of Concurrent Process Software, *Proc. COMPSAC 78*, Chicago, Nov. 1978, pp. 36–41.

TAYL83   R. N. Taylor, A General Purpose Algorithm for Analyzing Concurrent Programs, *Commun. ACM*, vol. 26, no. 5, May 1983, pp. 362–376.

THRW03   T. Thelin, P. Runeson, and C. Wohlin, An Experimental Comparison of Usage-Based and Checklist Based Reading, *IEEE Trans. Software Engineering*, vol. 29, no. 8, Aug. 2003, pp. 687–704.

TSDN93   M. Z. Tsoukalas, J. W. Duran, and S. C. Ntafos, On Some Reliability Estimation Problems in Random and Partition Testing, *IEEE Trans. Software Engineering*, vol. 19, no. 7, July 1993, pp. 687–697.

TSVK90   W. T. Tsai, D. Volovik, and T. F. Keefe, Automated Test Case Generation for Programs Specified by Relational Algebra Queries, *IEEE Trans. Software Engineering*, vol. 16, no. 3, Mar. 1990, pp. 316–324.

TYZP05   W. T. Tsai, L. Yu, F. Zhu, and R. Paul, Rapid Embedded System Testing Using Verification Pattern, *IEEE Software*, vol. 22, no. 4, July–Aug. 2005, pp. 68–75.

VANE79   M. H. van Emden, Programming with Verification Condition, *IEEE Trans. Software Engineering*, vol. 5, no. 2, Mar. 1979, pp. 148–159.

VEDA95   S. Venkatesan and B. Dathan, Testing and Debugging Distributed Programs Using Global Predicates, *IEEE Trans. Software Engineering*, vol. 21, no. 2, Feb. 1995, pp. 163–177.

VOMC98   J. Voas and G. McGraw, *Software Fault Injection: Inoculating Programs Against Errors*, Wiley, New York, 1998.

VOMM91   J. Voas, L. Morrel, and K. Miller, Predicting Where Faults Can Hide from Testing, *IEEE Software*, vol. 8, no. 2, Mar. 1991, pp. 41–48.

WATE79   R. C. Waters, A Method for Analyzing Loop Programs, *IEEE Trans. Software Engineering*, vol. 5, no. 3, May 1979, pp. 237–247.

WEGB74   B. Wegbreit, The Synthesis of Loop Predicates, *Commun. ACM*, vol. 17, no. 2, Feb. 1974, pp. 102–112.

WEGS94   E. Weyuker, T. Goradia, and A. Singh, Automatically Generating Test Data from a Boolean Specification, *IEEE Trans. Software Engineering*, vol. 20, no. 5, May 1994, pp. 353–363.

WEIS84   M. Weiser, Program Slicing, *IEEE Trans. Software Engineering*, vol. 10, no. 4, July 1984, pp. 352–357.

WEJE91   E. J. Weyuker and B. Jeng, Analyzing Partition Testing Strategies, *IEEE Trans. Software Engineering*, vol. 17, no. 7, July 1991, pp. 703–711.

WELL81   R. Welland, *Decision Tables and Computer Programming*, Heyden, London, 1981.

WEOS80   E. J. Weyuker and T. J. Ostrand, Theory of Program Testing and the Application of Revealing Subdomains, *IEEE Trans. Software Engineering*, vol. 6, no. 3, May 1980, pp. 236–246.

WEWH91   E. J. Weyuker, S. Weiss, and R. Hamlet, Comparison of Program Testing Strategies, *Proc. 4th Symposium on Testing, Analysis, and Verification*, Oct. 1991, pp. 1–10.

WEYU82   E. J. Weyuker, On Testing Non-testable Programs, *Computer J.*, vol. 25, no. 4, Nov. 1982, pp. 465–470.

WEYU83   E. J. Weyuker, Assessing Test Data Adequacy Through Program Inference, *ACM Trans. Programming Languages and Systems*, vol. 5, no. 4, Oct. 1983, pp. 641–655.

WEYU86   E. J. Weyuker, Axiomatizing Software Test Data Adequacy, *IEEE Trans. Software Engineering*, vol. 12, no. 12, Dec. 1986, pp. 1128–1138.

WEYU88   E. J. Weyuker, The Evaluation of Program-Based Software Test Data Adequacy Criteria, *Commun. ACM*, vol. 31, no. 6, June 1988, pp. 668–675.

WEYU93   E. J. Weyuker, More Experience with Data Flow Testing, *IEEE Trans. Software Engineering*, vol. 19, no. 9, Sept. 1993, pp. 912–919.

WHCO80   L. J. White and E. I. Cohen, A Domain Strategy for Computer Program Testing, *IEEE Trans. Software Engineering*, vol. 6, no. 3, May 1980, pp. 247–257.

WHIT00   J. A. Whittaker, What Is Software Testing, and Why Is It So Hard? *IEEE Software*, vol. 17, no. 1, Jan.–Feb. 2000, pp. 70–79.

WHIT03   J. A. Whittaker, *How to Break Software*, Reading, MA, 2003.

WHTH94   J. A. Whittaker and M. G. Thomason, A Markov Chain Model for Statistical Software Testing, *IEEE Trans. Software Engineering*, vol. 20, no. 10, Oct. 1994, pp. 812–824.

WIRT77   N. Wirth, Toward a Discipline of Real-Time Programming, *Commun. ACM*, vol. 20, no. 8, Aug. 1977, pp. 577–583.

XINO05   T. Xie and D. Notkin, Checking Inside the Black Box: Regression Testing by Comparing Value Spectra, *IEEE Trans. Software Engineering*, vol. 31, no. 10, Oct. 2005, pp. 869–883.

XUXU03   J. Xu, On Inspection and Verification of Software with Timing Requirements, *IEEE Trans. Software Engineering*, vol. 29, no. 8, Aug. 2003, pp. 705–720.

YEHR77   R. T. Yeh, Verification of Programs by Predicate Transformation, in *Current Trends in Programming Methodology*, vol. II; *Program Validation*, R. T. Yeh (Ed.), Prentice-Hall, Englewood Cliffs, NJ, 1977, pp. 228–247.

YOUR89   E. Yourdon, *Managing the Structured Techniques*, Prentice-Hall, 1989.

ZEIL83   S. J. Zeil, Testing for Perturbations of Program Statements, *IEEE Trans. Software Engineering*, vol. 9, no. 3, May 1983, pp. 335–346.

ZEIL89   S. J. Zeil, Perturbation Techniques for Detecting Domain Errors, *IEEE Trans. Software Engineering*, vol. 15, no. 6, June 1989, pp. 737–746.

ZWGO89   S. Zweben and J. Gourlay, On the Adequacy of Weyuker's Test Data Adequacy Axioms, *IEEE Trans. Software Engineering*, vol. 15, no. 4, Apr. 1989, pp. 496–500.

ZWHK92   S. Zweben, W. Heym, and J. Kimich, Systematic Testing of Data Abstractions Based on Software Specifications, *J. Software Testing, Verification, and Reliability*, no. 1, 1992, pp. 39–55.

INDEX

Software Error Detection through Testing and Analysis, By J. C. Huang
Copyright © 2009 John Wiley & Sons, Inc.

Printed in the United States
By Bookmasters